The History of Philosophy

ROYAL INSTITUTE OF PHILOSOPHY SUPPLEMENT: 78

EDITED BY

Anthony O'Hear

T0381882

CAMBRIDGE
UNIVERSITY PRESS

CAMBRIDGE
UNIVERSITY PRESS

University Printing House, Cambridge CB2 8BS, United Kingdom

One Liberty Plaza, 20th Floor, New York, NY 10006, USA

477 Williamstown Road, Port Melbourne, VIC 3207, Australia

314-321, 3rd Floor, Plot 3, Splendor Forum, Jasola District Centre, New Delhi - 110025, India

79 Anson Road, #06-04/06, Singapore 079906

Cambridge University Press is part of the University of Cambridge.

It furthers the University's mission by disseminating knowledge in the pursuit of education, learning and research at the highest international levels of excellence.

www.cambridge.org
Information on this title: www.cambridge.org/9781316626269

© The Royal Institute of Philosophy and the contributors 2016

A catalogue record for this publication is available from the British Library

ISBN 978-1-316-62626-9 Paperback

Contents

List of Contributors

David Sedley – Christ's College, Cambridge

S. Broadie – University of St. Andrews

A.A. Long – University of California

Brian Davies – Fordham University

Sarah Patterson – Birkbeck College, London

Susan James – Birkbeck College, London

Catherine Wilson – University of York

P.J.E. Kail – St. Peter's College, Oxford

Sebastian Gardner – University College London

Robert Stern – University of Sheffield

Simon May – King's College, London

Michael Beaney – University of York

Cheryl Misak – University of Toronto

Rupert Read – University of East Anglia

Preface

It is sometimes said that philosophy cannot be disentangled from its history, in the sense that the questions and topic studied in the 21st century have their roots and even their language in the past, near or distant. On the other hand, others will treat philosophy as if it is an entirely contemporary concern, with each new book or article arising new-born from the head, if not of Zeus, of its author. In this volume the authors attempt to show by implication at least that both these views are partial. The situation in philosophy today is indeed illuminated by a reflective return to the past, while those past thoughts and thinkers have new light shone on them by being viewed in the context of the way philosophy is conducted today.

The essays in this volume are based on the annual London lecture series of the Royal Institute of Philosophy for 2014–5. They are by philosophers whose distinction is to have made their mark both in their study of some of the great thinkers of the past and in their contributions to contemporary debate in philosophy.

While fourteen essays could not be said to encompass the whole history of philosophy, or indeed the whole universe of philosophical study, many of the key historical figures are here, from Plato to Wittgenstein, from Aristotle to the analytical revolution and twentieth-century pragmatism. Aquinas can be seen alongside Nietzsche, and Plotinus next to Hegel. The key moderns are here too, Descartes, Spinoza, Locke, Hume and Kant, And through the lenses provided by these figures from the past, our contributors range over metaphysics, matter, mind, religion, ethics, epistemology, aesthetics, politics and much else besides, including at the end, the notion of progress itself.

On behalf of the Royal Institute, I would like to thank our distinguished contributors for their lectures and also for their written papers, and I also thank Adam Ferner for compiling the index and for his help with organising the series along with James Garvey, the Secretary of the Institute. Finally, readers might be interested to know that podcasts of the lectures as originally delivered are available on the Royal Institute of Philosophy's website (http://royalinstitute philosophy.org/publications/video).

doi:10.1017/S1358246116000394   © The Royal Institute of Philosophy and the contributors 2016

An Introduction to Plato's Theory of Forms

DAVID SEDLEY

Abstract

This lecture was designed as an introduction to Plato's theory of Forms. Reference is made to key passages of Plato's dialogues, but no guidance on further reading is offered, and numerous controversies about the theory's interpretation are left in the background. An initial sketch of the theory's origins in the inquiries of Plato's teacher Socrates is followed by an explanation of the Forms' primary characteristic, Plato's metaphysical separation of them from the sensible world. Other aspects discussed include the Forms' metaphysical relation to sensible particulars, their 'self-predication', and the range of items that have Forms. Finally, the envisaged structure of the world of Forms is illustrated by a look at Plato's famous Cave simile.

Plato could well contend for the title of most celebrated Western philosopher, and the theory of Forms is probably his most celebrated theory. Yet even for historians of philosophy it is no easy matter to say just what a Platonic Form actually is. If the expression 'Platonic Form' has any current meaning for most of us, it is something like 'perfect exemplar'. Once in an undergraduate lecture I mentioned Plato's own question, is there a Form of everything, however ignoble? For example, I said, is there a Platonic Form of scum? 'Yes', shouted a girl in the audience, 'I've met him.'

My aim here is to present a conspectus of the theory, designed for a broad readership.[1] If you are a specialist, you will not need telling that a lot of what I say is controversial, even if I do not keep mentioning the fact. The interpretative literature on Plato's metaphysics – which will stay in the background on the present occasion – is huge, diverse, and riddled with controversy.

My first task will be to sketch the background from which the theory emerged.

In the early years of the 4th century BC, in the aftermath of Socrates' execution and virtual martyrdom, Plato was one of a group of his followers who took up writing Socratic dialogues – fictional or semi-fictional transcripts which tried to keep alive the unique magic of the searching conversations Socrates had spent his

---

[1]   Hence I have not attempted on this occasion to provide any guide to the massive bibliography on Plato's metaphysics, an addition which would have at least doubled the length of the paper.

doi:10.1017/S1358246116000333

David Sedley

life conducting on the streets of Athens. Plato's first dialogues were thus, in this sense, *about* Socrates. But Plato became increasingly dissatisfied with the negative outcomes of the interrogations Socrates was portrayed as conducting, and increasingly ready to represent Socrates as venturing positive ideas which promised to break the deadlock those dialogues standardly reached. One such idea was the theory of Recollection.[2] What is this?

When it comes to simple mathematical problems anybody, even with no prior expertise in the subject, can find the right answer out of their own inner resources, Plato contended, simply by answering questions. Mathematical knowledge is, as we might want to say, *a priori*: when you think about an item of such knowledge, you realise that it could not be otherwise. Take Plato's example,[3] our knowledge of equality. Something that you all already know, whether or not you have ever thought about it, is that equality is a transitive property: if two things are equal to a third thing, they are equal to each other. How do you know this? Not through your experience of the world, which often presents apparent counterexamples where two things look equal to a third thing but *not* to each other. Yet no amount of sensory counter-evidence could lead you to doubt the principle, because you already know it to be true: on reflection, that is, you see that it could not be otherwise. To Plato this can only mean that you were born already deep down knowing such truths. And what applies in the case of simple mathematical and logical truths must apply to philosophical discovery as well. In his view the reason why philosophers intuit that problems like the true nature of goodness can eventually be resolved by mere discussion is that the answers to these questions too are already present in our souls, waiting to be brought to the surface. Hence Plato's famous doctrine of Recollection: all learning is recollection.

Plato's deeply controversial further inference is that our souls must have acquired the knowledge before they entered our bodies, so as to be able to bring it with them, in however buried a form. Take, then, your buried knowledge of equality. If before your birth your soul could, when detached from the body, know the true nature of equality, the nature of equality must be directly accessible to the soul, without the mediation of the body's sense organs. And the same will apply to goodness, and to all the other concepts investigated in philosophical conversation. That then is Plato's first presupposition, namely that the key concepts investigated by mathematicians and

---

[2] *Meno* 81a-86c; *Phaedo* 72e-77a; *Phaedrus* 249b-250b.
[3] *Phaedo* 74a-c.

4

philosophers are intelligible, not sensible: they are accessible to the intellect directly, not via the senses.

The second presupposition is as follows. Our innate knowledge of concepts like equality and goodness could not be objectively *true*, as it certainly is, if the objects of which is true not even *exist*. This beguiling existential assumption is what we still sometimes call 'platonism', with a lower-case p.

From these first two presuppositions it already seems to follow that entities like equality and goodness exist in their own right as objects of pure intellectual enquiry, unmediated by the senses.

A third assumption connects this finding in turn with Socrates' own most prominent intellectual project, his constant search for definitions. According to Socrates in Plato's portrayal, you cannot know something unless you are able to say what it is, that is, articulate a successful definition of it. It seems to follow that the objects of pure intellectual enquiry can be equated with objects of definition. Getting to know such items as equality and goodness is, in whole or in part, a matter of arriving at their definitions.

In the light of this we may now return to the *objects* of knowledge and definition, those entities, like equality and goodness, with which our souls are presumed to have become acquainted before birth. Are they changeable, or altogether unchanging? Given that knowledge of them is founded on their definitions, Plato seems justified in his assumption that they are in fact unchanging. So far as knowledge as such is concerned, its objects might for all we know at this stage have been capable of change, in which case the knowledge of them would correspondingly become out of date: for example my knowledge that today is Thursday will be out of date tomorrow, its object having changed at midnight. But since our knowledge of equality, goodness and their like rests on our grasping their *definitions*, and given the further plausible assumption that those definitions are not such as to become out of date, Plato would seem to have confirmation that the objects of definitional knowledge are themselves unchanging. That definitions are eternally true, timelessly true, or at any rate true for all time, is easy enough to demonstrate. Consider two syllogisms.

First syllogism:

Henry VIII lived at Windsor
Windsor is near the M4 motorway
Therefore Henry VIII lived near the M4 motorway.

David Sedley

This is invalid, because of the change of tense: Windsor *is* near the M4, but wasn't near the M4 in Henry VIII's day. But now consider the second syllogism:

Henry VIII had six wives
A wife is a female spouse
Therefore Henry VIII had six female spouses.

This is valid *despite* the change of tense, because 'A wife is a female spouse' is a definition, and therefore true without regard to time. Plato seems on good ground in assuming, similarly, that the definitions of equality and goodness are not subject to change in truth value over time, and in therefore inferring that equality, goodness and the other *objects* of definition are themselves unchanging entities. Individual instances of equality, for example the equality of day and night at the equinox, may of course change to inequality with the passage of time, but *what equality itself actually is* is unchanging.

In assuming that equality and goodness can be treated in the same way as each other, I may seem to be making an unwarranted assumption. Surely, it will be said, whereas equality is a mathematical relation on which all cultures can be expected to agree in principle, goodness, being a value, unavoidably varies according to local cultural norms and fashions, in which case it will also change over time. Did Plato not see this? The answer is that he was familiar with that view, but decidedly rejected it. The intellectual culture in which Plato grew up made widespread use of a distinction between objective or absolute facts, said to exist 'by nature' (*physis*), and variable, culturally determined norms, said to depend on mere convention (*nomos*). Plato may seem to be recognising this very distinction in his dialogue *Euthyphro*,[4] when he has Socrates point out that no one need quarrel about weights, measures and the like, since there are agreed standards for settling such disputes, whereas it seems inevitable that there should be disagreements about such matters as the good, the beautiful, and the just. But Plato would certainly not approve the diagnosis of this in terms of the nature-versus-convention distinction, or of what has subsequently come to be known as the fact-value distinction. In his view, what makes disagreements about values like goodness and beauty unavoidable is not that these concepts are irreducibly subjective or relative, but that that they are extremely difficult to define and understand. Basic mathematical concepts are easy to master. In his dialogue *Meno* (82a-85b) Plato shows an uneducated slave, under interrogation, working out a

4   *Euthyphro* 7b-d.

simple geometrical theorem in just minutes; and he has Socrates readily formulate definitions of basic mathematical concepts like speed and shape[5] in order to illustrate what a proper definition should look like. His point is, again and again, that mathematical disciplines are comparatively easy to master and already successfully established. Ethics, by contrast, the science of the good, the beautiful and the just, is (a) incredibly difficult, and (b) still in its infancy. Indeed, it is Plato's own self-appointed task, in the wake of Socrates, to create precisely such a science. Let's fast forward for a moment to Plato's dialogue the *Republic*: there[6] he will calculate that the scientific study of goodness is so incredibly difficult as to require a preliminary ten years of mathematics, followed by a further five years of dialectical study.

In short, for Plato there is no fact-value distinction. Values *are* facts, just incredibly difficult ones. That is why simple mathematical concepts like equality and demanding ethical concepts like goodness can be treated under a single theory, and why mathematics, with its proven successes, can be seen as setting a model which a future science of ethics can be expected to follow.

We have now seen why it is that the objects of knowledge and definition, whether in mathematics or in ethics, must be unchanging entities. Given the widely agreed further assumption that all *physical* entities are subject to change, it follows for Plato that these objects of knowledge and definition are *non-physical*.

To sum up the results so far, the objects of knowledge must be eternal, changeless, non-physical entities, accessible directly to the intellect without reliance on the body and its sense organs.

We must now turn to a different consideration. According to Plato, special problems arise in connection with properties which have an opposite: largeness, equality, goodness etc. For these are found in perceptible objects only in an impure and ambiguous form, mixed with, or alternating with, their own opposites – respectively smallness, inequality and badness. Thus whatever perceptible object is large in one relation can also be seen in some other relation as small; whatever perceptible object is beautiful can also be seen as in some context ugly, depending on current fashions, what it is being compared with, and a variety of other factors; and so on for other pairs of opposite properties. To generalise: if 'F' and 'un-F' stand for any pair of opposites, then whatever sensible thing is in a way F is also un-F in some other *respect*, at some other *time*, for some

---

5   *Laches* 192a-b, *Meno* 74b-75c.
6   *Republic* 7.537b-d, 539d-e.

David Sedley

other *person*, or in some other *relation*. Pairs of opposite properties are thus no more than unstably present in the world around us. Any judgement about whether some given object is large or beautiful must be irreducibly provisional, context-dependent and contingent: there is no single undeniably right answer.[7]

This confirms that neither knowledge of largeness, a simple knowledge which we already have at our fingertips or can easily put there, nor knowledge of beauty, to which we at best may still aspire as a long-term goal, can possibly be empirical. It is a fundamental assumption of Plato's that knowledge, once acquired, cannot be subject to revision: if it were, it would not have been knowledge in the first place. Yet if it had as its aim the identification of largeness or beauty as we experience these in the sensible world, it would inevitably be subject to revision, these being inherently unstable properties which constantly jostle with their own opposites to manifest themselves. The largeness and beauty of which we can have knowledge are not, then, the largeness and beauty physically present in the world around us.

One more background assumption still needs to be added. In the many dialogues devoted to the definition of this or that concept, Plato's Socrates insists that the property in question, regardless of the multiplicity and variety of its manifestations, must itself be *one single thing*. However disparate in other regards the set of things called beautiful may be, the beauty in which they share must be a unitary, unvarying property. Although this principle of the Unity of Definition, a vital underpinning of Plato's theory of Forms, was already to be challenged by his own pupil Aristotle, its attractiveness is obvious enough. Barring the very unlikely supposition that the many things called beautiful owe this shared designation to a mere accident of language, as when we use the word 'toast' both for a celebratory drink and for a grilled slice of bread, it does indeed seem likely that they are linked by *some* single property that runs through all the instances.

In his early, Socratic dialogues Plato was already starting to call this unitary object of definition a 'form': the Greek word is *eidos* or *idea*. This was not yet a remotely technical term, just a convenient way of picking out the character or property that makes something the kind of thing that it is. What we call Plato's theory of Forms is expressed with this same term, but by a modern convention we tend for convenience to spell 'Forms' with a capital F. This spelling at a stroke turns 'Forms' into a technical term. What does the technicality add

---

[7]   See esp. *Symposium* 211a, *Rep*.5.479a-b.

or make explicit? That question brings me to my main topic. What is a Platonic Form?

The key is *separation*. The eternal and changeless 'forms' which as we have seen are sought in definitional inquiries and are the potential objects of pure knowledge, exist *separately from* all their sensible instances, rather than being *immanent* in them.

This is not at all to say that there are no immanent properties. To take the example of largeness, as well as the separate Form of Largeness there is also immanent largeness, such as your own particular largeness, or mine.[8] Largeness itself is apparently, according to Plato, definable as 'the power to exceed'.[9] Your particular immanent largeness is therefore *your* particular power to exceed, a different power to exceed from mine partly because of course it is in you, not in me, but also because, if we are of different heights, we anyway have different capacities to exceed, and thus different largenesses. For example there may be people short enough for you to exceed but too tall for me to exceed. So your largeness must be a different one from mine.

Nevertheless, when we *define* largeness what we are defining is not immanent largeness. Since immanent largeness is the capacity of some individual to exceed, it is volatile at least in the sense it may become inactive, depending on whom its possessor is being compared with, and is perishable in that it must perish when its possessor does. In contrast to this, the largeness that serves as the object of definition is largeness *itself* or *as such*, the capacity to exceed viewed in its own right independently of any individuals that might manifest it. Because this largeness, unlike all immanent largenesses, is independent of changeable bodies, it can be eternal and unchanging, and therefore, unlike them, is a suitable object of eternally true definitions and stable knowledge.

This is a metaphysical separation of the Form from the particulars that manifest it. But that metaphysical separation has a linguistic counterpart too. Suppose I say 'Tom and Bill are large'. The names 'Tom' and 'Bill' are jointly the *linguistic* subject, and the word 'large' is their *linguistic* predicate. What correspond to these metaphysically are Tom and Bill themselves, and an actual predicate or property, largeness, that they possess in common. This metaphysical predicate is not their own distinct individual largenesses, but largeness itself, which they both alike manifest. Suppose next that I want to tell you what this shared predicate *is* or *means*. What I do,

[8] *Phaedo* 102b-103a.
[9] *Parmenides* 150c-d.

David Sedley

linguistically speaking, is pick out the predicate large and turn it into a subject in its own right. The way to do that in Greek is to employ the expression 'large itself': Tom and Bill are large, and as for large itself, it is having the power to exceed. In Greek the expression for 'large itself' adds the definite article, 'the large itself', and this style of expression – 'the large itself', 'the beautiful itself', and so on – came to be Plato's most familiar way of referring to Forms.

However, actually almost as common in Plato's writings is the same expression but combined with the pronoun *ti* which serves in Greek as the *in*definite article: there is 'a large itself', 'a beautiful itself', and so on. This is usually his way of putting forward an existential hypothesis about Forms: Socrates is presented as claiming, hypothesizing, or even 'dreaming' that there are 'a beautiful itself', 'a good itself', and so on: that is, as positing that Forms of these various predicates actually exist.

Why should this existential question arise? To claim that there is, say, 'a large itself' is to claim that there is such a thing as largeness *independently of whatever subjects it happens to inhere in*. Or, to put the same metaphysical point in linguistic terms, it is to claim that the predicate 'large', as in the sentence 'Tom and Bill are large', can be picked out and used as a *bone fide* subject of predication in its own right. In the case of largeness, this is not really in doubt. As Plato has Socrates point out in the *Meno* (72d-e) everybody, adult and child, free and slave alike, in so far as they are large, are large in the same way. We know this, he means, because the predicates large and small are the objects of a simple and already successful science, that of measurement. But what about a so far undeveloped science, like that of beauty or goodness? For all we know at present, there may be nothing more to being beautiful than being a beautiful sunset, a beautiful painting, and so on, or being beautiful within this or that culture or value-system. That is, beautiful may for all we know be an irredeemably context-dependent predicate. Whether beautiful can also serve as a *bona fide* subject – whether, that is, there is such a thing as the beautiful itself, definable and knowable in its own right independently of all its manifestations – is a question we will not be able to answer affirmatively until a science of beauty has been established. When Plato has his Socrates posit or dream that there are a beautiful itself, a good itself, and so on, he is certainly expressing his deep-seated wish, conviction and aspiration, but he recognises that the jury is still out. His strongest ground for optimism in this regard lies in his confidence that simple mathematical Forms such as equality and largeness *have* already been successfully isolated as objects of definitional knowledge in their own right.

An Introduction to Plato's Theory of Forms

Even if in this regard the precise range of concepts that have Forms remains undetermined, it should be clear that a primary condition for qualifying as a separated Form is to be a *bona fide* subject of independent truths, not reducible to or dependent on facts about its sensible manifestations. Plato also gives many indications that, whereas facts about those sensible manifestations are contextual, unstable and contingent half-truths, about which our opinions are constantly subject to revision, the corresponding facts about the Forms are pure truths – independent of context, unchangeable, and, in that they could not have been otherwise, knowable with certainty.

This contrast between two distinct realms is linked by Plato to two competing means of cognitive access: the intellect, and the senses. Consequently, Plato is often and I think correctly credited with a 'two world' thesis. There are two worlds: the intelligible world, populated by Forms, and the sensible world, populated by sensible particulars. Inquiry about Forms is pure intellectual inquiry, which must minimise or eliminate the use of the senses. And since knowledge is in its nature permanently true and not subject to revision, the unchanging world of Forms constitutes a suitable object for knowledge. By contrast, the familiar world of sensible particulars is suitable only for opinion: opinion, being in its very nature capable of fluctuating between true and false, is the appropriate mode of cognition for inherently unstable objects. On this basis, Plato operates not only an epistemological distinction between the intelligible world and the sensible world, but also, and directly mapping onto this, an ontological distinction between a world of pure being and a world of pure becoming. Intellectual access to the world of being affords us an understanding of what such things as equality and beauty really and timelessly *are*, whereas sensory access to the world of becoming does no more than track the ebb and flow of the corresponding predicates – their *becoming*.

Plato is committed to the principle that sensibles not only share their names with the corresponding Forms but also owe their characters to those Forms: if a particular is properly called beautiful, such beauty as it possesses depends, not just linguistically but metaphysically as well, on the Form of Beautiful. It is in fact beauty – the Form – that causes things to be beautiful, and largeness that causes them to be large. That is, only if you know what beauty or largeness itself is do you know precisely what it is that makes this music beautiful or that building large.

In view of this causal role of Forms, the radical separation of the two worlds comes at a price. The more separate the two worlds are, the harder it becomes to understand how Forms can have any

David Sedley

causal or indeed other impact on the world we inhabit. To his eternal credit Plato, far from shirking this problem, devoted several intricate pages of his own dialogue the *Parmenides* (127d-134c) to airing it. The wise elder philosopher Parmenides, representing Plato's present self, is shown quizzing a very young Socrates, who on this occasion represents Plato's earlier 'classical' theory of Forms, now placed under close critical scrutiny. Their conversation comes to focus on the question, what does it mean for particulars to 'participate' or 'share' in these separated Forms?

Here it needs to be interjected that Plato does indeed sometimes speak of the Form-particular relationship as one whereby particulars 'participate' or 'share' in Forms. This corresponds to a perfectly ordinary Greek usage. If on the one hand you and I share a cake, we each get a portion of it. If on the other hand you and I both possess the same property, say baldness, it is equally normal in Greek to say that you and I 'share' that property, meaning this time no more than that we both have it, and not that we have shared the baldness out between us, each getting a portion of it. This same understanding of 'sharing' could equally well apply when it is said that two or more items share in one and the same Form, for example that all large things share in the Form of largeness. Of course Forms *have* to be shared, because each Form is a *single* thing, yet accounts for the common character of *many* like things.

The trouble is that, understood in this harmless way, the notion of participation or sharing is vacuous. It tells us nothing about how a set of particulars come to be characterised by a Form, just that they somehow do. It is therefore unsurprising that, in the dialogue named after him, Parmenides chooses to put pressure on this particular concept: what does participation actually mean? It turns out that the young Socrates has not given the matter any thought, so that when questioned he is ready to assume that participation in a Form will mean sharing it out bit by bit. As a result he is induced to admit all kinds of absurdities, such as that the Form of smallness will be parceled out into pieces smaller than smallness itself; or alternatively that a Form will, despite being indivisible, somehow be wholly present in each of the particulars it is set over. Critics often complain that Plato has made the young Socrates unnecessarily naïve here, but it is better to say that Plato is admitting, in the person of the young Socrates, that he has himself in the past left the notion of participation in Forms more or less unanalysed, thus inviting the literal-minded approach which in his dramatic portrayal Parmenides adopts and Socrates is initially powerless to resist.

12

An Introduction to Plato's Theory of Forms

In the end the young Socrates is driven to abandon his literal understanding of participation in Forms, telling Parmenides that the term should instead be understood as meaning resemblance. Forms are ideal paradigms, and particulars get their properties in virtue of their degree of resemblance to those paradigms. Although Parmenides proceeds to find a difficulty with this account of the Form-particular relationship as well, the fact is that the resemblance model is and remains by far Plato's favourite way of expressing that relationship, in a range of dialogues of which at least one is thought to postdate the *Parmenides*. We should therefore take the young Socrates' switch to the resemblance model as, from Plato's point of view, a mark of progress.

The idea that Forms are paradigms goes back to Plato's early dialogue the *Euthyphro* (6e). There Socrates, seeking a definition of piety, asks his interlocutor to tell him the 'form' which makes all pious things pious, so that by looking to this as a paradigm or model he can count as pious anything that is like it, and as impious anything that is not. Such talk in these dialogues has often given the impression that a Form is conceived by Plato as an ideal *exemplar* of the common property represented, rather than as being that property itself.

This impression that Forms are ideal exemplars is strengthened by Plato's notorious 'self-predication' assumption. To him, that is, it seems blindingly obvious that a property is truly predicable of itself: largeness is large, piety is pious, and so on for every property. As Socrates is already heard saying in Plato's early dialogue the *Protagoras* (330d-e), it is hard to see how anything *else* could be pious, if even piety itself is not pious. If piety itself really does have the strongest claim to be pious, it could once again seem plausible that Plato is conceiving piety itself as an ideal model or exemplar which paradigmatically manifests the property in question.

This temptation should be resisted. A Form, being the *one* thing shared by many diverse but like-named particulars, is a 'one over many': not a further particular but a universal. The sense in which the Form of, say, largeness is a paradigm against which all individual attributions of largeness are to be tested, and approved in so far as they resemble it, is not that largeness is a supremely large thing. It is that largeness itself, a universal, fully satisfies its own definition, and that other things are large precisely in so far as they too satisfy that same definition, that is, in so far as they resemble largeness itself. Largeness itself is definable as the power to exceed, and other things are large precisely in so far as they too, no doubt more episodically, manifest a property that satisfies that same description, namely their own individual power to exceed.

Although the way Forms serve as paradigms which sensible particulars imperfectly imitate is, for reasons I have tried to explain, different from the way in which a perfect specimen of some property is a paradigm of it, the notion of Forms as paradigms has proved useful as an aid to understanding why Plato takes the self-predication of Forms – that beauty is beautiful, largeness large, and so on – to be an obvious truth. Compare, as others have done, the paradigmatic role of the standard metre. In Paris there is a metal bar which serves as the paradigm for what counts as a metre. What we should, strictly speaking, compare to a Platonic Form is not that metre bar itself, but the length of the metre bar. Consider the functional parallelism. Plato sometimes speaks of Forms being 'present in' particulars, sometimes of particulars 'sharing' in the Form, and sometimes of particulars 'imitating' or 'resembling' the Form. All of these locutions will work equally well for the length of the metre bar. If a piece of string is one metre long, we might say, it has that property in so far as the length of the metre bar is *present in* it, or in so far as the string *shares* the length of bar, or in so far as the string, or perhaps rather its length, *resembles* the length of the metre bar. Under all these descriptions, the string's being one metre long is both contingent and subject to revision. Contrast with that the way in which the length of the metre bar is a guaranteed one metre long. We don't even need to measure it to know that it is one metre long: since it itself sets the standard, it could hardly fail to meet it. Likewise, it is tempting for Plato to say that Beauty itself sets the standard for what it is for things to be beautiful, in which case it, of all things, can hardly fall short of that standard.

In formulating this analogy on Plato's behalf, I permitted myself one small inaccuracy. Although it is true to say that the *metre bar* itself is one metre long, it was not strictly correct of me to say that *the length of the metre bar* is one metre long. Lengths do not have lengths: lengths *are* lengths. Thus the length of the metre bar is not one metre long; rather, the length of the metre bar is one metre. But in making that small change I have switched from the 'is' of predication ('is one metre long') to the 'is' of identity ('is one metre', i.e. 'is the same thing as one metre'). The standard metre is not self-predicating, but it is self-identical – and trivially so, since *everything* is likewise identical to itself. Similarly, it might be argued in reply to Plato, the Form of Large is not predicatively large: it is large merely in the sense of being, unsurprisingly, the same thing as the large.

However, such a riposte to Plato assumes that the distinction between the 'is' of predication and the 'is' of identity is a proven one. That would in all probability be strongly resisted by Plato, who almost never concedes that a single word may have multiple meanings. Even his pupil Aristotle, who by contrast distinguished at least ten senses of the verb 'to be', never distinguished the 'is' of identity from the 'is' of predication as far as I am aware.

Let's now return to the world of Forms and ask what its population is. If Forms are universals, is there a Form of every character that is actually or potentially shared between two or more individuals? Are there Forms of all natural kinds, including cat, cobweb and cucumber? Are there Forms of all types of artefact, including bucket, ballroom and basin? And are there Forms of bad things like ugliness and injustice? In the *Parmenides*, where as we have seen Plato is in confessional mood about possible weaknesses of the Form theory, he is particularly candid about the problem of the theory's scope – the range of the Forms (130b-e).

The young Socrates, representing Plato's past self, is confident of the first two groups of Forms that Parmenides puts to him:

Group a, e.g. likeness, one, many;
Group b, e.g. just, beautiful, good.

Of these, it is common to call the first group 'logico-mathematical' Forms, and the second group 'value Forms'. However, bearing in mind a distinction I noted earlier, it might be closer to Plato's intentions to say that the first group are the easy Forms that anyone can be expected to master after a minute's questioning, while the second group are the highly demanding ones that even philosophers may aspire to master only in the long run.

So much for how the two groups may be assumed to differ. But we also need to know what links unite the two groups, since these are between them the only Forms of whose existence Plato, in the mouth of the young Socrates, admits that he has in the past been fully confident. There are two links. The first is that the occupants of both groups are, in Plato's eyes, *a priori* concepts. Understanding what likeness, unity and plurality are does not in any way depend on information about the way the world happens to be, but solely on examination of our own innate concepts. That the same should apply to values like just, beautiful and good is perhaps less obvious to us, but, for reasons that I tried to bring out earlier, such is Plato's deep-seated conviction, born of his Socratic heritage according to which the study of values is best conducted by question and answer, rather than by any kind of empirical survey. To put it another way, there are such things as likeness, equality and largeness themselves, definable without reference to the subjects that happen to possess them; and similarly, according to Plato's philosophical dream, there are such things as goodness itself, justice itself and beauty itself, definable without reference to the subjects that happen to possess *them*.

What these Platonic definitions of value terms would be like, were Plato able to formulate them, is largely a matter for speculation. But there is not much doubt that they would look, to our eyes, like fundamentally mathematical analyses, embodying high-level principles of complex proportionality. According to well-authenticated reports, Plato once in his life announced that he would give a public lecture, and that it would be on the good. At the end, the reports continue, his audience went away deeply disappointed, because all that Plato had done in his lecture on the good was talk a whole lot of mathematics.

If, as I am suggesting, Plato's definitions of value terms were intended to be the outcome of high-level mathematical analysis, we have further confirmation that the first two groups of Forms listed in the *Parmenides* really do belong together. The first group - likeness, one, many — is typified by simple, entry-level mathematical and logical concepts; the second group – just, beautiful, good - represents the other end of the same spectrum: the highest level of mathematical analysis, to which no one, barring a few philosophers, is ever likely to gain access. No wonder, then, that between these entry and exit levels Plato required the trainee philosophers of Kallipolis, the ideal city depicted in his *Republic*, to spend ten years studying advanced mathematical sciences like astronomy and harmonics.

In asking what links these two groups of Forms to each other, I have so far emphasised the *a priori* nature that makes both types of Form alike objects of cognition quite independently of their material instantiations. However, a second characteristic that unites them is the fact that they are all *opposites*: like and unlike, one and many, just and unjust, beautiful and ugly, good and bad. As I mentioned earlier, in the sensible world, according to Plato, you never find just one opposite in isolation: it is always manifested along with its own opposite. This doctrine, that of the 'compresence of opposites', is a major underpinning of the theory of Forms. For if you can never expect to meet a pure case of largeness or beauty in the sensible world, either there simply is no such thing as pure largeness or pure beauty, or they do exist but independently of the sensible world. And the latter option amounts to saying that there are separated Forms of both. However, we should be wary of considering this criterion *sufficient* by itself to guarantee the existence of a corresponding Form. For Plato sometimes includes among the compresent opposites such empirical-sounding pairs as heavy and light, and hard and soft. There is no explicit evidence that he considers there to be separated, intellectually accessible Forms of heavy, light, hard and soft; and to insist that there are would pose an obvious threat to the *a priori* nature of the Forms. Here then we find ourselves pushing at the imprecise boundary of the world of Forms. Are its borders to be spread a little wider, so as to admit at least some items which cannot easily be said to be objects of pure thought?

It is with this question in mind that we now return to Parmenides' interrogation of the young Socrates about the range of Forms. Does Socrates suppose that there are Forms of such items as man, fire, and water, he next asks. These too will sound to a modern ear uncomfortably like empirical items, to be understood, if at all, at least partly in terms of flesh and blood in the case of man, heating in the case of fire, and so on. Moreover, this time we are dealing with items which have no opposite. Whereas sensible largeness is always encountered mixed up with its own opposite, smallness, there is no similar ambiguity about our experience of human beings. Hence, it might be argued, knowledge of man does not require intellectual access to a Form of Man, simply regular sensory experience of flesh-and-blood humans. One can therefore see why the young Socrates declares himself to be in a quandary about Forms of this type. Nevertheless, it is not hard to find reasons why he should not give up too readily on them.

One reason for sticking with them has to do with the role of Forms as models for craftsman to imitate. In some dialogues, Plato commits himself to the thesis that a good craftsman starts by turning his mind's eye to the Form of the artefact he is about to construct. Thus for example a good carpenter, setting out to make a table, focuses on the Form of table, and proceeds to embody it as best he can in the wood and other materials at his disposal. The Form of table is not to be thought of as an ethereal table complete with legs, etc., but rather as, if you like, the ideal function of a table, a function which can never be perfectly realised in matter, but which nevertheless constitutes a proper model for the craftsman to strive towards.

Now, this admission of mundane craft forms already by itself greatly expands the population of the world of Forms, again in a way that seems to call into question the *a priori* status of Forms. But it also, indirectly, ushers in a yet further class of Forms. According to Plato's late dialogue the *Timaeus*, the world and all its major components are themselves artefacts, albeit of a special kind, namely *divine* artefacts. Since it also goes without saying that the divine craftsman of the world was a *good* craftsman, it follows that in creating the world he, like any good craftsman, turned to the relevant Forms as his models. Plato is explicit, for example, that in order to make the world a living being the creator looked to the generic form of Living Being or Animal as his model. Since this generic Form of Animal is said contain all the individual species of animal, we can infer that there is, among these, a Form of Man. And Forms of Fire and Water are explicitly mentioned too in the *Timaeus*. In this way, Parmenides' question to the young Socrates as to whether there are Forms of man, fire, and water gets a very clear answer from Plato in his late work. The world of Forms is thus expanded yet again, to include, alongside models for human artefacts, those of most if not all natural kinds.

The implicit inclusion of a Form of man in the *Timaeus* can help dispel the worry about the surprisingly empirical nature of some Forms, the Form of man among them. According to the mythical narrative in Plato's *Timaeus*, the task of creating man was delegated to the lesser gods. And when they proceeded with the task, there is no suggestion that their knowledge of the Form of man already dictated what the flesh-and-blood structure of humans should be. Rather, it seems, that structure was devised by the gods as their own best attempt at realising the Form of man in matter. We can work out from this that Plato does not see the form of man as including such features as flesh and bone, two-leggedness, uprightness, or indeed any specific physical features. Rather, we may take it, the form of man specifies a function, probably that of housing a rational soul in a structure which enables it to make moral and intellectual progress during a prolonged but finite lifetime. The familiar human shape merely turned out to be, though not perfect, the best physical means of realising this function in matter. Such considerations may not make man an entirely *a priori* concept, but they do narrow the gap.

To resume, then, one reason why Plato has good grounds for retaining Forms of man, fire and water is that such items are divine artefacts, and their divine artificer will have needed a Form of each to look to as his model. I now turn to the second reason. Man, fire and water are *bona fide* objects of definition, and as I remarked earlier, definitions, being timelessly true, need objects which are themselves eternal and unchanging.

It is no doubt this last consideration, the role of forms as objects of definition, that leads Parmenides to test the young Socrates one more time. Does Socrates, he asks, consider there to be forms of things which might well be thought ridiculous, such as hair, mud and dirt? Socrates is aghast at the idea, but Parmenides predicts that he will in time grow out of this squeamishness – a clear enough signal by Plato that he has himself by now come to accept the inclusion of such Forms. In the first two cases, those of hair and mud, there is not much problem about explaining their inclusion in the world of Forms. According to the *Timaeus* hair has, at least in humans, the vital function of protecting the head from blows which might damage the workings of intelligence in the brain. As for mud, it actually is defined in a probably later dialogue, the *Theaetetus*, as 'earth mixed with water' (147c). Thus mud turns out to have as components of its definition two of the four elementary bodies – earth, water, air and fire – which, as we have already learnt, are included among the Forms, as proper models or paradigms for divine craftsmanship. It would be strange if there were Forms corresponding to earth and to water, but none corresponding to their combination, mud. Here it should be added that the Greek word for mud, *pēlos*, often means more specifically 'clay', referring to the basic material of the art of pottery, and thus to something with a defined function.

The final item in Parmenides list is the one that really pushes Socrates over the edge: dirt. Unlike hair and clay, dirt has no theoretical function whatsoever, being a mere by-product of processes which are themselves aimed at quite different ends. Dirt is neither an *a priori* concept, nor an opposite. Parmenides' insistence that it should not be excluded from the world of Forms must rely solely on the one remaining criterion of Formhood, namely that even dirt is a proper object of definition. But it must be admitted that, once this is conceded to be a sufficient criterion, the floodgates will have opened. If every general term is a legitimate object of definition, there will be a Form corresponding to every general term: not just a Form of dirt, but a Form of breakfast, a Form of boredom and a Form of beer.

There is every reason to assume that, at least at the time of writing the *Parmenides*, Plato really did intend to open wide the doors into the realm of Forms and admit all comers: hence the objects of definition were in Plato's late works to include such humble skills as angling and weaving. However, when putting this new licence into practice in those late dialogues, Plato very naturally downplayed any assumption that such objects of definition need be transcendent Forms. Hence, at least in those dialogues, the theory of transcendent forms was to give way to a general theory of universals, little concerned with the metaphysical status of its objects. That he had nevertheless not forgotten or abandoned his classical theory of Forms is attested by another late dialogue, the *Timaeus*, where the independent existence of the Forms is emphasized by a narrative according to which Forms were already there for the divine creator to use as paradigms even when he first set about creating the sensible world.

Thus in the end, it appears, the theory of Forms split into two branches. One branch, resting on no more than minimal metaphysical presuppositions, and by no means limiting itself to *a priori* concepts, became in effect a taxonomic map of the entire realm over which definitional inquiry may operate. The other branch, retaining the metaphysical transcendence that had been the hallmark of Plato's classical theory of Forms, was invoked in order to explain the ontological status of the physical world as a divine craftsman's best possible imitation, but still no more than an imitation, of an ideal set of paradigms.

Returning for one last time, in the light of this distinction, to the classical theory of forms, with its radical division between two worlds, let me end by examining the question, what the world of separated Forms is like. Is it really a structured world at all, in which some kind of intellectual tourism might be imagined, and not a mere warehouse or repository? Plato has tried to convey its nature to us in what is undoubtedly the most celebrated of all his images, the Cave simile in book 7 of the *Republic*. Let's take a brief look.

Ordinary people, living as they do in the sensory world, are to be compared to a row of prisoners, tied up and facing the wall at the bottom of a cave, where they have been since birth. The shadows that dance across the wall in front of them are fleeting representations of puppets that, unseen by them, are being carried along above a wall behind them. And those puppets are themselves in turn mere copies of the real beings that inhabit the world outside the cave. It is these last that symbolize the Forms. Ordinary people are like the prisoners for the following reason. Far from having any intellectual access to the Forms in their daily lives, they are barred by their culture from acquaintance even with entities in our own sensory world which are direct copies, that is, genuine instances or reflections, of the Forms, represented in the Cave image by the puppets carried behind them. Instead they must make do with fleeting shadows of those entities. As Plato will go on to explain in book 10 of the *Republic*, it is above all poetry, but also the other imitative art forms endemic to the civic culture, that grab people's attention and warp their view of reality. In our own age, the equivalent would probably be television or novels. For example a poet's, or as we might say a novelist's, portrayal of courageous behaviour can be at best no more than an external reflection of a genuinely courageous act, which is itself an imperfect likeness of the Form of courage. The culture in which we happen to find ourselves immersed keeps us as distant from the reality of the Forms as the prisoners are from the world outside the cave.

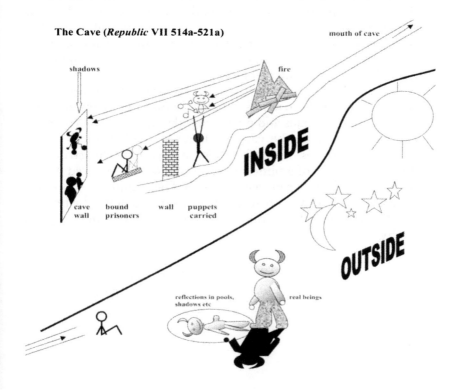

The Cave (*Republic* VII 514a-521a)

Plato's Socrates asks us to imagine the process of a prisoner somehow being released and dragged up into the world outside the cave; and then, in a subsequent phase, returning to bring the good news to its sadly uncomprehending residents. What this escape symbolizes is the educational journey of the intellect from the civic environment to the intelligible world, followed by its political journey back down again. That journey is a topic for another occasion. For present purposes, I just want to draw attention to the stratified structure of the intelligible world, as uniquely described here.

Owing to the dazzling light outside the cave, the newly escaped prisoner at first has to content himself with looking at shadows on the ground and reflections in pools. In the end, however he is able to look directly at the beings around him. Later still he is able to raise his eyes and look at the heavenly bodies in the night sky. And finally he is able to see the sun itself, and, working back down from it, to appreciate that all the beings in the world around him are causally dependent upon the sun and made visible by it.

As Plato has made explicit in the previous book of the *Republic*, the sun here represents the supreme Form, the Form of the Good. Just as the sun dominates the structures and processes of the visible world, so too the good dominates the intelligible structures of the world of Forms. Plato is here encouraging us to speculate about the interrelation of at least three distinct strata of forms: at the top, the sun represents the Form of Good; next, the lesser heavenly bodies almost certainly represent the remaining value forms; and below *them* the various genera of animals and plants outside the cave will symbolize, if nothing else, at least the various classes of mathematical Forms. The realm of Forms really is, then, a hierarchically structured world. The intellect of a philosopher, provided it is relieved of tiresome political duties, can according to Plato enjoy a supremely happy life in the world of Forms, travelling up and down the inferential paths that afford it unimpeded views of that metaphysical hierarchy.[10]

Christ's College, Cambridge
dns1@cam.ac.uk

[10] My thanks to audiences at the Royal Institute of Philosophy, London, in December 2014 and at Washington University, St Louis, in March 2015, for their probing questions.

Aristotle Through Lenses from Bernard Williams

S. BROADIE

Abstract

This paper looks at a theme in ancient Greek ethics from perspectives developed by Bernard Williams.[1] The ancient theme is the place of theoretical activity in human life, and I shall be referring to Aristotle. Williams is relevant through one strand in his scepticism about 'morality, the peculiar institution'.[2] His discussion suggests questions not merely *about* Aristotle but ones it would be interesting to put *to* Aristotle and see how he would or should respond to them.

1.

For Bernard Williams a major target was the way in which morality in its traditional self-presentation claims to set up sovereign demands: no conflicting consideration can trump the call of moral duty. This is not, of course, the thought that it is our duty always to obey a moral rule, e.g. to keep our promises, regardless of cost; for 'morality the peculiar institution' certainly allows in general that what counts as our actual duty in a given situation depends on the circumstances. The idea is that once moral thinking has determined what I in my situation should do so far as morality is concerned, there cannot be a good reason, let alone a better reason, for me to do something else. Kant seeks to make this a necessary truth by defining good fundamental practical reasoning *as* good moral reasoning. This aspect of Kantianism is shared by any normative system that teaches the over-ridingness of moral duty, even one that determines the dictates of duty in a manner alien or hostile to the Kantian way. Williams famously rejected this claim of necessary over-ridingness. He argued that human beings can be involved in non-moral projects

---

[1] This paper began life as a contribution to a conference at the University of Chicago, October 2011, on Bernard Williams's legacy for philosophy today. My remit was to present something on how our current study of ancient Greek ethics might benefit from thinking about themes from Bernard Williams.

[2] Bernard Williams, *Ethics and the Limits of Philosophy* (Cambridge, Mass.: Harvard University Press, 1985, 174–196).

doi:10.1017/S1358246116000242   © The Royal Institute of Philosophy and the contributors 2016

S. Broadie

and commitments which they may on occasion have good reason to pursue even at the expense of duty.

My first question for Aristotle is whether he should take comfort from this thesis of Williams. Is Aristotle's ethical stance on theoretical activity (the activity of theoretical wisdom, *sophia*) upheld, confirmed, corroborated by Williams's insistence that we may have good reason to pursue something even at the expense of our duties of justice and other duties in the sphere of ethical virtue? I should say a preliminary word on how this question arises in the first place. It arises because Aristotle maintains that the activity of *sophia* is more godlike and precious (or honourable, *timios*) than any other activity whether practical or recreational, and that the life devoted to it is the 'happiest' (*Nicomachean Ethics* X, 6–8). This position commits Aristotle to the view that the activity of theoretical wisdom is the highest of all human ends – and not only is he committed to this, but he eagerly affirms it. The position is developed rather fast and furiously in the penultimate chapters of the *Nicomachean Ethics* with little said in advance to prepare the reader for an ending so remote from common sense and so apparently disturbing. A number of twentieth-century interpreters worried that Aristotle implicitly condones or even supports the activity of *sophia* even at the expense of duties to fellow citizens, family members, and so forth, or else implicitly recommends a monk's or hermit's existence for those who aspire to the life of theoretical wisdom. This impression of an amoral or inhuman theoretical ideal prompted much scholarly effort to undercut its force, whether by arguing that it is based on textual misinterpretation or that it represents an immature view of Aristotle's which an ancient editor cobbled into the text of the otherwise mostly 'mature' (or anyway unintimidating) *Nicomachean Ethics*. However, the arguments of Williams may suggest another and more directly philosophical way to let Aristotle off this hook: namely, by lining him up with Williams's rejection of the necessary supremacy of morality. One does not have to be an amoral person to find good reason, in some situations, not to bow to claims of morality. One might care a great deal about morality without treating it as supreme no matter what else might be at stake. Thus (it might be argued) even if Aristotle's theoretical sage is neither a monk nor a hermit nor an alarmingly amoral person – even if he has accepted a life involving ordinary duties to city and family – it may still be reasonable and even perhaps very admirable of him to throw aside those duties when sticking to them would take him away from theoretical work. So my question now is: would we do well on Aristotle's behalf to vindicate him in terms suggested by Williams's famous rejection of the supremacy of morality?

24

Aristotle Through Lenses from Bernard Williams

The answer, I think, is 'No'. This is because we have no reason to view Aristotle's elevation of the theoretical ideal as needing the protection of Williams's umbrella. There is no evidence that Aristotle is committed to encouraging theoretical activity even when it would imply ignoring recognized moral duties. If anything, we have evidence for ascribing to him the contrary view. My claim here is based on the connection which Aristotle draws in the *Ethics* and the *Politics* between theoretical activity and leisure (*scholē*)[3]. He proposes theoretical activity as the supremely appropriate occupant of the leisure-sphere, a sphere which many people populate with nothing but trivial, even personally harmful, pleasures, or with pastimes that merely constitute a needed pause from practical toil.[4]). My point is that there is no reason why we should not take Aristotle to view leisure as something that kicks in only when there are no conflicting duties of justice etc. Aristotle's morally good person (the kind of person whose judgment is 'canonical' in such matters[5]) would not regard her- or himself as *being at leisure* at a time when he or she is supposed to be attending to some important practical duty, whether to the city, to the family, or perhaps of a prudential nature. Aristotle's highlighting of the theoretical *life* (this by contrast with particular episodes of theoretical activity) surely implies that those who take his lesson to heart will plan their lives so as to be free of a lot of the ambitious or strictly unnecessary social obligations in which many people immerse themselves. And in general it is possible to live according to such a plan without riding rough-shod over the basic core of moral duties. Thus nothing in the text forces us to see Aristotle as holding, in line with Williams, that the theoretical sage would have good reason to ignore items belonging to this core.

Interpreters who worried that Aristotle's elevation of the theoretical ideal condones neglect of family, dodging of burdens such as military service, and fraud committed to get money for research, were almost certainly working from a particular model of what it is to regard something as the highest human end. According to this model, given mileage by John Stuart Mill (and also in an indirect way by Kant[6]), for an end E to be highest is for it to be the

---

[3]   *Nicomachean Ethics* X, 1177b1–25; *Politics* VII, 1334a10–38; VIII, 1337b30–1338a13.

[4]   *Nicomachean Ethics* X, 1176b9–1177a1; *Politics* VIII, 1337b35–1338a1.

[5]   *Nicomachean Ethics* III, 1113a23–34.

[6]   The point is not that Kant's *summum bonum* plays the same part in his system as Mill's does in his, since this is clearly false. However, Kant

determinant of morally right action, i.e. an action is right (or subject-ively right) if and only if it is (or is reasonably judged) optimal for promoting E. The view that results from substituting 'E' with 'the activity of theoretical wisdom' is not only grotesque in itself but there is no independent evidence for ascribing it to Aristotle. That is: there is no independent evidence for ascribing to him the view that an action or type of action represents the morally right thing to do just if and when it is optimal for promoting the activity of theor-etical wisdom. If Aristotle appears to be committed to this position, the appearance almost certainly springs from the assumption that the only coherent way to treat E as the highest good is to assign it the role of *determinant of all right or morally appropriate action*. But this is a gratuitous assumption, for at least two reasons. (a) Philosophers can leave aside the question of *right*ness altogether and still ask, of the various goods in human life, which of them deserves to be considered the paramount good. Such philosophers may embrace the view that for E to be the paramount good is for E to be the good that ought to be maximally promoted. But this says only that the pursuit of *other goods* should always be subordinate to pursuit of E. It does not say that promotion of E should always take precedence over all practical considerations whatsoever. Thus the view allows for the moral necessity of keeping a promise simply because it is a promise (there being no extraordinary circumstances) regardless of whether keeping or breaking it leads to better results in terms of E. Moreover, (b) there can be and have been ways of treating E as the highest good that do not involve pursuing E to the maximum even as compared with other *goods*. Several philosophers have noted in recent years that there are ways of honouring something *most* – of re-garding it as most precious and valuable – that do not involve looking to maximize it, either in one's own life or in general. Arguably, for example, one would be honouring some end E most if one approaches it as the most godlike or perfect possibility available in human life, or as the good that most deserves to be pursued for its own sake alone. Aristotle sees the activity of theoretical wisdom as fitting these cri-teria. Another way of treating E as the highest good would be to treat it as the condition of value of all other goods, as Aristotle does

mistakenly thought that ancient theories of the *summum bonum* were heter-onomous accounts of moral rightness (*Critique of Practical Reason*, §§ 64–65). And Mill seems to have thought this too (see the beginning of *Utilitarianism*). All this has helped spread the impression that the ancient systems were consequentialist attempts to derive the right from the good.

in *Nicomachean Ethics* I. 12. Under these interpretations, regarding *E* as the highest good does not entail seeking to promote *E* in all circumstances even at the expense of recognized duties or to the neglect of all other goods. Here I only sketch some possible positions.[7] The main point for now is that if we allow Aristotle to be operating in terms of one or another of these alternative models of what it is for something to play the role of 'highest human end', and if in addition we understand 'leisure' intelligently, we can attribute to him large swathes of common-sense morality – including the assumption that the basic core of morality always has first claim on us – while allowing him to accord pre-eminence to the activity of theoretical wisdom.

That said, one can all the same point to an interesting resemblance between this Aristotelian ideal and Williams's scepticism about the necessary over-ridingness of moral duty. Each philosopher is seeking to liberate his audience from the grip of a stiflingly powerful idea which comes embedded in a mass of emotions and expressions widely shared or at least paid lip-service to throughout the respective culture. With Williams the adversary descends from a conception of morality as in fact a sort of religion or religion-substitute whose claim on its adherents (and all rational beings should be its adherents) annihilates any rival consideration, in the style of the monotheistic god. Aristotle's adversary is the notion that the pinnacle of human existence is successful political leadership (which itself can be and was interpreted in a range of more and less crude, and more and less subversive, ways), and that this is the only serious goal for those who entertain the ambition of leading superlative lives, so that anyone who sets it aside who might otherwise have pursued it is a wimp or an eccentric or not fully grown-up. There is considerable evidence from philosophical and non-philosophical literature of the period that this was the accepted view of many educated people.

The fact that Aristotle's theoretical ideal is put forward as an alternative to a certain notion of *the absolute pinnacle of human existence* shows that in this part of his *Ethics* he has moved beyond ethics for ordinary citizens: he is now promoting one kind of extraordinary and iconic achievement (or contribution) as against another. By contrast, the quasi-religious approach to morality which Williams is countering tends to focus away from extraordinary achievement. More important for this approach is the task of circumscribing carefully the scope of genuine moral duty. This is because without clear circumscription

---

[7] For more discussion, see S. Broadie, *Aristotle and Beyond: Essays on Metaphysics and Ethics*, (Cambridge: Cambridge University Press, 2007), chs. 9–12.

the demands of that kind of morality or attitude to morality can easily seem, or be, overwhelmingly consuming for all but a few. But attaching great importance to a clear boundary, and a special quasi-religious importance to what lies within it, can (though it certainly need not) lead to a sort of flattening out of everything outside. It can come to seem as if all external (the moralistic equivalent of 'profane') undertakings are at best straightforwardly optional, or of objectively neutral worth. And this can easily develop into the position that each is valuable (whether to the agent or absolutely) just to the extent of fitting in with a preference which the agent happens to have. Such a position would have been obviously repugnant not only to Aristotle but to those of his contemporaries who placed high political success above theoretical achievement in the scale of human values. Both sides in that ancient argument took it for granted that some pursuits objectively deserve to be taken immensely seriously, by contrast with others that are more or less worthless. Williams's position on this is (to me) less clear, but is certain to be more sophisticated. But I think he would be hard pressed to make it generally convincing that just *any* powerful, or to oneself deeply meaningful, preference could give one adequate reason for neglecting what would normally be considered a significant moral obligation. It may be that the plausibility of Williams's rejection of the overridingness of moral duty depends on our willingness to allow that some morally neutral projects or activities are objectively much more important than others.

Williams's dialectic about 'morality, the peculiar institution' crucially depends on the full secularization of morality. By accepting this through and through Williams was able to discern, as he thought, the real possibility that morality, such a deeply important but nonetheless fully human set of practices and attitudes, is something that individuals might on occasion reasonably set aside in pursuit of one or another other kind of deeply important human concern. By contrast and interestingly, Aristotle's dialectic in defence of his theoretical ideal depends in part on the argument that although the great political leader is indeed godlike, the brilliant philosopher or scientist is more godlike still.[8]

2.

I have been considering whether Williams-style scepticism about the over-ridingness of moral duty is a tool to be reached for by someone

---

[8]   *Nicomachean Ethics* I, 1094b9–9; X. 7–8.

who wants to defend Aristotle's stance on the theoretical ideal, and I have argued that the defender does not need that tool. I am now going to look at Aristotle's position in the light of another typically Williamsian question. In a general form this is the question of what we should say when there is possible divergence between the principles and type of motivation that control or even define a given practice, institution, attitude, or disposition, and the principles and type of motivation that come into play when the value of the entire practice or attitude etc. is up for assessment. The field to which Williams most famously applies this question is that of common-sense morality on the one hand, and, on the other, what he called 'government-house utilitarianism'.[9] In his picture, Government House for purely consequentialist reasons upholds the existence of commonsense or traditional morality complete with its beliefs that right action in signal instances is not determined by reference to the general consequences, and that we should do what is right just because it is right and should encourage and admire conduct from this motive in others. An interesting point about this situation, already discussed by Sidgwick, is that life on the commonsense level would run better (or so it seems plausible to think) if its participants remained locked in their belief that commonsense morality, with its emphasis on the pure motive of duty, is the whole story about how people should live.[10] If so, then Government House would need to keep its own position secret from the people. This follows because it is not enough, logically, for Government House simply to *have* its own aim. Government House cannot make sense to itself unless it endorses its aim as a practical 'ought' – but that amounts to endorsing a distinct morality of its own. Trying to keep this a secret would have political implications repugnant to most of us. This is in addition to difficulties arising for inmates of Government House with family or friends outside. The best solution to that (although hardly one that could be kept secret) would be the system of Plato's *Republic* whereby children with potential for government are separately educated from an early age; but like several other arrangements in the *Republic* this thankfully remains an impossible ideal. I am not so sure, however, that secrecy about the double standard is *in principle* necessary for things to run well. If the ordinary people could be counted on by everyone concerned to operate in terms of common-sense morality no matter what, and if Government House could be counted on by everyone

---

[9]   *Ethics and the Limits of Philosophy*, 109.
[10]   Cf. Sidgwick, *The Methods of Ethics* (London: Macmillan and Co., 1930), 489–92.

S. Broadie

concerned to continue to see this as the best means to achieving its own objectives, then both sides should find this a satisfactory symbiosis in which each operates exactly as it thinks it should, with each side regarding the other as deeply mistaken about morality, but with neither under any normative compulsion to try to convert the other. However, the 'ifs' of the previous sentence are as far removed from human reality as the assumptions of Plato's *Republic*.

I now want to ask whether similar questions arise when we look at some of Aristotle's remarks about theoretical activity. In *Politics* VII he writes:

> [Both in the case of individuals and in that of whole cities; cf. 1334a11–12] courage and endurance are required for the unleisurely part of life, and philosophy for leisure, temperance and justice for both, and especially in times of peace and leisure, for war compels people to be just and temperate, whereas the enjoyment of good fortune and the leisure that comes with peace tend to make them insolent. Those who seem to be the best off and to be in possession of every blessing, have special need of justice and temperance – for example, those (if such there be) who, as the poets say, dwell in the Islands of the Blest: they above all will need philosophy and temperance and justice, and all the more the more leisure they have, living in the midst of abundance. There is no difficulty in seeing why the state that would be happy and good ought to have those excellences. If it is disgraceful in people not to be able to use good things, it is still more so not to be able to use them in time of leisure – to show themselves excellent in unleisurely times and in war, but in peace-time and leisure no better than slaves (1334a22–40).[11]

Aristotle goes on to cite contemporary Sparta as an illustration of this kind of moral failure.

Now, is Aristotle here proposing theoretical activity ('philosophy') in the city as a safety valve for draining off the excess of material goods, and if so there is anything sinister in such a proposal? I have to admit that the passage by itself does not particularly prompt a suspicious reading; on the other hand, anyone who comes to it fresh from some of Williams's discussions might well want to pause and sniff round it for any possibly disturbing implication. This is what I shall do, but first we need to consider whether Aristotle would here

---

[11] *The Complete Works of Aristotle, The Revised Oxford Translation*, ed. Jonathan Barnes (Princeton: Princeton University Press, 1984), with some changes.

be contradicting things he says elsewhere about the activity of theoretical wisdom.

(i) In *NE* VI he raises this puzzle: given that *phronēsis* (practical wisdom) rules and gives orders about everything, doesn't it follow that it will be in charge of (*kuriōtera*) theoretical wisdom (*sophia*) – but how can this be, given (as he indicated earlier; cf. 1141a18–22), that of the two qualities *phronēsis* is the inferior? Aristotle's answer is that even if *phronēsis* gives orders *about* everything, it doesn't follow that it gives orders *to* everything. It does not use *sophia* for the sake of some further end as we use medicine for the sake of health, but on the contrary gives orders for its sake (1145a6–11). (ii) Then in *NE* X he emphasizes that political actions seek a distinct end beyond themselves, whether this end is power and honours or happiness for the leader himself and the citizens, whereas the exercise of theoretical wisdom seeks no end beyond itself and is therefore the more perfect form of happiness (1177b12–25; cf. I, 1097a28–b1). Both passages emphasize that 'philosophy' is free in the sense of not being subordinate to political objectives. Thus they may seem to be in tension with the thought that 'philosophy' serves a wealthy community by diverting some of the potentially *hubris*-generating material excess.

But on closer consideration the tension can be made to disappear. The *NE* VI passage can be taken as saying that it is not for *phronēsis* to tell *sophia* how to do research or what research to do. This embryonic version of the principle of academic freedom is, however, compatible with the idea that practical or political wisdom should be very glad to take advantage of, even exploit, theoretical activity's ability to soak up what might otherwise be a dangerous excess of leisure and material goods: which could be further developed into the idea that as far as wise rulers are concerned this safety-valve function is *the* reason why the state should look benignly on theoretical activity.[12] The typical theoretician might not agree with this managerial perspective, but what about Aristotle? Logically, he could agree with it – agree as a political philosopher, at least. And as a theoretical researcher himself into physics and metaphysics he logically need take no stand at all on this question. In a rather similar vein one can read the *NE* X passage as drawing a contrast between criteria of success: the success of excellent political action depends on its achieving whatever further good it was aiming at (e.g. military victory, provision against famine, etc.),[13]

---

[12]   Cf. Isocrates's approval of academic studies as at least keeping the young men from harmful pursuits (*Panathenaicus* 26–7).

[13]   Which does not, of course, entail that undertaking the political action does not count as meritorious unless it succeeds.

whereas the success of a piece of theoretical research depends entirely on whether it sets itself good questions and answers them well (or something like that), regardless of further consequences. On this interpretation, it is in principle an open question whether the theoreticians engage in the research just because they value this kind of activity only for its own sake or whether they do so as a service to the state – a hygienic service that helps keep the city free from the arrogance bred by wealth and idleness. Even where an activity's criterion of success is rigorously internal (Alistair MacIntyre's way of putting it), the motive for engaging in the activity at all, and the motive of outsiders in encouraging it, may look to the consequences of doing so.

Now even if Aristotle had distinguished between the motive for engaging in theoretical activity and the criterion for excellent engagement, (and whether he did make this distinction is far from clear), I am sure his actual view would be that true theoretical excellence engages in its own characteristic activity out of love of it for its own sake.[14] But would he have any good reason think this if he also admitted (what seems to be true) that bringing an 'impure' motive to bear does not entail lowering the standards of success? Should we saddle him with the view that although a lowering of standards is not *entailed*, experience shows that having the impure motive may very well lead to this decline? But is this true, and what is the evidence?

I believe that as far as Aristotle himself is concerned this worry about standards would be beside the point, or anyway would not be the main point. I think what would stick in his throat is the fact that a scientist or philosopher who engaged in the activity of *sophia* for the sake, ultimately, of order in the community, would after all be subordinating *sophia* to political wisdom or *phronēsis*: and this would be abhorrent to Aristotle even if it were somehow guaranteed to him that this form of subordination would never end by twisting the internal standards of theoretical research. It is less than godlike to engage in the activity of *sophia* from anything but the sheer love of it (since Aristotle's god can have no other activity and no other motive for engaging in it), and Aristotle wants human beings, or at least some human beings, to be as godlike as they can (*NE* X. 8). True, human theoretical activity is something that can function as a

---

[14]   My wording may seem to represent this love as a feature of theoretical excellence as such, but as a human disposition it can be shared by those who admire and support theoretical activity for its own sake without themselves taking part in it. Even so there is a difference between loving it from a distance and loving it from inside.

safety-valve for the superfluity of wealth, but Aristotle's line would be surely be that this is only a side effect, and that any theoretician who allowed it to be the central motive for leading the theoretical life would show abject misunderstanding. Such a stance would imply that theoretical activity is essentially a sort of blood-letting or a fire-blanket for stifling the natural consequences of material superfluity, and not necessarily more effective in this role than if the leaders used up extra wealth on mindless entertainments for the people – making sure, of course, that these were peaceful and did not incapacitate people for practical duties and cultivating practical virtues. Instead, Aristotle surely thinks that if peaceful and virtuous societies tend to over-generate wealth, this is because in the overall scheme of things such superfluity has a purpose, its purpose being to support philosophy and the theoretical sciences. This perspective, in rampant contrast with the reasons-internalism of Williams, assumes a natural teleology of leisure: human leisure has its own rightful end, whether or not most people aware of it and whether or not they desire that end.

Yes, *of course* theoretical occupations, in so far as they soak up some of the superfluity, can be looked on as means for preventing wealth from becoming an evil; but the right attitude reverses the means-end relationship so as to treat theoretical activity as an end that justifies and even glorifies the superfluity, not merely makes it safe. To expand on this point just a little: it is natural to treat prosperity as a great good – not just as a 'preferred indifferent', as the Stoics said. We expend so much effort in trying to avoid its opposite. But given the tendency to excess and the dangers consequent on that, how can we make it stably true that prosperity really is a good? That it is, is a basic assumption on which almost everyone every-where operates, including (of course) the poor and least educated. It seems to me that when Aristotle lines up theoretical activity as *the* preferred candidate for the role of occupying prosperity-funded leisure, he is giving a solution to the problem of how to make sure that that basic and natural human assumption is or remains true. We preserve its truth not by treating superfluous prosperity as a potential evil needing to be choked back so that from now on it has no effects or none that add anything to capture a sensible person's interest – but instead by looking for civic leaders who use excess to promote new noble enterprises – for example the pursuit of theoretical wisdom[15] – and to promote them just because they are

[15]   Other examples of 'higher' activities could be inserted into the argument, either in addition or instead.

noble. For consider civic leaders who approve of or tolerate the pursuit of theoretical wisdom simply as a safety valve: this attitude of theirs unconsciously calls into question the universal assumption that prosperity is a great good – and yet they invoke this very assumption at every turn in making and executing policy. Hence civic leaders escape self-contradiction only if they admire and value for their own sake the theoretical pursuits and any other noble enterprises.

There is a further Aristotelian reason why civic leaders should cultivate this attitude in themselves and the city at large. Given that a society at peace, and not crippled by poverty or some other major cause of backwardness, can be expected, if it practises the practical virtues, to increase its holdings and become much richer in just a few generations, people may easily draw the eventually corrupting lesson that the real value of general virtuous practice lies in its wealth-generating tendency. According to Aristotle something like this was what went wrong with the Spartans in the early 4th century. But if the civic mind accepts that the exercise of one noble quality, namely *sophia*, has its value entirely in itself since it explicitly and on every level aims to generate nothing beyond itself, then the city has one uniquely clear example to help it maintain a non-instrumentalist attitude towards virtuous activity in general, and hence towards virtuous practical activity. If leaders share this attitude, not only will they be less vulnerable to temptation to use their position to pile up personal wealth and power, but in their remit regarding the moral education of future citizens (ideally, for Aristotle and his audience, a central duty of leaders[16]), they will be bearers of an unconfused standard concerning the value of virtuous activity in general. To that extent they will be better as leaders – and the successful activity of the virtuous civic leader is beyond doubt a pinnacle of human life and happiness. But according to Aristotle there is a higher human pinnacle and a more perfect form of human happiness, and it belongs to the truly excellent leader to recognize that this is so, and to make provision for it for its own sake.[17]

Returning in conclusion to Bernard Williams, I shall briefly consider a situation quite different from this Aristotelian ideal, namely one in which on the one hand a philistine political leadership tolerates the theoretical life led by some of the citizens as harmless and usefully absorbing the otherwise dangerous energy of some of the Alcibiades-

---

[16]   It was a commonplace that the task of the *politikos* is to make the citizens virtuous; see e.g. *Nicomachean Ethics* I, 1099b28-32.
[17]   Theoretical excellence is godlike but still, for Aristotle, a thoroughly human ideal.

Aristotle Through Lenses from Bernard Williams

characters of this world, while on the other hand the theoreticians themselves value what they do just for its own sake. As will be obvious, this parallels government-house utilitarianism in relation to common-sense morality. In connection with that situation, I said that although the moral views contradict each other, knowledge of this fact on either side is perhaps not inevitably a threat, because we can conceive of a situation of such shared knowledge in which each side promotes the aims of the other simply by carrying on as it thinks it should. However, we can easily understand why in the real world Sidgwick would advise Government House to keep its policy secret. But is it so clear, in the parallel case, that it would be wiser for the philistine leaders (by their own standard of wisdom) to conceal from the theoreticians their own very different evaluation of theoretical activity? No doubt it would be better for *the theoreticians* if the politicians prized the activity of the theoreticians just for its own sake – they would be even more eager to fund it. But in the scenario I am considering, they tolerate it as a safety-measure in so far as it diverts the energy of very clever people who might otherwise make trouble for them. My question is whether the whole situation would be a better one for *the politicians*, i.e. from their point of view as political managers, if they, like Government House in the parallel case, hypocritically pretended to share the values of the theoreticians, despising them in secret rather than openly. Hypocrisy in this case would not be a matter of an elite pretending to respect the masses for the sake of the masses, but of one elite pretending to respect another elite for the sake of the masses. In both situations pretense is only worthwhile to the managers if it makes a positive difference to the welfare of the larger population for which they are responsible. But the likelihood of this seems much clearer in the case on which Sidgwick comments than in that of the theoreticians. In this latter ugly (although highly abstract) scenario, the theoreticians as such are instruments of state, not beneficiaries. Given that Government House *has* no respect for them it is not so obvious why it should *show* any.

University of St Andrews
sjb15@st-andrews.ac.uk

What is the Matter with Matter, According to Plotinus?

A.A. LONG

Abstract

Modern science is not linguistically original in hypothesizing the existence of *dark* matter. For Plotinus, the matter that underlies all perceptible objects, is essentially obscure and describable only in the negative terms of what it lacks by way of inherent properties. In formulating this theory of absolute matter, Plotinus took himself to be interpreting both Plato and Aristotle, with the result that his own position emerges as a highly original and equivocal synthesis of this tradition. Plotinus did not claim that matter is nothing, but the puzzling status he attributes to it can be aptly compared to Berkeley's doctrine that material substance is a self-contradictory notion.

1.

Matter, the most generic term for what physicists study, has become puzzlingly elusive in scientific parlance today. Everything in the cosmos consists of matter, but what is that? Some matter, we hear, is 'ordinary', consisting of atoms, but most of it is 'dark' and is indescribable in the standard model of particle physics. Together with the so-called 'dark energy' permeating space, dark matter accounts for 95% of the world's mass-energy content. We can infer its presence from the behavior of visible matter, but dark matter as such (hence its name) is of unknown composition.[1]

Plotinus, the latest ancient Greek philosopher of paramount genius, would have sympathized with the modern physicists' difficulties in describing and defining matter. He even anticipated them in calling *hyle*, his own term for matter, 'dark' (*skoteinos*).[2] Plotinus acknowledged the properties of perceptible matter, taking their presence to be straightforwardly evident from our experience of ordinary objects like trees, stones, and animals – bodily items, spatially extended, and endowed with qualities that impinge on our senses. If all that we mean by matter is the visible and tangible stuff of which ordinary

---

[1] I take this information from the Wikipedia article on 'dark matter', which is based on references dating to the year 2013.

[2] *Ennead* 2.4.10.

doi:10.1017/S135824611600028X   ©The Royal Institute of Philosophy and the contributors 2016

objects consist – the wood of the bed, the bronze of the spear, the flesh and bones of the animal – there is no linguistic or conceptual problem for Plotinus. But what are we to say or think, according to him, when we extend the scope of matter beyond ordinary objects?

Is there a further matter of which perceptible matter, in all its variety, is ultimately composed, a more or a most primitive feature of the world's physical make-up? The favourite ancient answer to this question had been affirmative – to wit, a set of four elements, comprising earth, air, fire, and water. Earth, air, fire and water were generally understood to be qualitative terms, each of them refer-ring not to a single, homogeneous stuff – water in the sense of H_2O for instance – but to the following set of primary qualities or combina-tions thereof: hot, cold, moist, and dry, all of which admit of change and degree. Qualities of what, we may ask, to continue the analysis? The classic answer – the answer of the Aristotelian school-had been 'prime matter'.[3]

Plotinus's problem, and its nominal affinity to the dark matter of modern physics, can now be stated. In order to serve as the physical foundation of everything, absolute matter cannot be identified with definite or determinate things, such as the four elements. For in that case it could not serve as their foundation too. Matter as such or matter *simpliciter,* to use Aristotelian language, must always be potential and analogical rather than actual, drawing its descriptive identity from the composite things of which it is the matter – for instance the bronze of the spear, the wood of the bed, etc. Is there, then, any such entity as prime matter if that expression signifies a completely indefinite and indeterminate foundation for things? How can we know that such matter is in any sense real and not a mere figment or convenience of our conceptual scheme?[4] I want to show how and why Plotinus grapples with these deep issues.

He is not willing to say outright that matter is nothing. Matter is, in his view, a precondition for the existence of bodies, three-dimensionally extended and perceptible objects; but taken by itself, matter,

---

[3] For the details and interpretative controversies, see M.L. Gill, *Aristotle on Substance* (Princeton, 1989).

[4] Aristotle had described matter *per se,* which he also calls the ultimate substratum, as 'neither a particular thing nor of a particular quantity nor spoken of in any of the other ways by which a being is determined' (*Metaph.* 7.3, 1029a20). Similarly, the Aristotelian commentator, Alexander: 'Absolute matter is a shapeless and amorphous nature, with no delineation according to its own account', *Comm. in De an.* p. 3, 27ff. Bruns. Plotinus frequently echoes these statements and adapts them to his own metaphysical scheme.

What is the Matter with Matter, According to Plotinus?

according to Plotinus, is not bodily or physical stuff or anything with determinate quality or quantity. Taken by itself, matter is completely imperceptible and amorphous. We know it only by a kind of inference from phenomena. Try, as we may, to imagine matter independently of form, we find ourselves completely in the dark, trying to picture the least accessible of the world's contents. And yet, however hard it is to specify, matter is there and is necessary. So much by way of introduction to the issues this paper will raise.

2.

I have chosen to discuss Plotinus because, at this late stage of my career, I find him one of the most challenging (and certainly the most difficult) of all the Greek philosophers (to whom I was first introduced in the years 1958–1960, as a Classics student at University College London, a few steps away from the home of the Royal Institute of Philosophy in Gordon Square). Plotinus, working on his grand metaphysical scheme in the first decades of the third century of our era, resists dividing the world dualistically into thought and extension, or animate and inanimate, or body and spirit. These binary categories are inapt, he postulates, because every existent thing has its primary source in everlasting and transcendent Unity, which he also calls God or Father or The Good. For everything that exists there is a corresponding idea, derived from Unity; or rather, existence (meaning determinate, stable reality), depends on what can be thought. Here Plotinus echoes Parmenides, one of his most hallowed predecessors, whom he takes (correctly, in my opinion) to identify being and thinking. Can ultimate matter be thought? If it cannot, it must exist only in some equivocal sense. Ultimate matter, as envisioned by Plotinus, is equivocal indeed, but it is not an incoherent notion. Its obscurity is essential to the queer role it plays in his metaphysical scheme.

I will now give a brief genealogy of the notions of matter that Plotinus inherited from earlier Greek philosophers.[5] I will then

---

[5]   My procedure is deliberately short on a vast range of exegetical questions, which typically predominate in treatments of Plotinus. As the interpreter of Plato that he took himself to be, Plotinus presupposed his readers' familiarity with the entire previous traditions of Greek philosophy. I will highlight only a selection of this background, to the extent that it is necessary for following his main argument in *Ennead* II.4. The essential historical details are excellently treated by P. Kalligas in vol. 1 of his commentary,

work through a selection of his statements, taking them mainly from his short essay *On Matter*.[6] This procedure will enable me to ask in more detail, 'What is the matter with matter?' from his stance. In conclusion, I will ask whether the dark matter of modern physics and the darkness Plotinus attributes to ultimate matter have anything more than a name in common.

3.

Plotinus begins his essay with the expression 'so-called matter'. This evasive-sounding phrase is appropriate because his Greek word *hyle*, conventionally translated by 'matter', starts its linguistic life meaning wood or timber; hence 'material' is often a better translation. Our English word 'matter' is derived from Latin *materia*. In Latin usage *materia*, like Greek *hyle*, primarily denotes wood or timber, deriving that name from the word *mater* in the sense of *mother* earth or parent.

From the outset, then, *hyle* is a metaphorical term standing generically for what things are made of (for instance wood) and then extended to signify the ultimate foundation of physical things. The earliest Greek cosmologists did not draw on the term, but they operated with comparable metaphors. Empedocles called earth, air, fire and water, which are his four primary beings, 'roots'. Soon this quartet was given the name 'elements' (*stoicheia*), a term which is also a metaphor for the world's basic physical components, taken from the Greek word for the letters of the alphabet. 'Seeds' (*semata*) or 'beginnings' (*archai*) were other metaphors that early cosmologists drew upon, to try to capture a notion like our idea of basic matter in ordinary speech. The point to emphasize here is that matter, signifying the world's physical foundations, was and always has been a metaphor-a theoretical notion lacking any fixed empirical reference in itself. Hence we are able to keep using the term even when our

---

The Enneads of Plotinus, trans. by E. Fowden and N. Pilavachi (Princeton and Oxford, 2014).

[6] *Ennead* 2.4. The title ascribed to the work by Porphyry, Plotinus's editor, is *On the Two Kinds of Matter*. I will be concerned here only with the kind of matter that Plotinus posits for the physical world as distinct from the non-physical matter that he calls 'intelligible'. The excerpts that I cite from *On Matter* are in my own translation. I am presently preparing a translation and commentary on the whole work for the series *The Enneads of Plotinus*, eds. J. Dillon and A. Smith (Parmenides Publishing).

scientific models have completely changed. You may care to reflect on the checkered history of modern attempts to give a final definite description to matter – the periodic table of elements; protons, neutrons, and electrons; quarks; strings etc.

Plotinus was familiar with the four Empedoclean elements and also with the atoms of Democritus and Epicurus. From our modern perspective these theories, especially Epicurean atomism, are among the most important antecedents of early European science with its understanding of matter as the ultimate physical make-up of everything. That is because elements and atoms were theoretical notions that envisioned the world's foundations in discrete corpuscular, or what we call 'material', terms. Plotinus, however, totally rejected corpuscular theories of ultimate matter. His cosmology, like that of Plato, Aristotle, and Stoic philosophers, invokes reason, structure, and design as the primary factors explaining the way the world is perceived to function. Unlike modern bottom-up, material models of explanation, with the world conceived as evolving from simpler to more complex states, Plotinus's philosophical ancestors largely proceeded by means of a top-down explanatory model. On their view, matter does not evolve, under its own causal power, into derivative elements and life-types. Rather, matter is taken to be the recipient of pre-existing *forms* or formative principles, and it is they (commonly called *logoi*, also translatable as formulae) that energize and characterize matter. (Thus, in Aristotle's understanding of sexual reproduction, the male parent's sperm endows uterine matter with specific animal form.)

Plotinus sets the scene by stating what he takes to be the shared view of Platonists, Aristotelians, and Stoics:

> Text 1: All who theorize about so-called matter (*hyle*) agree in describing it as a certain **substrate** (*hypokeimenon*) and **receptacle** (*hypodoche*) of **forms** (*eide*)... But they disagree ... as to what the substrate nature is, and how and of what it is receptive. (*Ennead* II.4.)

To unpack this difficult sentence, we need to clarify the words substrate, receptacle, and forms. All three of these terms are basic to Plotinus's own understanding of matter.

The first thing to emphasize concerning Text 1 is the absence of physical determinacy from this preliminary account of matter. Plotinus, as he continues, states that some of those who share the *substrate* and *receptacle* theory (he means Stoic philosophers) do attribute 'body' to matter, whereas other philosophers (Platonists and Aristotelians) take matter as such to be 'bodiless' (*asomatos*).

However, the Stoics' corporeal matter, is not an empirical entity but theoretical plasticine, as it were. This is how it is described by Calcidius in his commentary on Plato's *Timaeus*:

> Text 2: They (Stoic philosophers) say that what underlies everything that has qualities is matter, which is the prime substance (*essentia*) of all things, or their most primitive basis, [a body] without appearance by its own nature and without form.[7]

Here we can see how Stoic matter, corporeal though it is, fits Plotinus's generic description of matter as a substrate and receptacle of forms, i.e. a foundation of reality that is completely inert and amorphous.

'Substrate' (in Greek *hypokeimenon*) is an Aristotelian word. Plotinus explains the term as follows:

> Text 3: About the receptacle (*hypodoche*) of bodies, let it be said that there must be something underlying (*hypokeimenon*) bodies, which is different from the bodies themselves, as is made clear by the changing of the elements (*stoicheia*) into one another ... There is a change from one form (*eidos*) into another, and so there remains that which has received the form of the engendered thing and lost the other one. (*Ennead* II.4.6)

The 'remaining' item, what receives the form and persists through the change, is matter in the sense of *substrate*. Plotinus exemplifies this notion by reference to metallurgy – making a cup out of gold, and then smelting it down again: the cup comes to be and ceases to be, while the gold of which it is made persists. The gold, as *substrate* for the cup, exemplifies the proximate matter that ordinary objects are made of. Proximate matter explains how ordinary objects move and change, while also retaining their basic physical identity. In this account of proximate matter Plotinus follows Aristotle to the letter, borrowing Aristotle's instance of gold.[8] What, then are we to say about ultimate matter? Is there a persisting substrate for all things, even after they have been stripped bare, as it were, of all their perceptible properties?

This question brings us to Plotinus's other term for matter, *hypodoche*, translated 'receptacle.' Plotinus took this metaphor from Plato. Here is a portion of what Plato says about the term:

> Text 4: That nature which receives all the bodies ... has never in any way whatever taken on any characteristic similar to any of the

---

[7]   Calcidius, *In Tim.* 290 (*SVF* 1.86).
[8]   Cf. Aristotle, *Physics* 1.7.

What is the Matter with Matter, According to Plotinus?

things that enter it ... This is why we shouldn't call the mother or receptacle of what has come to be ... and of what is perceptible, either earth or air, fire or water, or any of their compounds or their constituents. But if we speak of it as an invisible and characterless sort of thing, one that receives all things and shares in a most perplexing way in what is intelligible, a thing extremely difficult to comprehend, we shall not be misled. (*Timaeus* 51a)

Plato introduces the obscure and characterless 'receptacle', which he also calls space, as the container of bodies, and therefore as extending throughout the physical world. This text along with its attendant doctrine was foremost in the mind of Plotinus when he attempted to clarify his own notion of ultimate matter. What I have called the Stoic plasticine notion, as cited in Text 2, was also influenced by Plato, but with the difference, observed by Plotinus, that the Stoic receptacle is not bodiless but taken to be a completely amorphous body.

Bodiless container, amorphous body – these are very obscure expressions. What philosophical thoughts are driving them? The answer has two related aspects, one I will call idealist and the other realist. The idealist aspect is the notion that ordinary things derive their identity, quality, and quantity from their forms or structures or intelligible natures, expressible in definitions or archetypes, principles that are fully accessible only to the mind. The realist aspect is the evident fact that ordinary objects are composites of a specific form (e.g. cat-form, daffodil-form) and of that in which the individual instance of that form is expressed or manifested – their particular physical and bodily make-up, like the wood of this bed or the gold of this cup. Ordinary objects are not bodiless containers or amorphous bodies, but in order for them to possess the specific identity, quantity and quality that they have, they each require, according to the theories I am discussing, a form-containing constituent entitled matter. The matter, then, is what *underlies* the form, or what *receives* the form, and enables the form to have magnitude or physical extension. In this analysis, then, form and matter are essentially correlative notions, presupposing one another, and not instantiated independently of one another. You cannot have form without matter or matter without form.

This co-dependence and correlativity fit Aristotle's and the Stoics' accounts of form and matter. When we study natural objects, we can focus either on what they are made of and on what persists throughout their life or existence, i.e. their material constituents, or on the forms that make them the particular things that they are – a cat or a tree etc., of a certain size, colour, etc. But Platonists such as Plotinus see a need to hugely complicate this analysis of form and matter. The complexity arises because, in their top-down analysis of reality, the forms that make natural objects particular cats or trees etc. are not fully and perfectly present in the objects' feline or arboreal matter. The matter of such objects is what makes them physical repositories of non-physical formative principles. Physical objects in Platonism are material copies of immaterial ideal substances, as David Sedley explained to this Institute in his December 2014 lecture on Plato's Theory of Forms. (You may care to recall Wordsworth's 'shades of the prison-house' that turn the 'light' of Plato's Forms into 'the light of common day' from his famous poem *Intimations of Immortality*). For Plotinus ultimate matter is an *insubstantial* substrate and receptacle of immaterial formative principles. In what follows we will see how he struggles to get this meaning across.

4.

In a systematic inventory of the perceptible world Plotinus sets out the following terms:

> Text 5: Matter, form, composite, simple bodies, composite bodies, accidents and attributes, relation, quantity, quality, and motion. (*Ennead* VI.3.2)

This list of originally Aristotelian terms would be quite straightforward if Plotinus, like Aristotle, had regarded individual things - this tree, this cat - as the physical world's primary beings or independent substances. Instead, as a Platonist, Plotinus treats *physis*, his name for the physical world of natural objects, as the domain of only derivative beings. He even calls perceptible objects such as stones, trees and cats, *images*, the originals of which are the supra-sensible Intelligible Forms. While Plotinus is quite ready to write on occasion as if perceptible things have intrinsic Aristotelian forms and corresponding matter, this is approximate language. The only unequivocal Plotinian beings, are purely incorporeal, intelligible and intelligent entities, objects and activities of divine thought. Perceptible properties and natures are projections into matter that fall short of full reality.

We can now see that Plotinus's two terms for his 'so-called matter', substrate and receptacle (Text 1), belong to two different earlier theories. One of these theories, the Aristotelian substrate theory, is well designed to identify the proximate material of natural or manufactured things such as trees or cups (the wood or the gold that underlies such forms) and to account for the primary elements of which wood and gold are formed. Neither proximate matter nor primary elements, however, account for the nature of matter as such, basic physical reality, as it were. The other theory, the Platonic receptacle and its Stoic successor, fulfill this latter role by positing a changeless, spatial container for all physical objects into which they come and go. This theory, however, does not explain the composition of proximate matter, what makes it golden or arboreal, nor does it explain why there are just four primary elements. In addition, neither theory fully faces the question of why there is a physical world, consisting of transient bodies, in the first place.

By synthesizing the substrate and the receptacle theories, Plotinus goes some way to responding to these points. In the process, however, he leaves us with an ultimate matter that is so dark that it is only describable in the negative terms of lack, or privation, or what it is not.

5.

The essay from which I drew Text 5 (*Ennead* VI.3) concerns the kinds of equivocal being that pertain to the physical world of change and flux. After positing matter as common to all bodies, Plotinus asks whether matter may be regarded as a genus. The Stoics had called their plasticine notion of material substrate 'primary substance' [Text 2] and so made it generic and foundational to everything that exists. Plotinus responds that matter cannot be a true genus because it has no essence; hence it does not confer anything substantive on objects. Substance, he argues, must exclusively be a function of form, intelligibility, structure.

May we, then, dispense with ultimate matter, and substitute for it a single genus of 'perceptible substance', call it body, that is essential and common to all terrestrial things – stones, earth, water, plants, and animals? The problem with that proposal, Plotinus urges, is that bodies are not uniform – some are complex and organic; others, like the four elements, are 'more matterish' (*hylikotera*), meaning less unitary and less determinate.[9] Body, in other words, is too diverse a notion to constitute the ultimate foundation of all perceptible objects. Ultimate matter on this view must be something more primitive and inchoate than even the simplest body. To get at it, we have to resort to the mental operation of trying to separate all form, even the simplest determination, from embodied things and physical elements.

[9] *Ennead* VI.3.9.

A.A. Long

Plotinus's notion of ultimate matter seems to face two paradoxes, one conceptual and the other ontological. The conceptual paradox is the indispensability of an essentially imperceptible and indescribable substrate to the analysis of perceptible objects. Plotinus explains his position thus (*Ennead* II.4.5):

> Text 6: Intellect discovers the doubleness of bodies. For it divides them until it arrives at something simple that cannot be further analyzed. But as long as possible, it proceeds into the depth of body. The depth of each body is matter. Therefore all matter is *dark*, because the formula (*logos*) is light. Intellect too is a formula. In seeing the formula that is on each thing, intellect takes what is below to be *dark* because it is beneath the light. It is like the way the eye, whose form is light, when it gazes at the light and at colours, which are lights, states that what lies beneath the colours is *dark and material*, concealed by the colours.

To do philosophical justice to this passage, we need to take light and dark quite literally, albeit with reference to mental vision. The obvious aspect or component of a body is its perceptible form. But bodies also have imperceptible depth. How do we know? By analogy with dark as the absence of light, Plotinus infers that bodies have a dark underside, consisting of the absence of what we can actually perceive of their make-up. Ultimate matter, on this account, is essentially something that defies description and perception.[10] We know of it only in the way that we know that if we turn off a light, dark supervenes. Dark simply is the absence of light; there is nothing else to it.

Plotinus articulates the ontological paradox in the following passage (*Ennead* III.6.7. 3):

> Text 7: Matter is an image and a phantom of bulk (*ongkos*), a striving for substantiality, a stable instability ... it has no strength but is lacking in all being. Whatever announcement it makes, therefore, is a lie, and if it appears great, it is small, if more, it is less; its apparent being is not real, but a sort of fleeting frivolity; hence the things that seem to come be in it are frivolities, nothing but phantoms in a phantom, like something in a mirror which really exists in one place, but is reflected in another; it seems to be filled, and holds nothing; it is all seeming.

Bulk or solidity is basic to any notion of body, but whence do bodies derive their bulk? From their matter, surely? But ultimate matter as

---

[10] Cf. *Ennead* 1.8.9 where Plotinus repeats the notion of seeing the dark by cutting off the light of intellect.

What is the Matter with Matter, According to Plotinus?

such has no *real* bulk or solidity? Ultimate matter is a mere phantom of bulk. How do we deal with this regress? Does it mean that bulk or mass is in some sense illusory, a mere figment of our imagination?

Rather than answer that pressing question now, let me step back and say where I take Plotinus to be coming from in his mystifying statements about ultimate matter. Given his Aristotelian background, might we remove suggestions of paradox by interpreting the two quoted passages as rhetorical rather than doctrinal? As the substrate of the four elementary bodies, Aristotle's 'prime matter' is best interpreted as a purely conceptual or logical notion with no directly physical referent. The elementary qualities hot, cold, dry, and wet are basic to the simplest instances of Aristotelian matter that we can experience. There is no such Aristotelian *thing* as prime or ultimate matter. May we explain Plotinus correspondingly, as he himself sometimes suggests our doing?

Only up to a point, I respond, because ultimate matter, as understood by Plotinus, is absolutely necessary to the nature of the physical world. Ordinary objects, unlike ideal objects, are embodied. Embodiment is a function of ultimate matter as distinct from form. We cannot get at such matter, to examine it in the laboratory, because ultimate matter, as distinct from proximate matter, does not exist as a separable component of things. Yet it furnishes ordinary objects with the basic bodily properties that distinguish them from the ideal objects of thought, viz. spatial extension, changeableness, multiplicity, impermanence, and imperfection.

Plotinus also differs profoundly from Aristotle in crediting ultimate matter with supreme negative value – not as being 'evil', as some scholars like to say – but because ultimate matter negates the supreme positive value he attributes to determinate unity, identity, and intelligibility.[11] What makes ultimate matter bad, illusory, phantomlike, for Plotinus is its complete lack of substantive identity, determinacy, and unity. Its badness is a function of what it lacks.

Plotinus also differs from Aristotle in the way he distinguishes between intelligible, proximate, and ultimate matter. All three of these types of matter satisfy the generic concept of being 'a substrate and receptacle', but they fit the concept in the distinct ways that

---

[11] 'Evil' has inappropriate theological connotations. Hence I disagree with parts of D. O'Brien's account in his paper, 'Plotinus on matter and evil', in L.P. Gerson, ed. *The Cambridge Companion to Plotinus* (Cambridge, 1996), 171–95. For a more balanced interpretation of matter's badness, even to the point of granting it 'an element of goodness', see G. van Riel, 'Horizontalism or verticalism? Proclus vs Plotinus on the procession of matter', *Phronesis* 46 (2001), 129–53.

pertain to the three distinct levels of Plotinus's overall metaphysical scheme, to which I now turn.

Intelligible matter, as the substrate of Intelligible Forms, belongs to the level of Nous/Intellect and is therefore unqualifiedly good.[12] Proximate matter, as the substrate of perceptible forms, belongs to the level of Soul/Nature. Its value is correspondingly relative to the kind of phenomenal matter that it is, for instance, flesh, bone, bronze. Ultimate matter pertains to the bottom of this scheme, where forms have run out of all claims to substance, leaving only the residue of indeterminate substrate. In his essay on matter, Plotinus presents the topic in exactly this order, starting with the generic concept, and then passing, in turn, to intelligible matter, proximate matter, and finally, and at greatest length, ultimate matter.

Headed by the transcendent One, Plotinus's philosophy involves both a vertical and a horizontal dimension. The horizontal dimension has three aspects, ontological, cognitive, and axiological. The vertical dimension has five levels, ranging from the One down to ultimate matter, with a radical gap dividing the three incorporeal and eternal levels (One, Nous, and Soul) from the corporeal and mortal domain of Nature and the shadowy domain of ultimate matter.

I represent this scheme in the following diagram.[13]

Ontological status	**Mode of cognition**	**Value**
The One transcendence	immediate union	perfection

The One projects intelligible matter as substrate of **Nous**, so as to constitute the noetic realm of Intelligible Forms.

Nous being/actuality	intellection	goodness

Nous projects **Soul** as generator of perceptible form copies.

Soul intermediacy	discursive thought	variability

Soul projects form copies into matter, to constitute embodied **Nature**.

Nature appearance/body/animate things	perception	inferiority
Ultimate Matter privation	illusion	badness

---

[12] See *Ennead* II.4.5.

[13] For a clear introduction to Plotinus's metaphysical categories, see P. Remes, *Neoplatonism* (Berkeley & Los Angeles, 2008), 47–59.

What is the Matter with Matter, According to Plotinus?

According to this hierarchical scheme, ontology, cognition, and value are so related to one another that unity and stability are their common measure at the top and complete privation of stability and determinacy are their common measure at the bottom, as signified by ultimate matter. Plotinus's scheme states, then, that as things or levels become less unitary and stable and determinate, they become less real, less cognitively accessible, and less good. The scheme is an obvious successor to Plato's famous Sun, Line, and Cave analogies (*Republic* 6–7) but it differs importantly from these prototypes by its explicit incorporation of the principles One, Soul, and Matter. Plato presupposes the existence of bodies, and the inferior status of bodies as perceptible, non-knowable, changeable items, but he does not clearly explain why the world contains them. In Plotinus, Soul, the principle of animate life, creates bodies by generating perceptible images of Intelligible Forms in ultimate, formless matter. To put it another way, ultimate matter is the wall of Plato's cave, distorting true ideas by reflecting imperfect images of them.

The physical world, then, according to Plotinus, is an inferior embodied counterpart to the purely Intelligible and immaterial Forms. This secondary status does not make the physical world unreal or bad; Plotinus takes the physical world to be a trickle-down product of Intelligible Forms and as good as it can be, relative to its derivative status, but its contents, owing to their embodiment and matter, lack the unity and stability of the Intelligible Forms. Particular human souls simultaneously live a life of thought and of sense perception. They (i.e. we) convert apprehension of incorporeal thinkable and thinking realities into the corporeal, perceptible, and animated images that constitute ordinary objects. These objects, like the gold cup or the tree or the cat, lend themselves to analysis in terms of matter and form. But what can we say about matter, when we try to conceptualize it below the level of its proximate vegetable matter or animal matter or metallic matter, or below the level of such matter's constituents, such as the four elements?

6.

Plotinus starts his account of ultimate matter by reaffirming its complete tractability and inherent lack of quality and quantity. Whence, then does matter acquire colour, temperature, weight, size, and shape, which are the basic attributes of bodies Not from itself, evidently, but from

> Text 9: The giver of shape and size ... that supplies everything, as it were from the realities (*ta onta*)... If the maker is prior to matter, matter will be just as the maker wants it to be, accommodating to everything including size ... The form supplies matter with everything that goes with and is caused by the formative principle (*logos*). (*Ennead* II.4.8)

How are we to understand 'the giver of shape and size' and 'the will of the maker'? The answer, supplied by the text, is form, in the sense of 'formative principle'. But formative principles do not simply float down, as it were, to matter from Nous, the Intelligible level of Plotinian reality. Formative principles [we may perhaps compare DNA, digital information, encoded algorithms] are mediated to matter; they are projected on to it, as I was just saying, by soul, in the sense of World Soul, the providential principle of embodied life. It is tempting to align Plotinus's World Soul and its will with the divine Demiurge of Plato's *Timaeus*, who imposes mathematical form on the corporeal traces that flit in and out of the 'receptacle'.[14] But this Platonic precedent can only be a loose approximation to what Plotinus is saying here. His ultimate matter is neither a set of corporeal traces nor an independently existing region of empty space. It is something so abstract and amorphous that mind, the mind of the World Soul, can make of it anything it chooses from the stock of Intelligible Forms. Matter only comes into consideration, as we have had occasion to note before, in the light of its correlativity to form.

Next Plotinus asks: 'How can one grasp an entity that has no size'? His response to this question amplifies the points just made concerning form and soul. Matter independently of form simply lacks size.

> Text 10: The formative principle gave [*edoke;* note the tense] it a size that was previously absent. (*Ennead* II.4.9)

To conceptualize absence of size, Plotinus says, we need to invoke 'the soul's indefiniteness' (*aoristia. Ennead* II.4.10). By way of clarification for this expression, Plotinus first repeats his earlier assertion about the way the eye, in the absence of colour, can be said, in a way, to be affected by the dark. But is this really seeing? It can only be so described if the eye sees not nothing, but the absence of everything visible. By analogy,

> Text 11: When the soul thinks nothing, it says nothing, or rather experiences nothing. But when it thinks matter (*hylen noei*), it is affected by an impression, as it were, of the amorphous. (*Ennead* II.4.10)

---

[14] See Plato, *Timaeus* 53b.

What is the Matter with Matter, According to Plotinus?

During normal perceptual consciousness the soul thinks its perceptual objects in terms of their shape, size, and so forth, that is to say, in terms of their perceptible forms and proximate matter, such as the golden cup. The soul can recognize these things because, thanks to its rational faculty, it has the corresponding concepts. But when it comes to thinking of matter as such, ultimate matter, the soul arrives at an impasse, bringing us back to the ontological and conceptual paradoxes I brought up earlier. To continue with Plotinus's own extraordinary words (*Ennead* II.4.10):

> Text 12: Having abstracted and removed everything in the whole composite item, the soul *obscurely* thinks this *obscure* non-rational residue, a *dark* thing that it thinks *darkly* and thinks non-thinkingly. And since matter itself does not remain amorphous, but is shaped in things, the soul too immediately thrusts on it the forms of things, from distress at the indefiniteness, as if it were afraid of being outside of beings and could not bear to spend any time on that which is not.

The soul cannot accept a representation of absolute indefiniteness, so it always bestows some form, however minimal, on matter.

Can ultimate matter, then, in view of its obscure and illusory status, be an objective constituent of the physical world? Bodies need bulk or mass (*ongkos*) to be the recipient of their magnitude and qualities. But since ultimate matter has no magnitude, how can it provide bulk or mass?

Plotinus answers this question by seeming, for the first time, to assign a positive function to ultimate matter. Drawing on his original description of matter as an incorporeal substrate, he says:

> Text 13: What matter receives from forms, it receives *in extension*, because it is receptive of extension (*Ennead* II.4.11)... It is not a mass, but it is pictured as a mass because its primary attribute is the capacity for mass ... Matter is necessary both to quality and magnitude, and therefore also to bodies. It is not an empty name, but something that underlies even though it is invisible and without magnitude. (*Ennead* II.4.12).

What matter receives from forms, it receives *in extension*, and thus it becomes bulk or mass. How are we to take this claim? Is ultimate matter just empty space? That suggestion could fit its description as pure recipient and substrate. But ultimate matter cannot be empty space in our modern sense of the term, with its objective designation. How, moreover, could empty space endow bodies with mass?

A.A. Long

The indefiniteness of ultimate matter gives it its capacity to receive the forms constitutive of bodies. Otherwise, if matter had its own magnitude, it would impose that magnitude on the forms it receives. By its reception of bodily forms 'matter becomes mass', or at least we imagine it so. When the forms of things that are naturally embodied encounter ultimate matter, they cause matter to acquire the magnitude appropriate to such bodies. As such, however, ultimate matter is always sheer void – 'an illusion of mass' – incapable of being credited with any size of its own. Ultimate matter is a *privation*, knowable or thinkable by what it is not, and hence something unavoidably dark in a metaphysical scheme that posits the identity of form and intelligibility.[15]

Rather than shirk this conclusion Plotinus revels in it, as the following dizzying passage exemplifies (*Ennead* II.5.5):

> Text 14: Since matter is nothing in itself, except what it is by being matter, it is not in actuality. For if it is going to be something in actuality, it will be what that thing is in actuality and not be matter. So it would not be matter absolutely, but only in the way that bronze is... So it is in actuality an illusion (*phantasma*), in actuality a falsehood ... Therefore, if it must be, it must not be in actuality, so that, in departure from true being it may have its being in non-being.

Plotinian matter is neither nothing nor something. He can call it a phantom, a mirage, a privation, but even these characterizations are meaningful only by courtesy of what matter actually lacks, namely any kind of form or describable or intelligible reality. In light of his Aristotelian inheritance, why didn't Plotinus take ultimate matter to be a purely conceptual substrate, separable only in thought from the primary bodies, the four elements? There are many possible answers to this question. Here are two.

7.

First, Plotinus the Platonist cannot avail himself of the robust Aristotelian notion that embodied beings are basic substances.

---

[15] Plotinus insists (Ennead II.4.14) that absolute matter is always privation and essentially 'not-being' in response to Aristotle's position (*Physics* I.9) that matter loses its privation when the privation is replaced by its contrary.

What is the Matter with Matter, According to Plotinus?

Embodied things can only be diminished beings, according to him, because they are shadowy reflections of Intelligible Forms. Corporeality is their least substantive attribute. Bodies require matter, in order to be bodies, meaning occupants of space, but this material consistency deprives them of any claim to be unequivocal substances. Rather than underpinning the firm existence of bodies, matter accounts for bodies' impermanence and changeableness, and so prevents their being full-fledged entities.

My second rejoinder is to propose that Plotinian matter brings him quite close to George Berkeley's notorious doctrine that material substance is a self-contradictory notion of which there can be no idea and no knowledge. Recall what Plotinus says concerning the soul's vain attempts to achieve a positive and intelligible representation of matter. What our individual souls can actually think or perceive is the *formed* aspect, not the *material* aspect, of bodies. Plotinus presumes that there is more to perceptual things than we can perceive of them, namely their matter, but this is such a strange sense of 'more' that it is tantamount, as he repeatedly says, to indefiniteness or 'not-being'.

The perceptible form/matter compounds that he takes bodies to be are not self-subsistent and independent beings that simply exist in their own right 'out there', as it were. They are also, at a prior level, already in the soul, because, as he likes to say, soul is not 'in' body, but body is 'in soul' (*Ennead* IV.3.20–2). This dependence of body on soul also goes some way to anticipate Berkeley's rejection of a mind-independent world of material things.[16] Plotinus verbally agrees with Aristotle that perceptible objects are composites of matter and form, or substrate and qualities. Yet for Plotinus the matter, taken by itself, is not even a potential being but only a privation – an amorphous receptacle that contributes nothing except receptivity to the forms and qualities constitutive of bodies. Matter as such is a non-entity. That is what is the matter with it.

To return to our modern physicists' dark matter, are we to speculate that what is so called will eventually become clear to the eye of experimental reason? Or may it be the case that science is running out of resources to provide a fully intelligible account of what we have traditionally taken to be out there? If Plotinus has any cognitive relevance to physics, it will not be thanks to a resurgence of

[16] For a different view, see M. Burnyeat, 'What Descartes saw and Berkeley missed', *Philosophical Review* 90 (1982), 3–40.

A.A. Long

Platonic ontology, I suppose, but to the challenge he presents, like Berkeley, to our capacity to conceptualize a completely mindless physical space.[17]

University of California, Berkeley
aalong@berkeley.edu

[17]   I thank Christian Wildberg and Lloyd Gerson for their helpful criticism of a version of this paper that I delivered in Princeton and Toronto. They should not be presumed to endorse all my readings of Plotinus. I also thank the officers of the Royal Insitute for giving me the opportunity to present a paper in this series on ancient philosophy.

Aquinas on What God is Not

BRIAN DAVIES

Abstract

It is often said that if God exists, he is strongly comparable to what is not divine. In particular, it has been claimed that for God to exist is for a person to exist. In what follows I show how, esteemed theologian though he is commonly taken to be, Thomas Aquinas adopts a strongly different line of thinking according to which we seriously do not know what God is. In doing so, I draw attention to his use of nominal definitions in his arguments for 'God exists'. I also highlight his teachings that God is simple and that words used to talk about God in subject-predicate sentences always 'signify imperfectly'.

Early in his *Summa Theologiae*, Aquinas writes: 'We cannot know what God is, only what he is not. We must therefore consider the ways in which God does not exist rather than the ways in which he does'.[1] You may think that this seems an odd thing for a Christian philosopher to assert. So, you might suppose that Aquinas does not here mean what he appears to be saying. But I shall now try to explain why this supposition would be wrong and that Aquinas's philosophy of God is shot through with the conviction that, in a truly serious sense, those who speak about God do not know what they are talking about, regardless of whether they say 'God exists' or 'There is no God'.

Some theologians and philosophers seem to suppose that we have a fairly clear idea what it means to say that God exists. Take, for example, Professor Richard Swinburne, one of the best known of contemporary philosophers of religion.[2]

He tells us that someone 'who believes that there is a God' is a theist. By a 'God', Swinburne goes on to say, theists understand 'something like a "person without a body (i.e. a spirit) who is eternal, free, able to do anything, knows everything, is perfectly

---

[1]   I quote from Brian Davies and Brian Leftow (ed.), *Thomas Aquinas:* Summa Theologiae *Questions on God* (Cambridge University Press: Cambridge, 2006), 28. In what follows, I quote from this volume using the abbreviation 'Davies and Leftow'.

[2]   In what follows, I make reference to Professor Swinburne only since I take him to be an especially famous representative of a way of thinking about God that is currently much in vogue among contemporary Anglo-American philosophers of religion. In philosophical jargon, I take Swinburne to be a token of a type.

doi:10.1017/S1358246116000230

Brian Davies

good, is the proper object of human worship and obedience, the creator and sustainer of the universe"'.[3] According to Swinburne, 'theology uses only ordinary words in their ordinary senses'. When talking about God, he says, 'the theologian uses ordinary words to denote ordinary properties' but 'claims that the properties cited are manifested in unusual combinations and circumstances and to unusual degrees'.[4] On this account, God, though different from us, is also rather like us since God is a person who knows and acts.

Some theologians have held that God is immutable and outside time, but Swinburne thinks that such theologians are both philosophically mistaken and unfaithful to biblical teaching.[5] Persons are mutable and temporal, he says; so if God is a person, God is mutable and temporal. Indeed, suggests Swinburne, we can, in a serious sense, understand what it is like to act as God does in the light of his 'basic powers'. 'We can imagine finding ourselves having a basic power not merely to move objects, but to create them instantaneously.'[6] Swinburne takes it as obvious that, if God exists, then God resembles what Descartes took himself to be when claiming that he was essentially a thinking thing. Of course, Swinburne holds that God is much more powerful than Descartes understood himself to be. He also thinks of God as more knowing than we are and as much better behaved. On Swinburne's account, however, God is different from us in a quantitative way. God is not *radically* different from us.

I refer to Swinburne at this stage since I want, at the outset, to provide some context for understanding Aquinas's approach to God. And I want to stress that Aquinas is as far away from Swinburne as it is possible to get when it comes to the word 'God'. Aquinas would not have agreed with anything that I have just quoted Swinburne as saying. One can begin to see how this is so by looking at the way in which he presents arguments for God's existence in several of his writings.

Aquinas holds that we can come to know that the proposition 'God exists' is true. Indeed, he thinks that we can *demonstrate* the truth of

---

[3] Richard Swinburne, *The Coherence of Theism* (Revised Edition, Clarendon Press: Oxford, 1993), 1. In this book Swinburne focuses on what God is. In its sequel, *The Existence of God* (Revised Edition, Clarendon Press: Oxford, 1991), Swinburne offers arguments in favor of theism.
[4] *The Coherence of Theism*, 52.
[5] Swinburne argues for these conclusions in Chapter 12 of *The Coherence of Theism*.
[6] Richard Swinburne, *Is There a God?* (Oxford University Press: Oxford, 1996), 5.

'God exists'. Following Aristotle, Aquinas takes a demonstration to be an argument with true premises that entail its conclusion, and he thinks that knowledge that God exists can only be gained from demonstration. More precisely, Aquinas takes a demonstrative argument to have the form: (1) 'All X is Y' (e.g., 'All human beings are mammals'); (2) 'All Y is Z' (e.g., 'All mammals breath air'); (3) 'Therefore, All X is Z' (e.g., 'Therefore, all human beings breath air').

Aquinas is aware that some people have claimed that 'God exists' is somehow self-evident to us, but he rejects that position largely because of what he thinks concerning our ignorance when it comes to God. For example, in response to the suggestion that God has to exist given that the word 'God' means 'that than which nothing greater can be signified', he says 'because we do not know what God is, the proposition is not self-evident to us and needs to be demonstrated by things more known to us ... that is, by God's effects'.[7] Here Aquinas is arguing that we can know, as opposed to truly believe, that God exists only because we can reasonably claim that God produces effects from which we can reason to God as one who brings things about.[8]

Yet Aquinas recognizes two kinds of causal demonstration: (a) from cause to effect, and (b) from effect to cause.

Suppose we reason thus:

(1)   Hydrogen is the element with atomic number one.
(2)   The element with atomic number one is the lightest gas.
(3)   So, hydrogen is the lightest gas.
(4)   Any balloon filled with the lightest gas rises in air.
(5)   So, any balloon filled with hydrogen rises in air.

Here we start from a definition of what something is, and we end up arguing syllogistically for the occurrence of a visible effect. Our procedure here is an example of what Aquinas takes to be an argument from cause to effect starting with a grasp of the nature of the cause.

However, suppose we reason:

(1)   This balloon is rising in the air.
(2)   Every rising balloon is full of something that makes it rise.

---

[7]   Davies and Leftow, 21.
[8]   Aquinas tends to distinguish sharply between knowledge and belief. He takes belief to involve conviction without seeing, and he takes knowledge to amount to recognizing that a proposition is true and *why* it is true. In the *Summa Theologiae*, this distinction surfaces particularly clearly in Aquinas's discussion of what he calls the theological virtue of faith (*Summa Theologiae*, 2a2ae,1–7).

(3)   So, this balloon is full of something that makes it rise.
(4)   Everything that fills a balloon and makes it rise must be lighter than air.
(5)   So, this balloon is full of something lighter than air.

Here we make no appeal to what it is precisely that fills this balloon rising in the air; we do not claim to know what exactly that is. Is it hydrogen, helium, or just hot air? But we do try to account for what we perceive in terms of a cause of some sort. We reason from effect to cause.

Now, according to Aquinas, if we know that 'God exists' is true, that can only be by virtue of a demonstration from effect to cause. He thinks that demonstration from cause to effect is impossible when it comes to 'God exists' since we lack an understanding of what God is, since we do not know God's nature or essence. This means that Aquinas's various arguments for 'God exists' presuppose that we do not know what God is. They positively rely on the idea that we do not have a grasp of God's essence or nature.

In that case, however, why does Aquinas present them as arguments for it being true that God exists? Does not the question 'Does God exist?' already depend on an understanding of what God is? In turning to this question Aquinas distinguishes between two kinds of definition, which I shall refer to as 'real' and 'nominal'.

According to Aquinas a real definition tells us what some existing thing is by nature or essence. So, in his view we can reasonably aim at a real definition of what, say, a cat or a rose is. What, though, of wizards or hobbits? Can these be defined? Since they do not exist, Aquinas denies that we can arrive at a real definition of them. Yet 'wizard' and 'hobbit' are genuine words, and it is possible to explain what they mean. So, as well as acknowledging that there are real definitions, Aquinas also agrees that there are nominal ones; and his arguments for the truth of 'God exists' are grounded only in a series of nominal definitions.

Aquinas, of course, does not think that the word 'God' signifies something unreal. But, when formally arguing that God exists, he employs only nominal definitions. This is what accounts for the fairly minimalistic understandings of the word 'God' in his famous Five Ways to demonstrate that God exists as found in his *Summa Theologiae*. When presenting these arguments, all Aquinas claims to have shown is that there is (1) 'a first cause of change that is not itself changed by anything', (2) 'a first cause that is not itself caused in any way ', (3) 'something that owes its necessity to nothing else, something which is the cause that other things must be', (4) 'something that causes in all other beings their existence, their goodness and whatever other perfection they have', and (5) 'something with intelligence that directs all natural things to ends'.[9] Aquinas is here only employing what he takes to be nominal definitions, ones that he derives from what he believes to be traditional talk about God coming from Jews, Muslims, and Christians.

Critics of Aquinas have often said that people mean a lot more by the word 'God' than Aquinas does in his Five Ways. Yet Aquinas, Christian theologian that he was, did not need to be told this. However, in his 'from effects to cause' arguments for 'God exists', he sticks to what he takes to be non-controversial nominal definitions of 'God', ones that do not rely on an understanding of God's actually existing nature or essence, this being something that Aquinas takes us to lack.

Why, though, does he say that we do not know what God is? Here we need to note the drift of *Summa Theologiae*, Part 1, Question 3, and comparable texts, in which Aquinas notes ways in which God cannot be thought of as composite. Like Aristotle, Aquinas thinks that there are various ways in which something can be composite. On the other hand, however, Aquinas has a notion of composition that goes beyond anything that Aristotle presented.

As it begins, *Summa Theologiae*, 1,3 remains on familiar Aristotelian ground since Aquinas employs the idea that some things are composite by having both form and matter.[10] Among other things, Aquinas argues that being corporeal is being something with potentiality or ability for change, a potentiality that must be lacking in God. He writes: 'The first being must of necessity be actual and in no way potential'. He continues:

Although in any one thing that passes from potentiality to actuality, the potentiality precedes the actuality, actuality, absolutely speaking, precedes potentiality, for nothing can be changed from a state of potentiality to one of actuality except by something actual. Now we have seen that the first being is God. So there can be no potentiality in God. In bodies, however, there is always potentiality, because the extended is as such divisible. So, God cannot be a body.[11]

---

[9] Davies and Leftow, 25–26.
[10] Roughly speaking, Aquinas takes a thing's form to be what we refer to when saying what kind of thing it is or what it is like in various ways. And (again roughly speaking) he takes matter to be what allows something to change either by passing out of existence or by being modified somehow. So, for example, being feline is a form had by my cat, and my cat's being able to perish is due to it being material.
[11] 1a,3,1 (Davies and Leftow, 30).

Brian Davies

Armed with this conclusion, Aquinas thinks that he has no problem in going on to assert that God cannot be 'composed' of matter and form. He says, 'Since having dimensions is one of the primary properties of matter, anything composed of matter and form must be a body. As I have shown, however, God is not a body. So, he is not composed of matter and form'.[12]

In *Summa Theologiae*, 1,3,3 however, Aquinas goes on to argue that in God there is no composition of *suppositum* and nature, thereby digging deeper into what he takes God not to be.

By the word *suppositum* Aquinas means '*this* individual thing as opposed to another one'. So, he would say, for example, that Socrates is a *suppositum* and is, as such, an individual subject. He is Socrates and not Plato or any other human being. Aquinas would also say that beings such as Socrates, like all material substances, are composites of *suppositum* and nature (*natura*) or essence (*essentia*) – meaning that they display or have a nature or essence that is not simply to be identified with the individual subjects that they are. Socrates is a human being. Yet, thinks Aquinas, there are many things with the same nature or essence as Socrates. Such things, says Aquinas, are, like Socrates, not to be identified with the nature or essence that they have. Rather, they are a composition of *suppositum* and nature. Yet, Aquinas maintains, in God there is no such composition. So, says Aquinas, God (the individual that God is) and God's nature (what God is) are one and the same immaterial thing.

In propounding this teaching, Aquinas is first of all saying that God is not an individual in the sense of 'individual' that we have in mind when saying that an individual is one of a kind of which there is or could be more than one member. Now, as I have noted, Professor Swinburne thinks it important to insist that God is a person. Aquinas, however, does not think that God is a thing of a kind. He does not think it possible to classify God. One might suppose that Aquinas would at least concede that God and everything other than God add up to a definite number of beings. Yet Aquinas believes that '___ is a being' does not tell us what something is. He does not think that there is any such class of things as *things that simply are*.[13] Aquinas is not even willing to say that God

---

[12]   1a,3,2 (Davies and Leftow, 32).
[13]   Cf. *Summa Theologiae*, 1a,3,5: 'Since the genus of something states what the thing is, a genus must express a thing's essence. But God's essence is to exist ... So, the only genus to which God could belong would be the genus of being. Aristotle, however, has shown that there is no such genus: for genera are differentiated by factors not already contained within those genera, and no differentiating factor could be found that did not

60

is a substance. In *Summa Theologiae*, 3,6 he observes: 'The word "substance" does not mean baldly that which exists of itself, for existence is not a genus ... Rather, "substance" means "that which is possessed of an essence such that it will exist of itself, even though to exist is not its essence". So, it is clear that God does not belong to the genus of substance'.[14]

In *Summa Theologiae*, 1,3,3 Aquinas is defending the idea that God is a subsisting form, not something exemplifying or possessing a form. This, of course, means that he is trying seriously to distinguish between God and those objects of which we can claim knowledge concerning what they are essentially. He takes these to be objects of sensory experience which allows us to pick them out as individuals and to ascribe natures to them, this implying a distinction in them of individuality and nature. Yet Aquinas takes God to be a single non-corporeal and subsisting nature. He thinks of God as something whose individuality has to be thought of as its nature, something that does not *have* a nature but *is* a subsisting nature. So, he argues, 'God is identical with his own divinity, his own life, and with whatever else is predicated of him'. Aquinas means that, say, God's goodness is not something different from God's power, and that neither of these is different from God.

I think we can put this point by saying that Aquinas thinks that the logic of our language fails us when we try to talk or think about God. Our language, and, therefore, our thinking, is heavily grounded in a distinction between subject and predicate, and our understanding of things in the world reflects this. For Aquinas, however, God does not have properties. Aquinas agrees that, for example, God is living, knowing, good, and powerful. Yet he does not think of God's life, knowledge, goodness, and power as aspects of God or as attributes that God happens to have as you and I happen to have various attributes. Nor does he think of them as being really distinct *in* God, as they are in us, or as distinct *from* God. His view is that terms like 'God' and 'the power of God' both refer to one and the same reality, which is one reason why he says that we do not know what God is. For how can we claim to understand the nature of something that, in reality, is not material and not one of a kind lacking properties or attributes distinct from itself?

You might say that there is nothing here to understand since Aquinas is talking nonsense while claiming that God lacks

---

already exist (it could not differentiate if it did not exist). So we are left with no genus to which God could belong'. I quote from Davies and Leftow, 37.
[14]   Davies and Leftow, 38.

Brian Davies

composition. However, and as Peter Geach once noted, there is a comparison to hand which might give us pause when consigning *Summa Theologiae*, 1,3,3 to the flames as obviously incoherent. What Geach says is worth quoting in full. He writes:

> The difficulty here is to exclude from one's mind the Platonism that Aquinas combats – the 'barbarous' misconstruction of 'the wisdom of God' as 'wisdom', which belongs to, is a property of, God; if we do think along these lines, Aquinas will appear to be saying that wisdom and power are different, but God possesses both, and in him they are not different but identical – which is sheer self-contradiction. The analogy of mathematical functions … proves valuable here … 'The square of ___' and 'the double of ___' signify two quite different functions, but for the argument 2 these two both take the number 4 as their value. Similarly, 'the wisdom of ___' and 'the power of ___' signify different forms, but the individualizations of these forms in God's case are not distinct from one another; nor is either distinct from God, just as the number 1 is in no way distinct from its own square.[15]

I would add that, even if we reject the comparison to which Geach refers, Aquinas's claim that God is all that God has (that there is no distinction in God of *suppositum* and nature) does not seem to be manifestly absurd since it is not offered as a *description* of God. In *Summa Theologiae*, 3 Aquinas is concerned to *deny* various things when it comes to God, not to paint a portrait of God. He wants to say is that God is *not* to be thought of as being like those things the nature of which can be distinguished from the individuals that they are, that God is *not* one of a kind, that God is *not* something having distinct properties. You may think that in 1a,3 Aquinas is describing God in positive terms. But he is actually noting what *cannot* be thought when it comes to God. That is because he is merely trying to flag ways in which God does *not* exist on the understanding that to say that God is not X, Y, or Z is not to be committed to any account of what God positively is.

So much, then, for *Summa Theologiae*, 1,3,3. In 1,3,4, however, Aquinas introduces another thought that runs through his writings in general. This is not at all an Aristotelian one, and it amounts to the claim that God is non-composite since in God there is no distinction of essence (*essentia*) and existence (*esse*). As he dwells on this notion, Aquinas suggests that our knowledge of God is even more

---

[15] G.E.M. Anscombe and P.T. Geach, *Three Philosophers* (Basil Blackwell: Oxford, 1961), 122.

limited than we might take it to be even if we concede that in God there is no composition of *suppositum* and nature.

Here Aquinas is drawing on his claim that God is the first cause of all creatures *from nothing* (*ex nihilo*). By this he means that the existence of everything other than God derives at all times from God directly and without intermediaries. He also means that what God is, God's nature, cannot be caused to exist by anything and can therefore be spoken of as 'subsisting existence' lacking any conceivable potentiality. So, says Aquinas, God is not just his own essence. God 'is also his own existence'.[16] Hence, and drawing on the reasoning of *Summa Theologiae*, 1, 3, 4, Aquinas can say in 1, 13, 11 that the 'most appropriate name for God' is 'He who Is' (*Qui Est*). 'Since the existence of God is his essence', argues Aquinas, 'and since this is true of nothing else ... It is clear that this name is especially fitting for God, for we name everything by its form'.[17] He continues:

> All other names are either less general or, if not, they at least add some nuance of meaning which restricts and determines the original sense. In this life our minds cannot grasp what God is in himself; whatever way we have of thinking of him is a way of failing to understand him as he really is. So, the less determinate our names are, and the more general and simple they are, the more appropriately do we apply them to God. That is why Damascene says 'The first of all names used of God is "The One who Is", for he comprehends all in himself, he has his existence as an ocean of being, infinite and unlimited'. Any other name selects some particular aspect of the being of the thing, but 'The One who Is' fixes on no aspect of being but stands open to all and refers to God as to an infinite ocean of being.[18]

The philosophical value of this way of talking has been challenged by a number of authors, especially those anxious to defend the claim that 'being' or 'existence' cannot be attributed to individuals. According to this claim, 'X exists' tells us something about concepts, not objects, and is equivalent to sentences of the form 'Something or other is F' where F is equivalent to expressions such as '___ is canine' or '___ is hungry'.[19] Be that as it may, however, Aquinas

---

[16] Davies and Leftow, 35.
[17] Davies and Leftow, 163.
[18] Davies and Leftow, 163.
[19] For a trenchant defense of this position drawing on Gottlob Frege (1848–1925), see C.J.F. Williams, *What is Existence?* (Clarendon Press: Oxford, 1981). Williams applies this position, while explicitly targeting

certainly wants to speak of God as 'existence itself', and his putting that wish into practice contributes to his consistent teaching that we do not know what God is. That is because, as I have said, Aquinas does not think that 'exists' can enter into a real definition of something that expresses what we know it to be. When speaking of God as 'Being itself' Aquinas is not trying to define God. He is saying that, since God accounts for the existence of everything other than God, God is not something derived from anything. In short, he is saying that God is not created.

At this point I should pay some attention to what Aquinas means when he speaks about God being the Creator, for this is something that does not just lead Aquinas to say that we do not know what God is but is part and parcel of his teaching to that effect.

As I have said, Aquinas argues causally for the truth of 'God exists'. In doing so, he claims that God accounts for there being change, numerous secondary causes of different kinds, and things which exist but do not themselves account for their actually existing. We might put all this by saying that Aquinas argues that God exists and is the Creator of all things other than God.

The belief that God is the Creator of all things is often taken to mean only that God, so to speak, got the universe going some time ago. So, some people who believe that God exists think it critical to reject any theory that seems to suggest that the universe had no beginning. Yet Aquinas is not of their mind. He maintains that for God to create is for God to make something to exist for as long as it exists and whether or not it had a beginning of existence. As it happens, Aquinas believed that the world did begin to exist, but, like Aristotle, he did not think that this fact can be established philosophically.[20] For Aquinas, that the universe had a beginning is a matter of faith. Yet Aquinas does not think that we should reject belief in God as Creator should we happen to conclude that the universe had no beginning. For, he holds, to speak of God as Creator is to speak of God as accounting for the sheer existence of things at any time.

In other words, Aquinas's view is that God is the Creator of everything since God accounts for there being *something* rather than *nothing at all*. So, at one point he says:

Aquinas for criticism, in Chapter 27 of Philip L. Quinn and Charles Taliaferro (ed.), *A Companion to Philosophy of Religion* (Blackwell: Oxford, 1997).
[20] Aquinas's most detailed defense of this conclusion comes in his *De Aeternitate Mundi* ('On the Eternity of the World'). In the *Summa Theologiae* he touches on the conclusion in 1a,46,2.

It is not enough to consider how some particular being issues from some particular cause, for we should also attend to the issuing of the whole of being from the universal cause, which is God; it is this springing forth that we designate by the term 'creation' ... If we consider the coming forth of the whole of all being from its first origins we cannot presuppose to it any being. But no-being and nothing are synonymous. As therefore the begetting of a human being is out of that non-being which is non-human being, so creation, the introduction of being entirely, is out of the non-being which is nothing at all.[21]

In Aquinas's view, God is the cause of things that have being but do not exist by nature. So, in *Summa Theologiae*, 1,46 he can say 'The world exists just as long as God wills it to, since its existence depends on his will as on its cause'.[22] We need to realize that, in Aquinas's thinking, '___ is *being created* by God' is truly to be affirmed of any creature at any time. We also need to note the extent to which Aquinas maintains that 'creates', in 'God creates', takes us beyond causality as he thinks that we understand it. In speaking of God as Creator, Aquinas, while drawing on Aristotle's thinking about causes, is focusing on God as an efficient or agent cause, something that produces one or more effects in something. On the other hand, he also holds that God cannot be an efficient or agent cause in what we might call 'the usual' or 'the Aristotelian' sense.

Following Aristotle, Aquinas thinks that talk about efficient or agent causes has its roots in our recognition of change in the world and our looking, so to speak, for culprits. If I start running a temperature, I ask 'What is responsible for this?'. If I return to my apartment to find it robbed, I ask 'Who did this?'. Aristotle and Aquinas have no inclination to construe talk about efficient causation as deriving from our experience of what David Hume called 'constant conjunction'. They think that causal explanation aims at understanding why this or that thing is producing a result of a certain kind, regardless of how often it seems to be doing so.

Also, and abstracting from our experience of what tends to follow from what, they think of efficient causes as agents active in their effects, and they conclude that an efficient cause and its effect are, in a sense, one thing. As Aquinas puts it, 'what the agent does is what

---

[21] I quote from Volume 8 of the Blackfriars edition of the *Summa Theologiae* (Eyre and Spottiswoode: London, and McGraw Hill: New York, 1967), 27.
[22] I quote from Volume 8 of the Blackfriars edition of the *Summa Theologiae*, 69 and 71.

the patient undergoes' so that 'action and passion are not two changes but one and the same change, called action in so far as it is caused by an agent, and passion in so far as it takes place in a patient'.[23] If I cause the drapes on my window to be drawn, that is because they *are being drawn* because of me, because my act of causing the drapes to be drawn amounts to the drapes being drawn by me.

Yet this account of efficient or agent causation is an account of it as it occurs in the universe, and it diverges from what Aquinas has in mind when it comes to God making the difference between there being something and nothing. That is because Aquinas does not think of God's creating as making any difference to anything and, therefore, as bringing about a change in something.

In short, though Aquinas takes God's creating to be a form of making, and an instance of efficient or agent causation, he also takes it to be making that is not to be understood as we understand making in general. It is making that brings about something from *nothing*, not making that results in a transformation of some kind. It is making that does not *modify* anything but makes things to be what they are. It is making by a maker that is not a thing as objects in the universe are things. It is making that is thoroughly mysterious to us.

One might, of course, say that if that is what 'creating' as ascribed to God is, then 'making' has undergone what Professor Antony Flew once referred to as 'the death by a thousand qualifications' and that Aquinas is incoherent in what he says about God as Creator.[24] Flew's point, intended to be critical of belief in God, is that those who make assertions about God typically allow nothing to count against them and end up saying nothing of significance since the words they use when talking about God are deprived of their original meaning. Unlike Flew, however, Aquinas welcomes this death by a thousand qualifications when it comes to talk about God since he takes it to be a positive consequence of rightly seeking to account for there being something rather than nothing, since he takes it as implied by his basic reason for supposing God to exist in the first place.

As I have said, when trying to say why we should think that 'God exists' is true, Aquinas does not start from an understanding of what

---

[23] This is what Aquinas argues in his commentary on Aristotle's *Physics*. I quote from Timothy McDermott (ed.), *Thomas Aquinas: Selected Philosophical Writings* (Oxford University Press: Oxford and New York, 1993), 83 and 84.

[24] For Flew, see Antony Flew, 'Theology and Falsification' in Antony Flew and Alasdair MacIntyre (ed.), *New Essays in Philosophical Theology* (SCM Press: London, 1955), 97.

God is. He starts from questions that he thinks to arise when it comes to what is in the universe, questions that lead him to a question about the very existence of the universe. Wittgenstein once said 'It is not *how* things are in the world that is mystical, but *that* it exists'.[25] Aquinas seems to agree with Wittgenstein here. However, while Wittgenstein goes on to say that when wondering why the world exists we should resort to silence, Aquinas, tries to keep talking, albeit that he recognizes that he is using language that is being stretched to breaking point, to the point where he is trying to say more than he can mean, to the point where he ends up seriously asserting that we do not know what God is and are better informed when it comes to what God is not.[26] Aquinas thinks that we have some (albeit limited) knowledge when it comes to what created things in the universe are. But he also holds that God is not a created thing having existence as an effect and is, therefore, not a knowable thing at all. Why not? Because God is not one among the beings in the universe that exist as created. In his Commentary on Aristotle's *Peri Hermeneias*, Aquinas says that 'God's will is to be thought of as existing outside the realm of existents, as a cause from which pours forth everything that exists in all its variant forms'.[27]

Yet is Aquinas not well known for holding that some of the words we use when talking about creatures can be applied to God in a literal and non-figurative sense? Indeed he is, and in various places he argues that some words can be used both of God and creatures *analogically* while taking analogical predication to be a literal mode of discourse and not a figurative one. Be that as it may, however, when arguing in this way Aquinas does not go back on anything that I have been ascribing to him. He claims that certain affirmative statements about God can be known to be literally true for quite precise reasons. So, he holds that when talking of God or arguing about God's nature we are not always engaging in pure equivocation since pure equivocation spoils arguments.[28] Again, Aquinas also

---

[25] *Tractatus Logico-Philosophicus*, 6.44.

[26] This point is developed by Herbert McCabe in Chapter 2 of Herbert McCabe, *God Still Matters* (Continuum: London, 2002).

[27] The Latin text here reads: 'Voluntas divina est intelligenda ut extra ordinem entium existens, velut causa quaedam profundens totum ens et omnes eius differentias'. I quote from Timothy McDermott, *Thomas Aquinas: Selected Philosophical Writings*, 282–283.

[28] In 1a,13,2 Aquinas rejects the view that all positive sounding statements about God are to be construed as denials. Perhaps wrongly, he attributes this view to Maimonides (1135–1204) while understanding it to amount to the claim that sentences like 'God is F' should be understood as

holds that God is not composite, so he reasons that when we say that God is such and such, when we say, for example 'God is good', we are not speaking of God and of things in the world univocally – since things in the world can be distinguished from the properties or attributes that they have while God cannot be so distinguished. In *Summa Theologiae*, 1,13 Aquinas explicitly says that in 'This creature is F' and 'God is F' we cannot construe F as univocal or purely equivocal, though its use in both cases can *sometimes* be justified with reference to causal reasoning from creatures to God. And this is where Aquinas's notion of analogical predication enters in. When it comes to some words signifying perfections, says Aquinas, we can 'name' God from creatures without speaking metaphorically, or by means of simile, since God accounts for the existence of perfections in creatures who can, therefore, be said to resemble God to some extent (on the principle that you cannot give what you do not have).[29] In spelling out these points, however, Aquinas never casts aside his claim that we do not know what God is. Indeed, he reiterates it by saying:

> We cannot see God's essence in this life. We know him only from creatures. We think of him as their source, and then as surpassing them all and as lacking anything that is merely creaturely. So, we can designate God from creatures, though the words we use do not express the divine essence as it is in itself ... Since we come to know God from creatures, and since this is how we come to

---

always denying something of God, that, for example, 'God is good' means 'God is not bad', or that 'God is living' means 'God is not inanimate'. Aquinas rejects this view, though without giving up on his claim that we do not understand what God is. For what seems to be a different reading of Aquinas here, see Eleonore Stump, 'God's Simplicity', which is Chapter 10 in Brian Davies and Eleonore Stump (ed.), *The Oxford Handbook of Aquinas* (Oxford University Press: Oxford and New York, 2012).

[29]   Aquinas thinks that *omne agens agit sibi simile* (which we might translate as 'every agent cause acts so as to produce what reflects it'). He does not mean that, for example, when I poach an egg I have to look like a poached egg. He means that poached eggs produced by me can, once we have made the right causal connection, be thought of as reflecting what I am as a potential poacher of eggs.   He means that, typically, a cause (an agent or efficient cause) is something exerting *itself*, something that has an influence and imposes its character in some way, albeit not always in a way that results in a look-alike of itself (as, say babies, literally look like their parents by being human).   For a short but reliable account of Aquinas on causality see Appendix 2 to Volume 3 of the Blackfriars edition of the *Summa Theologiae* (Eyre and Spottiswoode: London, and McGraw Hill: New York, 1964).

refer to him, the expressions we use to name him signify in a way that is appropriate to the material creatures we ordinarily know ... God is both simple, like a form, and subsistent, like something concrete. So, we sometimes refer to him by abstract nouns (to indicate his simplicity) while at other times we refer to him by concrete nouns (to indicate his subsistence and completeness) – though neither way of speaking measures up to his way of being, for in this life we do not know him as he is in himself.[30]

Aquinas goes on to say:

The difference between subject and predicate represents two ways of looking at a thing, while the fact that they are put together affirmatively indicates that it is one thing that is being looked at. Now, God, considered in himself, is altogether one and simple, yet we think of him through a number of different concepts because we cannot see him as he is in himself. But although we think of him in these different ways we also know that to each corresponds a single simplicity that is one and the same for all ... Our minds cannot understand subsisting simple forms as they are in themselves. We understand them in the way that we understand composite things, in which there is the subject of a form and something that exists in that subject. And so we apprehend a simple form as if it were a subject, and we attribute something to it.[31]

As I have said, Aquinas thinks that attribution such as this always fails to represent God adequately. When we talk about God affirmatively, says Aquinas, we are always 'signifying imperfectly'. We may, he thinks, speak literally and positively about God while ascribing certain perfections to God. Indeed, 'as far as the perfections signified are concerned, we use the words literally of God, and in fact more appropriately than we use them of creatures, for these perfections belong primarily to God and only secondarily to other things'. Yet, Aquinas immediately adds: 'But so far as the way of signifying these perfections is concerned, we use the words inappropriately, for they have a way of signifying that is appropriate to creatures'.[32]

It is the purpose of texts like *Summa Theologiae*, 1,13 'to show in what way theological language must differ from ordinary usage'.[33]

---

[30]   Davies and Leftow, 139–140.

[31]   Davies and Leftow, 165–166.

[32]   Davies and Leftow, 144.

[33]   Volume 3 of the Blackfriars edition of the *Summa Theologiae* (Eyre and Spottiswoode: London and New York, and McGraw-Hill: New York, 1964), 104.

Brian Davies

This is because Aquinas is deeply struck by our ignorance concerning what God is, ignorance that leaves Aquinas effectively saying that we do not know what the word 'God' really signifies, albeit that we can provide nominal definitions of the word. Or, as my late friend Herbert McCabe once said:

> St Thomas thought that things in some way pointed beyond themselves to something which is not a thing, which is altogether outside the universe of things and cannot be included in any classification with them. Given this idea it is not too difficult to understand his notion that words can point beyond their ordinary meanings, and this he thought is what happens when we talk about God. We can use words to mean more than we can understand.[34]

If McCabe is right here, we should conclude that when Aquinas talks about God he is doing something seriously different from what Professor Swinburne seems to be doing when he tells us that God is a person, albeit one better and more powerful and knowledgeable than us.[35] And I take this fact to mean that Aquinas represents a challenge to what many contemporary philosophers of religion, whether or not they believe in God, have to say when it comes to what 'God exists' means. Were he alive today, Aquinas would be appealing to a text like *Summa Theologiae*, 1,13 as one that, if cogent in its reasoning, ought to lead those who talk about God as if God were some understandable member of a kind to think again. An appeal like this, coming from someone who can reasonably be taken to be one of the greatest of western philosophers and theologians, ought, perhaps, to be taken very seriously, if only to be thought of as setting up an approach to God that atheists might bear in mind when saying that there is no God. Aquinas's treatment of God's

[34] Herbert McCabe, Appendix 3 to Volume 3 of the Blackfriars edition of the *Summa Thelogiae).*

[35] For what it is worth, I would note that the formula 'God is a person' does not appear in the Bible, though, of course, the Bible is full of personal and other imagery when it comes to God. As far as have been able to discover, its first occurrence in English appears in the report of a heresy trial held in Gloucester, UK, in 1664. The accused individual was someone called John Biddle. The charge against him was that he claimed that God is a person. This claim was taken to be heretical as contradicting the orthodox doctrine of the Trinity according to which God is three persons in one substance. For more on this, see Philip Dixon, *Nice and Hot Disputes: The Doctrine of the Trinity in the Seventeenth Century* (T&T Clark: Edinburgh, 2003).

unknowability might be full of mistakes. It might be wrong for some philosophical or theological reasons. But I think that it is something that should be borne in mind by anyone who wants to understand what his teaching on God amounts to in general.[36]

Naturally enough, I suppose, people often tend to think of God as the biggest thing around, the Top Person, and so on. Aquinas, however, definitely does not think in this way. He is very much an agnostic, not because he does not believe that God exists, but because, while 'modern agnosticism says simply "We do not know, and the universe is a mysterious riddle"', Aquinas says 'We do not know what the answer is, but we do know that there is a mystery behind it all which we do not know, and if there were not, there would not even be a riddle. This Unknown we call *God*. And if there were no God, there would be no universe to be mysterious, and nobody to be mystified'.[37]

Fordham University
bd01725@gmail.com

[36] The *Summa Theologiae*'s teaching on God amounts to much more than I have just reported since, in spite of what I have been saying and because it is the work of a teacher of *sacra doctrina* ('holy teaching' or teaching concerning what Aquinas took to be divine revelation), it is grounded in belief in the doctrine of the Trinity. So, for Aquinas, God is not just the incomprehensible creator but is also and from eternity Father, Son, and Spirit. See *Summa Theologiae*, 1a,33-43. As Aquinas develops his account of the Trinity, the differences between him and those who think of God as a relatively understandable person simply leap off the pages that he writes, though I have no space to dwell on them here.

[37] Victor White, *God the Unknown* (Harvill Press: London, 1956), pp.18–19. For a magisterial account of Aquinas and what we can know God to be, one which ranges over many of Aquinas's writings, see Chapter XIII of John Wippel, *The Metaphysical Thought of Thomas Aquinas* (The Catholic University of America Press: Washington, D.C., 2000).

Descartes on the Errors of the Senses[1]

SARAH PATTERSON

Abstract

Descartes first invokes the errors of the senses in the *Meditations* to generate doubt; he suggests that because the senses sometimes deceive, we have reason not to trust them. This use of sensory error to fuel a sceptical argument fits a traditional interpretation of the *Meditations* as a work concerned with finding a form of certainty that is proof against any sceptical doubt. If we focus instead on Descartes's aim of using the *Meditations* to lay foundations for his new science, his appeals to sensory error take on a different aspect. Descartes's new science is based on ideas innate in the intellect, ideas that are validated by the benevolence of our creator. Appeals to sensory error are useful to him in undermining our naïve faith in the senses and guiding us to an appreciation of innate ideas. However, the errors of the senses pose problems in the context of Descartes's appeals to God's goodness to validate innate ideas and natural propensities to belief. A natural tendency to sensory error is hard to reconcile with the benevolence of our creator. This paper explores Descartes's responses to the problems of theodicy posed by various forms of sensory error. It argues that natural judgements involved in our visual perception of distance, size and shape pose a problem of error that resists his usual solutions.

1. Sensory error and scepticism

Descartes first appeals to the errors of the senses in pursuing his plan of demolishing all his opinions through doubt. The rationale he gives for this plan in the opening sentences of the *Meditations* is that he acquired many false beliefs in childhood:

> Some years ago I was struck by the large number of falsehoods that I had accepted as true in my childhood, and by the highly doubtful nature of the whole edifice that I had subsequently based on them. I realized that it was necessary, once in my life, to demolish everything completely and start again right from the foundations...[2]

[1]   An earlier version of some of this material was presented to a Birkbeck work-in-progress seminar. I am grateful to my colleagues, especially Stacie Friend, for helpful comments and questions on that occasion.

[2]   AT VII 17, CSM II 12, tr. alt. References to AT are references by volume and page number to C. Adam and P. Tannery (eds), *Oeuvres de Descartes*, 11 vols. (Paris: Vrin, 1904). References to CSM are references

doi:10.1017/S135824611600031X   © The Royal Institute of Philosophy and the contributors 2016
Royal Institute of Philosophy Supplement **78** 2016

Sarah Patterson

The fact that we acquired some false beliefs in childhood hardly seems to justify wholesale demolition of our current beliefs through doubt. That can fuel the thought that this is simply a pretext for a project that is actually motivated by the threat of scepticism. On this traditional view, Descartes's project in philosophy is to try to defeat the threat of scepticism once and for all, and he pursues it by advancing the strongest sceptical arguments he can muster in the hope of finding a form of certainty that is proof against any doubt. In the First Meditation he points out that the senses sometimes deceive, that we are often deceived in dreams, and finally that for all we know we might be subject to wholesale deceit by God or an evil demon, so that we go wrong all the time. In the Second Meditation, he finds his first certainty in knowledge of his own mind; even if he is being deceived, he is still thinking, and if he thinks he must exist. But knowledge of one's own mind is a pretty slender foothold from which to rebuild knowledge of the world; and so, in the Third Meditation, Descartes has to appeal to a benevolent God as a *deus ex machina* to slay the evil demon and so pull him out of the sceptical hole he has dug for himself.

This, I think, is a familiar reading of the progress of the first three *Meditations*; and, I think, it is easy to feel that there is something unsatisfactory about Descartes's progress, so described. After the exhilarating doubt and recovery of the first two Meditations, the sudden appearance of God comes as rather a let-down. The image of a solitary iconoclastic thinker striking out into the unknown seems very modern, indeed appealing; a shamefaced rescue by appeal to a traditional deity seems quite the opposite. In one sense, this juxtaposition is not surprising. Descartes is not called the father of modern philosophy for nothing; he is plausibly seen as having one foot in the medieval world of the Aristotelian schoolmen and one foot in the modern world of the scientific revolution.[3] But we can find a more satisfactory role for Descartes's appeal to a benevolent creator if we read the *Meditations* not as a heroic quest against scepticism, but as an attempt to lay foundations for a new science, a new

---

by volume and page number to J. Cottingham, R. Stoothoff and D. Murdoch (eds), *The Philosophical Writings of Descartes* Vols. I and II (Cambridge: Cambridge University Press, 1984).

[3]   This is aptly reflected in the title of John Carriero's recent study of the *Meditations, Between Two Worlds* (Princeton: Princeton University Press, 2009).

way of understanding the world and our place within it.[4] For Descartes, the blueprint for this new understanding comes from ideas that are innate in us, placed in our minds by God.

2. Cartesian physics and the prejudices of the senses

But for the condemnation of Galileo, Descartes's first published work would have been a work of science. In 1633 Descartes was about to publish a book entitled *The World* in which he aimed to 'explain all the phenomena of nature – i.e. all of physics' – when he heard that Galileo had been condemned for maintaining the movement of the earth.[5] This movement was central to the physics of *The World*, and Descartes preferred to withdraw it rather than 'publish it in a mutilated form'.[6] Instead he set out to create the conditions for the favourable reception of his physics. First, in 1637, he published the *Discourse on the Method* with essays on optics, meteorology and geometry, samples of the results could be achieved using his method. Then, in 1641, he published the *Meditations*. In a now famous passage, he wrote to Mersenne:

> ...I may tell you, between ourselves, that these six Meditations contain all the foundations [*fondemens*] of my physics. But please do not say so, because those who favour Aristotle would perhaps have more difficulty in approving them. I hope that those who read them will imperceptibly [*insensiblement*] become accustomed to my principles, and recognize the truth in them before they notice that they destroy those of Aristotle.[7]

---

[4]   This approach to the *Meditations* has gained prominence in recent decades. For influential examples of it, see Margaret Dauler Wilson, *Descartes* (London: Routledge & Kegan Paul, 1978), Daniel Garber, *'Semel in vita*: The Scientific Background to Descartes' *Meditations'* and Gary Hatfield, 'The Senses and the Fleshless Eye: The Meditations as Cognitive Exercises', both in A. O. Rorty (ed.), *Essays on Descartes' Meditations* (Berkeley and Los Angeles: University of California Press, 1986), and John Carriero, 'The First Meditation', *Pacific Philosophical Quarterly* 68 (1987), 222–48.
[5]   Letter to Mersenne of 1629, AT I 70, CSMK 7. References to CSMK are references to J. Cottingham, R. Stoothoff, D. Murdoch and A. Kenny (eds.), *The Philosophical Writings of Descartes* Vol. III (Cambridge: Cambridge University Press, 1991).
[6]   Letter to Mersenne of 1633, AT I 271, CSMK 41.
[7]   Letter of 1641, AT III 298, CSMK 173, tr. alt.

Sarah Patterson

The metaphysics in the *Meditations*, then, provides the foundations for Cartesian physics. If we think of them as part of Descartes's campaign to replace the principles of Aristotle with the principles of Cartesian physics, the progress of the first three Meditations looks very different. According to Cartesian physics, the physical world consists of matter divided into parts of different shapes and sizes, moving in different ways. The nature of this matter is simply to be extended in three dimensions, to take up space. In Descartes's view, our grasp of the fundamental nature of the physical world comes not from our senses but from an innate intellectual idea placed in our minds by God, the idea of matter as extension that enables us to understand geometry. We also have innate ideas of thought, substance and God. But these ideas are obscured by a pre-occupation with the senses that begins in childhood and persists into adult life. This preoccupation gives rise to many 'prejudices of the senses' that obstruct our understanding of the true natures of body and mind.[8] Descartes writes:

> *The senses often impede the mind* in many of its operations, and in no case do they help in the perception of ideas. The only thing that prevents all of us noticing equally well that we have these ideas [sc. innate ideas of mind and God] is that we are too occupied with perceiving the images of corporeal things.[9]
>
> In metaphysics...there is nothing which causes so much effort as making our perception of the primary notions clear and distinct...they conflict with many *prejudices derived from the senses* which we have got into the habit of holding from our earliest years...[10]

One of the primary notions placed in our minds by God is the idea of matter as extension. According to this,

> ...nothing whatever belongs to the notion of body except the fact that it is something which has length, breadth and depth and is capable of various shapes and motions.[11]

However, our grasp of this idea is obstructed by our preoccupation with the sensory images of corporeal things. Thanks to this, we all believe that the bodies around us have qualities of colour, heat, cold and so on that exactly resemble our sensations. To counteract

[8] See AT VII 440–1, CSM II 296–7.
[9] AT VII 375, CSM II 258, emphasis added.
[10] AT VII 157, CSM II 111, tr. alt., emphasis added.
[11] AT VII 440, CSM II 297, tr. alt.

these prejudices of the senses, which 'offer only darkness', Descartes seeks to steer his readers' minds away from opinions that they have 'never properly examined – opinions which they have acquired not on the basis of any firm reasoning but from the senses alone'.[12]

Moreover, in Descartes's view, Aristotelian philosophy simply codifies this naïve preoccupation with the senses. As Aquinas puts it, citing Aristotle, the principle of knowledge is in the senses.[13] The senses receive the likenesses of sensible things, and our intellectual understanding of their nature is abstracted from these. On this view, all the materials of thought come from the senses; since there is nothing in the intellect that was not first in the senses, there are no innate ideas.[14]

If we read the first sentence of the *Meditations* against this background, we can see Descartes's talk of the many false beliefs acquired in childhood not as a reference to casual infantile mistakes, but as a reference to the prejudices of the senses we have got into the habit of affirming from our earliest years. And when he says that what we take to be most true is acquired from the senses, Descartes is voicing the view of childhood prejudice and Aristotelian philosophy. This is the view he expects his readers to bring to their reading of the text, the view he seeks to unseat. So it is not surprising that Descartes should speak of the benefit of the First Meditation doubt as he does in the Synopsis:

> Although the usefulness of such extensive doubt is not apparent at first sight, its greatest benefit lies in *freeing us from all our prejudices*, and providing the easiest route by which the mind may be *led away from the senses*.[15]

Undermining our naïve faith in the senses helps to free us from the prejudices of the senses imbibed in childhood, while drawing the mind away from the senses enables us to turn inwards and discover the intellectual ideas of mind and body innate in our minds, as we begin to do in the Second Meditation. Once in our lives, as Descartes says in the opening sentences of the *Meditations*, we need to demolish the views based on the prejudices of childhood and

---

[12]   AT VII 158, CSM II 112.
[13]   Thomas Aquinas, *Summa Theologiae*, Part I, question 84, article 6.
[14]   Descartes alludes to the Aristotelian slogan, 'Whatever is in the intellect must previously have been in the senses' when describing his pre-meditative views in the Sixth Meditation (AT VII 75, CSM II 52).
[15]   AT VII 12, CSM II 9, tr. alt.

Sarah Patterson

start again from new foundations, the foundations provided by innate ideas.

3. Innate ideas and the origin of our nature

If we read the First and Second Meditations in this way, in the context of a new science based on innate ideas, the appeal to God's benevolence in the Third Meditation takes on a different cast. God is brought in not to slay the evil demon, but to respond to a question that arises when we consider the ideas we find within ourselves.[16] Ideas that are innate, that come not from the senses but from within, are ideas we possess by nature. But what is their provenance? Where does our nature come from? We need to know this to know whether ideas we have by nature can be trusted.[17] This question of the origin of our nature is raised explicitly in the First Meditation:

> ...firmly rooted in my mind is the long-standing opinion that there is an omnipotent God *who made me the kind of creature that I am*. How do I know that he has not brought it about that there is no earth, no sky, no extended thing, no shape, no size, no place, while at the same time ensuring that all these things appear to me to exist just as they do now? What is more, since I sometimes believe that others go astray in cases where they think they have the most perfect knowledge, may I not similarly go wrong every time I add two and three or count the sides of a square, or in some even simpler matter, if that is imaginable?[18]

Here, God is specifically identified as our author of our natures, as the creator who made us the kind of creatures that we are. How do we know that this creator has not given us a nature that makes us subject to constant error? One might object that this would be incompatible with God's benevolence. But Descartes has a response:

[16] The evil demon doubt (on which the traditional reading focuses) is differentiated in the text from the doubt based on ignorance of the origin of our nature. Worries about the origin of our nature are introduced as a reason for doubt; the evil demon is introduced simply as a device to counteract habitual tendencies to belief (AT VII 22, CSM II 15). This point is stressed by Carriero, op. cit. note 3, 57–8.

[17] Carriero, op. cit. note 4, argues for interpreting Descartes's concern with the origin of our natures in light of his innatism.

[18] AT VII 21, CSM II 14, emphasis added.

...perhaps God would not have allowed me to be tricked in this way, since he is said to be supremely good. But if it were inconsistent with his goodness to have created me such that I am deceived all the time, *it would seem equally foreign to his goodness to allow me to be deceived even occasionally*; yet this last assertion cannot be made.[19]

If occasional deception is compatible with God's goodness, why not constant deception? Moreover, the prospect of constant deception is not removed by denying that we are the creations of an omnipotent God:

Perhaps there may be some who would prefer to deny the existence of so powerful a God rather than believe that everything else is uncertain. ...yet since to be deceived and to err seem to be imperfections, the less powerful they make my original cause, the more likely it is that I am so imperfect as to be deceived all the time.[20]

In sum, an all-powerful God could surely make us such that we go wrong all the time, while a less powerful cause might also produce the kind of nature that is constantly mistaken.[21] To assuage these worries about our nature, we need what might be called an origin story; we need to know where our nature comes from, how we come to be the kind of creatures that we are. The Third Meditation provides this origin story by arguing that we are the creations of a perfect being, God, 'who is subject to no defects whatsoever'.[22] This removes both the worry that our originating cause is lacking in power, and the worry that we are the creations of a deceiver. A perfect being 'cannot be a deceiver, since all fraud and deception depend on some defect'.[23]

Descartes's innatism makes sense of his concern with the origin of our nature. But once we have discovered that our creator is benevolent and non-deceiving, the problem raised in the First Meditation returns. How can this origin story be reconciled with the fact that we are sometimes deceived, that we are sometimes in error? Without a satisfactory answer to this question, the suspicion may

[19]   AT VII 21, CSM II 14, emphasis added.
[20]   AT VII 21, CSM II 14; tr. alt.
[21]   The significance of this dilemma argument is stressed by Carriero, op. cit. note 4, and by Robert Stoothoff, 'Descartes' Dilemma', *The Philosophical Quarterly* 39 (1989), 294–307.
[22]   AT VII 52, CSM II 35.
[23]   AT VII 52, CSM II 35.

remain that God's benevolence is compatible with our having a nature that is inherently flawed, a nature that disposes us to embrace falsehoods. Moreover, this question arises with particular force for Descartes, since he holds that many of the opinions we take for granted are in fact erroneous. The main task of the Fourth Meditation is to explain how the benevolence of our creator is compatible with the fact that he has given us a nature that enables us to make erroneous judgements. In doing so, Descartes takes pains to show that our capacity for judgement error can be explained without attributing any flaw to the faculties bestowed on us by the author of our nature.

4. Judgement error and the goodness of God

It might seem that the existence of judgement error is easy to reconcile with the benevolence of our creator. We are finite, imperfect creatures, so of course we make mistakes. But Descartes rejects this solution as unsatisfactory. We have already seen that for strategic reasons, Descartes could not rest content with attributing our errors to the imperfection of our nature. If we err simply because our nature is imperfect, our nature may be so imperfect as to contain false innate ideas, or positive propensities to affirm falsehoods. If our having such a nature were compatible with God's benevolence, appeals to that benevolence would be useless as a guarantor of the veracity of our innate ideas and propensities.

A satisfactory solution to the problem of judgement error, Descartes argues, must do justice to the fact that error is a privation: 'error is not a pure negation, but rather a privation or lack of some knowledge that somehow should be in me'.[24] A negation is simply the absence of something that could have been present. God could have given us wings, for example, but he has not done so. A privation is more than this; it is the absence of something that should be present.[25] If we judge wrongly only through lack of some knowledge that should be present, that suggests that we might be able to avoid error by repairing that lack. Descartes's explanation of our judgement errors makes good on this suggestion by attributing them to our

[24]   AT VII 55, CSM II 38.
[25]   For helpful discussion of the negation/privation distinction and its role in Descartes's argument, see Lex Newman, 'The Fourth Meditation', *Philosophy and Phenomenological Research* 70 (1999), 559–91, especially sections 1.1–2.

incorrect use of our freedom of will. The intellect perceives ideas, the contents of potential judgements; the ideas are affirmed or denied by an act of will. Erroneous judgements come about when we use our freedom of will to assent in cases where our perception is not sufficiently clear and distinct to discern the truth.[26]

> If I simply refrain from making a judgement in cases where I do not perceive the truth with sufficient clarity and distinctness, then it is clear that I am behaving correctly and avoiding error. But if in such cases I affirm or deny, then I am not using my free will correctly. …In this incorrect use of free will may be found *the privation which constitutes the essence of error.*[27]

The privation involved in judgement error arises from our incorrect use of free will; we fail to take account of the fact that 'the [sc. clear] perception of the intellect should precede the determination of the will', and so we assent in cases where we do not fully understand.[28] We are responsible for the incorrect use of freedom that constitutes the essence of error; 'the privation, I say, lies in the operation of the will in so far as it proceeds from me'.[29]

Descartes's explanation of our errors of judgement is designed to show that they do not arise from any defects in the faculties given to us by God. Our power of willing is not the source of our errors, since it is 'extremely ample and also perfect of its kind.'[30] The intellect is not to blame; since it comes from God, everything we understand, we understand correctly.[31] Indeed, at the end of the Fourth Meditation Descartes derives the truth of clear and distinct ideas directly from the nature of God:[32]

---

[26]   As is often noted, Descartes's solution to the problem of judgement error parallels a traditional solution to the problem of evil. That solution reconciles the evil of human sin with the perfection of our creator by attributing it to our misuse of our freedom of will.

[27]   AT VII 59–60, CSM II 41, emphasis added.

[28]   AT VII 60, CSM II 41.

[29]   AT VII 60, CSM II 41.

[30]   AT VII 58, CSM II 40.

[31]   AT VII 58, CSM II 40.

[32]   Descartes says in the Third Meditation that ideas considered solely in themselves, and not referred to anything else, cannot strictly speaking be false (AT VII 37, CSM II 26). This might suggest that ideas considered solely in themselves cannot be true either. However, the Fourth Meditation passage is one of several places in which Descartes speaks of ideas as being true. See also AT VII 46, CSM II 32, where he describes the idea of God as true. See Carriero, op. cit. note 3, 309–11, for helpful discussion.

...every clear and distinct perception is undoubtedly something and so cannot be from nothing, but necessarily has God for its author, God, I say, who is supremely perfect, who cannot be a deceiver on pain of contradiction; and therefore it is undoubtedly true.[33]

If what comes from God must be true, the story of our divine origin seems to vindicate our innate ideas and innate propensities. Surely nothing that we receive from a God who is 'supremely good and the source of truth'[34] could lead us astray.

5. The errors of the senses and the goodness of God

But this is not the end of the matter. The faculty of sensation is also part of our God-given nature. In the context of his campaign against naïve-cum-Aristotelian views, Descartes warns us of the deceitfulness of the senses and the error of trusting the senses rather than the intellect. But in the context of his story about the benevolence of our creator, the deceitfulness of the senses seems to pose a problem of theodicy that parallels the problem of judgement error. If our creator is no deceiver, why has he equipped us with what seems to be a deceitful faculty of sensation?

As a first step towards answering this question, we need to unpack Descartes's talk of the errors, deceptions and prejudices of the senses. Let us turn to a passage from the Sixth Replies in which Descartes clarifies what he means by saying that the senses are less reliable than the intellect. This is a passage in which Descartes draws an important distinction between three grades of sensation.

6. Errors of sensation and errors of judgement

The authors of the Sixth Objections pose a challenge to Descartes's claim that the reliability of the intellect is much greater than that of the senses.[35] 'How', they ask, 'can the intellect enjoy any certainty unless it has previously derived it from the senses when they are working as they should?'.[36] They cite the example of a stick that is straight, but looks bent in water because of refraction. Here, they

---

[33] AT VII 62, CSM II 43, tr. alt.
[34] AT VII 22, CSM II 15.
[35] AT VII 418, CSM II 281–2.
[36] AT VII 418, CSM II 282.

claim, the sense of touch corrects an error made by the sense of sight, a correction that the intellect could not make on its own.[37]

Descartes responds that there is in fact no error of sensation in this case; rather, there is an erroneous judgement that is corrected by another judgement. He supports this diagnosis by distinguishing three grades in what is called 'sensation'. The first is purely corporeal; it consists in the stimulation of the bodily organs by external objects, and subsequent motions in the nerves and brain.[38] The second grade

> comprises all the immediate effects produced in the mind as a result of its being united with a bodily organ that is affected in this way. Such effects include perceptions of pain, pleasure, thirst, hunger, colours, sound, taste, smell, heat, cold and the like, which arise from the union and as it were intermingling of mind and body.[39]

The third grade of sensation 'includes all the *judgements* about things outside us which we have been accustomed to make from our earliest years on the occasion of the movements of these bodily organs'.[40] Descartes goes on to explain that nothing beyond the second grade 'should be referred to sensation, if we wish to distinguish it carefully from the intellect.'[41] Nonetheless, he says,

> when from our earliest years we have made judgements, and even rational inferences, about the things that affect our senses...we refer them to sensation, because we reason and judge so quickly because of habit, or rather we remember judgements we made earlier about similar things, so *we do not distinguish these operations from a simple sense perception.*[42]

According to Descartes, then, sense-perception proper ends with the perceptions of pain, thirst, colour, heat and so on that occur in the mind as the immediate effects of movements in the brain. However, these perceptions are followed by inferences and judgements that go unnoticed, because they are so fast, habitual and familiar. Since they go unnoticed, they are confused with simple sense perceptions.

This confusion of habitual judgement with sensation, Descartes argues, lies behind the objectors' claim that the sense of touch

---

[37]   Ibid.
[38]   AT VII 436–7, CSM II 294–5.
[39]   AT VII 347, CSM II 294.
[40]   AT VII 437, CSM II 295, tr. alt., emphasis added.
[41]   Ibid,, tr. alt.
[42]   AT VII 438, CSM II 295, tr. alt., emphasis added.

corrects an error made by the sense of sight. Strictly speaking, there is no error of sensation here:

> we are not here dealing with the first and second grades of sensation, because *no falsity can occur in them.*[43]

This is a striking claim. Descartes insists that no falsity can occur in the perceptions of pain, pleasure, thirst, hunger, colours, sound, taste, smell, heat, cold and the like that occur at the second grade of sensation. Though this claim it may sound odd in view of his talk of the deceptions of the senses, it is just what we should expect, given that the faculty of sensation is part of our nature as embodied minds. Sensory perceptions are simply the natural effects of movements occurring in the body. Since they are a consequence of the workings of a nature created by a benevolent God, Descartes has good reason to say that there is no falsity in them.[44]

Where, then, is the error that the objectors attribute to the sense of sight? According to Descartes, it is the product of judgements occurring after the second grade of sensation. He explains that 'when people say that a stick in water "appears bent because of refraction"', they mean that 'it appears to us in a way which would lead a child to judge that it was bent', and may even cause us to make the same judgement, if we follow our childhood prejudices.[45] The correction of the error is also the work of judgement rather than of the senses. First we judge that the stick is straight as a result of touching it, then we judge that the judgement based on touch is to be preferred to the judgement based on vision.[46] So when the senses are said to be less reliable than the intellect, 'the senses' means habitual childhood judgements occurring at the third grade of sensation. To say that the intellect is more reliable than the senses, then, is to say that

---

[43] AT VII 438, CSM II 295–6, tr. alt., emphasis added. The claim that there is no falsity in the senses has a long pedigree. Aristotle writes in *De Anima* III.6 that the senses cannot be deceived about their proper objects (418a11). However, error is possible about objects perceived by more than one sense, such as size (*De Anima* III.3, 428b17).

[44] As we will see in sections 8 and 9 below, Descartes holds that sensations of thirst and pain occurring at the second grade of sensation can be erroneous when conditions are abnormal, and he has a story to tell about how this comports with God's goodness. The objectors to whom he is responding in the Sixth Replies explicitly limit their discussion to cases where the senses are working as they should, which may be why he does not mention these errors here.

[45] AT VII 438–9, CSM II 296.

[46] AT VII 439, CSM II 296.

mature, considered judgements are more reliable than infantile, unconsidered judgements; and this, Descartes says, is true.[47]

This passage provides important clarification of Descartes's talk of sensory error. It is not sensation proper that is in error, he says, but judgements that we have habitually made since childhood and that we do not distinguish from sensation. This recasting of errors of sensation as errors of judgement puts a different spin on Descartes's talk of the malign influence of the senses. The so-called 'prejudices of the senses' are evidently judgements, precisely because they are prejudices (pre-judgements) – judgements made before the intellect has examined the matter. Opinions acquired on basis of the senses, and never properly examined, are also judgements. But 'errors of the senses' that are actually errors of judgement can be dealt with by the account given in the Fourth Meditation.[48] The defect leading to these errors is not a defect in the faculty of sensation that God has given us, but consists in our wilful assent in cases where we do not perceive sufficiently clearly and distinctly.

7. A natural propensity to false resemblance judgements?

If Descartes's talk of errors of the senses can be recast as referring to erroneous judgements, they do not pose a further problem of error. However, Descartes not only speaks of the prejudices of the senses, he speaks of erroneous judgements that we seem to be 'taught by

[47]   AT VII 438, CSM II 295.
[48]   Some interpreters hold that third-grade judgements are not judgements in the full-blooded sense of the Fourth Meditation. This is the view taken by Alison Simmons, 'Descartes on the Cognitive Structure of Sensory Experience', *Philosophy and Phenomenological Research* 67 (2003), 549–79, 566–7 and by Cecelia Wee, *Material Falsity and Error in Descartes's* Meditations (London and New York: Routledge, 2006), 69–70. Since Descartes attributes third-level judgements to the intellect *alone*, they read him as referring to an act of combining ideas that involves only the intellect and not the will. I read Descartes's talk of the intellect *alone* as designed to emphasise that the senses are not involved, rather than to exclude any role for the will. This reading gains support from the fact that Descartes associates judgements in the full-blooded sense with the 'intellect alone' at the end of the Second Meditation, where his point is also to contrast judgement with the senses and imagination (AT VII 33, CSM II 22). Here Descartes uses 'intellect' as an umbrella term to cover intellect and will, the faculties of pure mind, when a contrast is being made with the faculties of the embodied mind.

Nature' to make, and this threatens to pose another problem of error. It is as hard to see how a veracious God could give us a natural propensity to make false judgements as it is to see how such a God could give us a deceitful faculty of sensation.

What are these false judgements that we seem to have a natural propensity to make? As noted earlier, we all believe that the bodies around us have qualities of colour, heat, cold and so on that exactly resemble our sensations. And early in the Third Meditation, Descartes identifies what he calls 'the chiefest and most common mistake' in our judgements, that of judging that external bodies wholly resemble our sensory perceptions.[49] He gives some examples in the Sixth Meditation: we judge that 'heat in a body is something exactly resembling the [sensory] idea of heat that is in me', that 'when a body is white or green, the selfsame whiteness or greenness which I perceive through my senses is present in the body', and that 'stars and towers and other distant bodies have the same size and shape which they present to my senses.'[50] By Descartes's lights, the belief that heat in a body is something exactly resembling the idea of heat that is in me, and the belief that stars have the same size which they present to my senses, are false. Heat as it exists in a body, for example, is to be understood in terms of the motions of matter. A star is a distant sun, many times larger than the earth. Nevertheless, Descartes depicts the tendency to form these false beliefs as universal; we all have a tendency to form what we might call 'resemblance judgements' – to believe that bodies exactly resemble the sensory perceptions they cause in us. Moreover, in the Third and Sixth Meditations he alludes to the idea that we are 'taught by Nature' to believe that external bodies wholly resemble our sensory perceptions of them.[51] Not surprisingly, then, many commentators read Descartes as holding that we have a natural propensity to form these false resemblance judgements.[52]

[49] AT VII 37, CSM II 26.
[50] AT VII 82, CSM II 56–7.
[51] AT VII 38, CSM II 26; AT VII 76, CSM II 53.
[52] See for example, Gary Hatfield, *Routledge Philosophy Guidebook to Descartes and the* Meditations (London: Routledge, 2003), 262. He writes that 'we have a natural inclination to affirm the resemblance thesis' and that 'He [God] has given us a tendency to believe that things are as they appear to us'. Deborah Brown, 'Descartes on True and False Ideas' in J. Broughton and J. Carriero (eds), *A Companion to Descartes* (Oxford: Blackwell, 2008), speaks of the senses as disposing us to judge incorrectly that the world is a certain way (197), and of our having 'a very natural and useful inclination' to externalize the content of our sensory ideas (214).

If God has given us a tendency to form a host of false beliefs, that surely poses a problem of theodicy. How could a non-deceiving God have given us such a propensity to error? This would be hard to reconcile with Descartes's claim that

> Since God is the supreme being, he must also be supremely good and true, and it would therefore be a contradiction that anything should be created by him which positively tends towards falsehood.[53]

Moreover, Descartes's argument for the existence of material things is based on the premise that a propensity to belief that is given to us by God must be trustworthy. Descartes argues that God has given us a 'great propensity' to believe that our sensory perceptions are caused by material things, and since God is no deceiver, this belief must be true.[54] He goes on to make the more general claim that

> ...everything that I am taught by nature contains some truth. For if nature is considered in its general aspect, then I understand by the term nothing other than God himself...and by my own nature in particular I understand nothing other than the totality of things bestowed on me by God.[55]

It is hard to see how these claims about God's veracity could be squared with the claim that we have a natural propensity to form a host of false beliefs about the resemblance between external bodies and our sensory perceptions.

Fortunately, Descartes does not face the task of reconciling these two claims. He does not hold, and indeed explicitly denies, that we have a natural propensity to form resemblance judgements. Far from being something we are taught by nature, he claims, such beliefs are prejudices that we affirm through habit. Descartes writes:

> ...there are many other things which I may appear to have been taught by nature, but which in reality I acquired *not from*

Raffaela De Rosa, *Descartes and the Puzzle of Sensory Representation* (Oxford: Oxford University Press, 2010), 26, claims that according to Descartes, our nature as a combination of mind and body erroneously teaches us that heat in a body is something exactly resembling the idea of heat which is in us, and so on.

[53] AT VII 144, CSM II 103.
[54] AT VII 80, CSM II 55.
[55] AT VII 80, CSM II 56.

nature but from *a habit of making ill-considered judgements*; and it is therefore quite possible that these are false.[56]

Descartes takes pains to emphasise that these habitual resemblance judgements do not derive from any real or positive propensity:

> ...although a star has no greater effect on my eye than the flame of a small light, *that does not mean that there is any real or positive propensity in me* to believe that the star is no bigger than the light; I have simply made this judgement from childhood onwards with out any rational basis.[57]

Given his views on what follows from God's veracity, he has good reason to emphasise this. A real propensity to believe would come from God, since 'everything real which is in us must have been bestowed on us by God'.[58] But a real propensity to believe that a star is no bigger than a small light would be a real propensity to believe a falsehood, and a non-deceiving God would not give us such a propensity.

For Descartes, then, we have no natural propensity to form resemblance judgements; we cannot, given the veracity of our creator. How, then, do we come to make them? Well, we already know from the Fourth Meditation that we form false beliefs because we judge where we do not perceive the truth sufficiently clearly and distinctly. When we do so, we forget that 'the perception of the intellect should always precede the determination of the will'.[59] That is just what we are doing, Descartes explains in the Sixth Meditation, when we draw conclusions from sensory perceptions about things located outside us 'without waiting until the intellect has examined the matter'.[60]

But this still leaves something unaccounted for. Our capacity to jump to conclusions explains how we are able to make ill-considered judgements, but it does not explain why we form *these particular* ill-considered judgements, nor why we all jump to the same conclusions. Without an account of this, Descartes's account looks incomplete. Descartes does have a story to tell here, one which begins with his diagnosis of where we go wrong in these cases:

> ...I see that I have been in the habit of misusing the order of nature. The proper purpose of the sensory perceptions given

---

[56] AT VII 82, CSM II 56, emphasis added.
[57] AT VII 83, CSM II 57, tr. alt., emphasis added.
[58] AT VII 144, CSM II 103.
[59] AT VII 60, CSM II 41.
[60] AT VII 82, CSM II 57.

me by nature is simply to inform the mind of what is beneficial or harmful for the composite of which the mind is a part; and to this extent they are sufficiently clear and distinct. But I use them as reliable rules for immediately discerning the essence of the bodies located outside us, about which they signify nothing that is not obscure and confused.[61]

Descartes claims that this habit of misusing sensory perceptions begins with our childhood preoccupation with the senses. As he depicts it in the Sixth Meditation, because we know external things only on the basis of our sensory ideas, we suppose that external things resemble these ideas.[62] Moreover, we take the supposition of complete resemblance to be something we are taught by nature; hence, Descartes initially describes it in the Third Meditation as something we are 'apparently' taught by nature. In the Sixth Meditation, the supposition is revealed as habitual, rather than natural. Our nature as embodied beings teaches us to avoid things that cause pain and seek things that cause pleasure, but it does not teach us to draw conclusions about external bodies from sensory perceptions without proper intellectual examination.[63] Beliefs reflecting the assumption that external objects wholly resemble our sensory perceptions are made through habit, not through natural propensity.

8. True errors of nature

All the so-called 'errors of the senses' discussed so far have been reduced to errors of judgement. They are errors we make by judging too hurriedly, by affirming what we are in the habit of affirming; they do not indicate any deceit in the faculties, propensities or ideas that we possess by nature. However, Descartes's claims about what our natures teach, about the purpose for which God has given us sensory perceptions, point us towards cases of genuinely sensory error.

Internal sensations of pain, thirst, hunger are given to us to inform us of harms to the mind-body composite, and of what would be beneficial to the composite. These occur at the second grade of sensation, so they are part of sensing proper. But these sensations can mislead.

[61]   AT VII 83, CSM II 57–8, tr. alt.
[62]   AT VII 75, CSM II 52.
[63]   AT VII 82, CSM II 57. I discuss teachings of nature in more detail in 'Descartes on Nature, Habit and the Corporeal World', *Aristotelian Society Supplementary Volume* 87 (2013), 235–58, secs. 2 and 3.

Sarah Patterson

In the second part of the Sixth Meditation, Descartes discusses the cases of the person with pain in a limb that no longer exists, and of the person with dropsy who feels thirst when drinking would be harmful. Descartes signals clearly that such cases present a new problem of theodicy, not reducible to the problem of judgement error.

> I have already looked in sufficient detail at how, *notwithstanding the goodness of God*, my *judgements* are false. But *a further problem* now comes to mind regarding those very things which nature presents to me as objects which I should seek out or avoid, and also regarding the internal sensations, where I seem to have detected errors...[64]

He identifies two forms of error here: cases in which nature presents something as beneficial when it is in fact harmful, and cases of error in the internal senses. The dropsy case is an example of the first kind of error, while phantom limb pain is an example of the second.[65] How is the existence of these errors to be reconciled with the goodness of our creator? This is the problem that Descartes faces, and it is one he takes very seriously. It cannot be dismissed, he argues, simply by saying that the nature of the person with dropsy is disordered by the disease:

> A sick man is no less one of God's creatures than a healthy one, and it seems no less a contradiction to suppose that he has received from God a nature which deceives him.[66]

He takes pains to emphasise that in a case of dropsy, the human being or mind-body composite is subject to what he calls a 'true error of nature' in being thirsty when drinking will cause it harm.[67] Here our God-given nature leads us astray. So 'it remains to inquire how it is that the goodness of God does not prevent nature...from deceiving us'.[68]

---

[64]   AT VII 83, CSM II 58, emphasis added.

[65]   Phantom limb pain is also mentioned earlier in the Sixth Meditation as an example of error in the internal senses, when Descartes is surveying reasons for doubting the senses (AT VII 77, CSM II 53). He presents it alongside cases of error in 'the judgements of the external senses', such as errors about the shape of distant towers (AT VII 76, CSM II 53).

[66]   AT VII 84, CSM II 58.

[67]   AT VII 86, CSM II 59.

[68]   AT VII 86, CSM II 59.

Descartes's explanation of how these errors can occur in a nature created by a perfect God is very different from his theodicy of judgement error. Judgement error is made possible by the difference in scope of will and intellect, and made actual by our misuse of freedom of will. What Descartes calls 'true errors of nature' are erroneous sensations; and since sensations are involuntary, the misuse of our wills cannot be responsible for them. Instead, Descartes offers a theodicy of these errors of nature that exploits his account of human beings as composites of mind and body.

9. Natural deceptions of the senses and the goodness of God

Descartes's explanation of what he calls 'natural deceptions of the senses' turns on his account of our nature as minds united to mechanical bodies. He compares the human body to a clock, depicting it as 'a kind of machine equipped with and made up of bones, nerves, muscles, veins, blood and skin'.[69] The mind united to the body is affected by motions in only one part of it, the part of the brain that contains the common sense (elsewhere identified with the pineal gland).[70] Moreover, motions in the brain are paired one-to-one with sensations in a fixed correspondence. A given motion in the gland causes 'just one corresponding sensation' in the mind.[71] This holds true no matter how the motion in the pineal gland has been produced. Given these constraints, Descartes says, the best system that could be devised is that a given motion in the gland should produce 'the one sensation which, of all possible sensations, is most especially and most frequently conducive to the preservation of the healthy man'.[72] Furthermore, he claims that

> experience shows that the sensations which nature has given us are all of this kind; so there is absolutely nothing to be found in them that does not testify to the power and goodness of God.[73]

Although God has devised the signalling system that best conduces to the preservation of our health, occasional errors are inevitable: 'notwithstanding the immense goodness of God, the nature of man as a

[69]   AT VII 84, CSM II 58.
[70]   See the *Optics*, AT VI 129 and the *Treatise on Man*, AT XI 175, CSM I 105.
[71]   AT VII 87, CSM II 60.
[72]   AT VII 87, CSM II 60.
[73]   AT VII 87, CSM II 60.

combination of mind and body is such that it is bound to mislead him from time to time.'[74] It is possible for motions in the pineal gland to be caused by neural events other than those they are intended to signal to the mind, and when they are, the resultant sensation is 'naturally deceptive'.[75] This is what happens in the cases Descartes singles out, those of phantom limb pain and dropsy. Suppose a foot has been amputated. Motions can still occur in the nerves that used to lead from the foot to the brain, and when they are transmitted to the brain they produce a sensation of pain as in the foot. Suppose that in dropsy, the throat is dry because fluid is accumulating elsewhere in the body. The dryness of the throat will cause motions in the nerves and in the brain that induce a sensation of thirst. The fact that God has given us a nature that is subject to these errors is not inconsistent with his goodness, because God has paired sensations with pineal motions in the way that works for the best in the typical case.[76]

10. The errors of the senses and the goodness of God revisited

The question we are concerned with is whether Descartes manages to reconcile the fact that we are subject to sensory error with the perfection of our creator. And it seems that he does. Consider again the three grades of sensation. No falsity can occur in the first grade, since this is just a matter of motions in nerves. No falsity occurs in the perceptions of the second grade, though sensations of thirst, hunger and pain can be deceptive when conditions are out of the ordinary. But as we have seen, Descartes argues that this occasional misrepresentation is an inevitable consequence of an internal signalling system that is the best it can be, given the limitations of a being composed of mind and body. Error at the third grade of so-called sensation is actually error in judgement. We have no natural propensity to make false judgements on the basis of sensory perceptions; our tendency to do so is the result of habits formed in childhood, when we lacked the use of reason.

---

[74] AT VII 88, CSM II 61; tr. alt., emphasis added.

[75] Ibid.

[76] Descartes implies both that it is better for God to design the system to preserve the healthy ('well-constituted') body, and that the circumstances for which the system is designed are more common than those for which it is not (the motion signalling damage to the foot more frequently arises from such damage than from another cause).

Descartes seems to be home and dry; he seems to have strategies for reconciling all our putatively sensory errors with the perfection of our creator. However, I think it would be premature to think that this is the end of the matter. According to Descartes's account of vision, our perception of the size, shape and position of objects is very often erroneous. On a natural reading of his account, these errors are due to erroneous judgements that contribute to the construction of our visual experience. (Recall the discussion in the Sixth Replies of how we perceive the shape of a stick.) Since they form part of the natural processes responsible for visual perception, they would seem to be judgements we have a natural propensity to make. If this is so, this poses a further problem of error for Descartes, a problem that has received little attention from commentators.[77] To see how these errors arise, we need to turn to Descartes's account of how visual perception works.

11. Descartes's account of how we see position, distance, size and shape

Descartes's fullest account of vision appears in the *Optics*, published in 1637.[78] This is the account to which he refers the reader in the passage in the Sixth Replies in which he distinguishes between the three grades of sensation. The *Optics* explains how light rays reflected by an object are focussed on the back of eye, tracing its image on the retina as a pattern of motion. This image is transmitted by nerves to

[77] Celia Wolf-Devine does recognize that these erroneous judgements threaten to pose a problem of error. She writes that Descartes's assigning our perceptual errors to erroneous judgements helps him to reconcile those errors with God's benevolence. See *Descartes on Seeing: Epistemology and Visual Perception* (Carbondale and Edwardsville: Southern Illinois University Press, 1993), 87. I argue below that these judgements are ones we are have a natural propensity to make, and that the problem of reconciling them with God's benevolence therefore remains.

[78] For further discussion of Descartes's account of vision, see op. cit. note 77, Gary Hatfield, 'Descartes' Physiology and its Relation to his Psychology' in J. Cottingham (ed.), *The Cambridge Companion to Descartes* (Cambridge: Cambridge University Press, 1992) and Celia Wolf-Devine, 'Descartes' Theory of Visual Spatial Perception' in S. Gaukroger, J. Schuster and J. Sutton, *Descartes' Natural Philosophy* (London: Routledge, 2000).

the brain, where it appears as a pattern of motion on the surface of the pineal gland.[79] As in the explanation of sensory signalling in the Sixth Meditation, these patterns of motion in the brain naturally produce certain sensations in the mind:

> it is the movements composing this picture which, acting on our soul insofar as it is united to our body, are ordained by nature to make it have such sensations.[80]

We are now at the second grade of sensation, that of the immediate effects in the mind of motions in the body. Discussing the example of seeing a stick in the Sixth Replies, Descartes says this grade 'extends to the mere perception of the colour and light reflected from the stick'.[81] He explains in the *Optics* that the *force* of the movements in the relevant part of the brain makes the soul have a sensation of light, while the *manner* of these movements makes it have sensations of colour.[82] So Descartes appears to think of the immediate mental effect of brain motions at the second grade as a perception of a two-dimensional pattern of colour.[83]

Nonetheless, light and colour are not the only qualities we see; we also perceive 'position, distance, size and shape' by sight.[84] To perceive the position, distance, size and shape of objects, the mind needs more information than is present in the two-dimensional image alone. Information about location is crucial, as Descartes recognises, since we need it to determine the size and shape of objects on the basis of the two-dimensional image. A small object located near the eye can project the same image as a large object positioned further from the eye. So how do we determine an object's distance from us?

Descartes details four methods we use. Firstly, the shape of the eye varies depending on whether it is focussing light from an object close to us or from an object further away. These changes in the shape of the eye are accompanied by a change in the brain which is 'ordained by

---

[79] AT VI 128, CSM I 167.
[80] AT VI 130, CSM I 167.
[81] AT VII 437, CSM II 295.
[82] AT VI 130, CSM I 167.
[83] Descartes says in the *Optics* that we can only discriminate the parts of the bodies we look at if they differ in colour (AT VI 133, CSM I 168), and speaks in the Sixth Replies of a perception of 'the extension of the colour and its boundaries' (AT VII 437, CSM II 295). So, as Simmons notes, expanses of colour are represented at the second grade (op. cit. note 48, 558).
[84] AT VI 130, CSM I 167.

nature to make the soul perceive this distance'.[85] Secondly, we can determine the distance of an object 'as if by a natural geometry'.[86] Imagine a line drawn between our two eyes A and B. This line AB forms the base of a triangle with X, the object seen, at its apex. If we know the length of the line AB and the size of the visual angles XAB and XBA, we can calculate how far the object X is from our eyes. The magnitudes of the line AB and the angles XAB and XBA combine together in our imagination and enable us to perceive the distance of X by an action of thought which although 'a simple act of the imagination, implicitly contains a reasoning quite similar to that used by surveyors'.[87]

The third way of perceiving distance is through 'the distinctness or indistinctness of the shape seen, together with the strength of weakness of the light'.[88] Objects further or nearer than the object X are seen less distinctly. If they reflect light more strongly than they would if they were at the same distance as X, we judge (*jugeons*) them to be nearer; if they reflect light more weakly, we judge them to be further.[89] Fourthly and finally, when we 'already imagine' the size or position of an object, or the distinctness of its shape and its colours, or merely the strength of the light that comes from it, this can enable us to imagine, though not to see, its distance.[90] For example, Descartes says, if we look from afar at something we are used to seeing close at hand, 'we judge [*jugeons*] its distance much better than we would if its size were less well known to us'.[91] If we look at a sunlit mountain beyond a forest in shadow, 'it is only the position of the forest that makes us judge [*juger*] it the nearer'.[92] If we look at two ships out at sea, one smaller than the other but proportionately closer so that they appear equal in size, 'we will be able to judge [*juger*] which is farther away' by the difference in their shapes and colours and the light they send to us.[93]

---

[85]   AT VI 137, CSM I 170.
[86]   Ibid.
[87]   AT VI 138, CSM I 170. I quote from the translation of the *Discourse on Method, Optics, Geometry and Meteorology* by Paul J. Olscamp (Indianapolis: Hackett, 2001), 106.
[88]   Ibid.
[89]   AT VI 138, CSM I 172.
[90]   AT VI 138–40, CSM I 172, Olscamp 107.
[91]   AT VI 140, CSM I 172, Olscamp 107.
[92]   Ibid. In this case, presumably, the greater brightness of the mountain would lead us to judge it to be nearer than the forest, if we did not already know that the forest was in front of it.
[93]   Ibid. It is not completely clear what is meant to be going on in this example, but perhaps Descartes's point is that we will judge a ship to be nearer if we perceive its shape and colour more distinctly. (He has already

As this summary indicates, Descartes accords processes of judging a central role in our perception of distance. The same is true of our perception of the size and shape of objects, since he holds that the perception of these is 'wholly included' in the way we see the distance and position of their parts.[94] He explains that

> we judge [*s'estime*] their size by the knowledge or opinion we have of their distance, compared with the size of the images they imprint on the back of the eye.[95]

Moreover, he thinks it equally obvious that 'shape is judged [*se juge*] by the knowledge, or opinion, that we have of the position of the various parts of the object'.[96] He cites the fact that retinal images usually contain only ovals and rhombuses when they make us see circles and squares. Because we know (or believe) that the object we are looking at is positioned at an angle to our line of sight, we judge it to be circular rather than elliptical, even though it produces an elliptical image in the eye.[97]

These passages from the *Optics* indicate the extent to which processes of reasoning and judgement are involved in seeing.[98] The size, distance and shape of distal objects cannot be determined on the basis of the two-dimensional image alone. The visual perception of these features depends on processes of reasoning and judging that combine information present in the image with information from other sources.[99] These judgements occur beyond the second grade

---

explained why different colours cannot be discriminated in distant objects, AT VI 134, CSM I 168–9.)

[94] Ibid.

[95] Ibid. Descartes explains the phenomenon of size constancy by appeal to the nature of these judgements. We obviously do not judge the size of objects by the absolute size of the retinal image alone, he says, because we do not see objects as a hundred times larger when they are close to us, even if the image they produce on the retina is a hundred times larger than the one they produce when ten times further away. Instead, we see them as the same size, but far away.

[96] Ibid.

[97] Ibid.

[98] This is emphasised in the Sixth Replies, where Descartes writes that he explained in the *Optics* 'how size, distance and shape can be perceived by reasoning alone, which works out any one feature from the others' (AT VII 438, CSM II 295).

[99] Alongside these references to judgement, Hatfield sees Descartes as presenting an account of distance perception as purely psychophysical (op.

of sensation, but are nonetheless involved in the construction of visual experience. Borrowing a term from Simmons, I call them 'constructive judgements'.[100] Why should constructive judgements be thought to pose a further problem of error?

12. Erroneous constructive judgements and the goodness of God

Firstly, the constructive judgements that figure in the seeing of position, distance, shape and size are very often wrong. This is inevitable, since 'all our methods for recognising distance are highly unreliable'.[101] Consider, for example, the first and second methods of estimating distance, which depend on the shape of the eye and the visual angles respectively. The shape of the eye varies hardly at all, Descartes says, when the object is more than four or five feet away, and even when it is closer it varies so little that 'we cannot have any precise cognizance of it'.[102] If we are looking at an object at all far way, there is very little variation in the visual angle. This, he claims, is why the moon and the sun look so much smaller than they are. Our methods for registering distance represent them as no more than one or two hundred feet away, and this false estimate leads to a false constructive judgement of their size. We see them as one or two feet across at the most, he says, although we know through reason that they are very much larger.[103]

Secondly, a case can be made for regarding constructive judgements as ones that we have a natural propensity to make. This point can also be illustrated by the perceived size of the sun. The constructive judgement of size responsible for our visual experience of

---

cit. note 78, 356–7). In the *Treatise on Man* (AT XI 170, CSM I 106), he depicts perceptions of distance as depending directly on changes in the pineal gland. In the *Optics* (AT VI 137, CSM I 170), he says that changes in the shape of the eye are accompanied by changes in the brain 'ordained by nature' to make the soul perceive distance. Even on this psychophysical account, processes of reasoning and judgement would presumably be needed to yield perceptions of shape and size, but vision would involve fewer (erroneous) judgements.

[100]   Op. cit. note 48, 569. Though I disagree with it on some details, I have learned much from Simmons' paper.

[101]   AT VI 144, CSM I 173.

[102]   Ibid.

[103]   Ibid.

the sun is made on the basis of the size of the two-dimensional image the sun projects, combined with information about distance gleaned from sources that are unreliable. The knowledge that the information is false, that the sun is very far away and very large indeed, does not enable us to stop making the constructive judgement; the sun goes on looking as it always did. This is reason to think that the constructive judgement is dictated by our nature – that it is a consequence of the way we mind-body composites are set up to perceive distance, size and shape. But if God has given us a natural propensity to make erroneous constructive judgements, that poses a problem of error distinct from any discussed so far.

However, a case can also be made for the contrary view that our tendency to make constructive judgements is due to habit, not natural propensity. After all, in the Sixth Replies Descartes associates visual error about the shape of a stick with judgements made through habit. If these false judgements are habitual, they are our responsibility, and our tendency to form them is no more problematic from the point of view of God's goodness than our tendency to form false resemblance judgements. To weigh the case for regarding constructive judgements as natural, we need to consider the case for the contrary view.

13. A natural propensity to false constructive judgements?

Speaking of how we see the size, shape and distance of a stick in the Sixth Replies, Descartes speaks of 'judgements, or even rational inferences, about the things that affect our senses' that are made at great speed because of habit, judgements made since childhood.[104] This may seem to provide clear evidence that he regards constructive judgements about size, shape and distance as made through habit.[105] But the discussion in the Sixth Replies is open to differing interpretations. Does it concern resemblance judgements, which are acknowledged to be habitual, or constructive judgements, the status of which is in question? To say a stick in water appears bent because of refraction, Descartes claims, is to say that it appears in a way that would lead a child to judge it to be bent. But is he speaking here of the constructive judgement that determines how the stick visually appears, or of

[104] AT VII 438, CSM II 295.
[105] For example, see Hatfield, op. cit. note 78, 357–8 and Alison Simmons, 'Spatial Perception from a Cartesian Point of View', *Philosophical Topics* 31 (2003) 395–423, 398.

the resemblance judgement that the child may make on the basis of that appearance? The fact that he says that we adults may also judge it to be bent, *if* we follow the prejudices of childhood, suggests that he is referring to a judgement that can be corrected. This is most plausibly taken to be the resemblance judgement. We adults know that the stick in water is straight despite its visual appearance, so we can correct the false childhood judgement that it is bent. But even if we do, the visual appearance of the stick in water remains the same. So the judgement we correct is not the constructive judgement that determines the visual appearance of the stick, but the resemblance judgement – the rash childhood judgement that the stick is just as it appears. This would make the point that Descartes is aiming for here: that adult judgements are more reliable than childhood judgements.

Later in the Sixth Replies, Descartes speaks of astronomers who know that the sun is larger than the earth, but cannot prevent themselves from judging it to be smaller when they turn their eyes to it.[106] He compares them to those who have an inveterate habit of affirming judgements made since childhood.[107] Does this not show that he regards the constructive judgement of the sun's size as habitual? Again, the text is open to differing interpretations. There are two false judgements in this case, the false constructive judgement responsible for the visual appearance of the sun, and the false resemblance judgement that the sun is as small as it appears. Descartes uses the case to illustrate the difficulty of abandoning an habitual judgement. Is it the constructive judgement that is the habitual judgement in question, or the resemblance judgement? The text tolerates both readings. Here as elsewhere, though, Descartes's concern is with false resemblance judgements. He uses the passage to illustrate how difficult it is to relinquish false habitual opinions about the natures of mind and body. Clearly he thinks these opinions can be corrected; the arguments of the *Meditations* are designed precisely to correct them. So the illustration better serves Descartes's purposes if these opinions are compared to the astronomer's habitual resemblance judgement, which can be altered, rather than the constructive judgement, which cannot.

Of course, this consideration is not decisive if Descartes himself holds the view that the constructive judgement of the sun's size

[106] AT VII 440, CSM II 296.
[107] AT VII 446, CSM II 300. The same comparison appears in the later *Principles of Philosophy*, section I.72, AT VIIIA 36–7, CSM I 219–20.

Sarah Patterson

resists alteration only because it is entrenched by habit.[108] But that
view is extremely implausible. Descartes clearly regards it as possible
to correct errors in habitual judgements as a result of rational reflection, even though it is difficult to do. The error in the constructive
judgement of the sun's size is not difficult, but impossible to alter
through rational reflection. This is not surprising, since the errors
in these different judgements originate in very different ways. The
error in the habitual judgement that the sun is the size it visually
appears to be is due to lack of reflection; it is a resemblance judgement
made without good grounds in childhood, and thoughtlessly affirmed through habit since then. The error in the constructive judgement of the sun's size is due to false information derived from
unreliable methods of judging distance. Our judgements of distance
are unreliable not because they are based on childhood habits, but
because of limitations in the way the visual system works. That is
good reason to regard the errors in our constructive judgements as
errors we are disposed to make by the nature God has given us,
rather than errors we make because we have not yet corrected the prejudices of childhood.[109]

14. Constructive judgements and natural deceptions of the senses

If these erroneous constructive judgements flow from our nature, can
they be handled in the same way as so-called errors of nature, such as
sensations of pain in a missing limb? Since these natural errors are explained as the inevitable consequence of the way we mind-body composites are constituted, so this proposal may seem promising at first.

[108]   The fact that Descartes speaks of the difficulty of 'imagining' the
sun and stars as being larger than we are accustomed to do may be a sign
that he is tempted by this view, if 'imagine' is read as an allusion to experience. This terminology appears in the Sixth Replies, AT VII 446, CSM II
300 and the *Principles*, AT VIIIA 37, CSM I 220.
[109]   As noted earlier (note 48), Simmons denies that constructive judgements involve the will. She takes them to involve mental operations falling
'somewhere between the mere perception of ideas and the affirmation by
the will of whatever those ideas present to the mind' (op. cit. note 48,
566). These operations yield sensory experience, which cannot be revised,
rather than belief, which can (see 567). Some kind of affirmation still
seems to be involved here, even if it does not involve the will; so even on
this view, we are so constructed as to naturally affirm falsehoods, though
not because of a natural propensity to believe.

100

However, Descartes's solution to the problem of errors of nature does not generalise in any straightforward way to the problem of error in constructive judgements. The explanation of errors of nature turns on the claim that although God has benevolently devised the signalling system that best preserves health in usual conditions, misleading sensations can still occur when the body is damaged or diseased. In these unusual conditions, sensations can be caused by bodily conditions other than the one they are intended to signal to the mind. But erroneous constructive judgements do not fit this model. False estimates of distance and erroneous constructive judgements about shape and size do not happen occasionally, when conditions are unusual or when the body is damaged or diseased. They occur routinely, as a consequence of the ordinary functioning of the visual system. Moreover, the claim that a visual system that functions in this way is the best that could be devised seems hard to defend. It is not difficult to imagine changes to the system that could produce more reliable estimates of the distance of objects, such as greater variation in the shape of the eye, or in the visual angle. Finally, unlike naturally deceptive sensations, the visual errors we are concerned with are errors in judgement. It seems more troubling to suppose that the routine operation of our God-given visual system compels us to act incorrectly, by affirming falsehoods, than it does to suppose that God has created an internal signalling system that occasionally produces erroneous sensations.

Even though the model Descartes uses to reconcile natural errors with God's goodness does not fit error in constructive judgements, the focus on sensations may suggest a more promising line of thought. Descartes emphasises that our senses are given to us for the preservation of life, to present bodies to us in ways that indicate their potential to help or harm us. So, we might think, there is no surprise, and no conflict with God's goodness, in the occurrence of false judgements in the operation of a visual system that aims at preservation rather than truth. According to this line of thought, the putative problem of error simply dissolves when we take account of the true function of the senses.

This solution has been used to explain how Descartes reconciles our supposed natural propensity to form false resemblance judgements with the goodness of God. It is fine for the senses to dispose us to false judgements, the thought goes, since the senses aim at survival rather than truth.[110] I have argued that the reconciliation is

---

[110]   For example, Brown writes, 'We learn from the Sixth Meditation that the primary function of sensation is to deliver us the world not so as to know it but so as to navigate it as embodied agents. ...Take seriously

unnecessary, since Descartes denies that we have such a natural propensity. But if we do have a natural propensity to form false constructive judgements, why not apply the solution here?

Though the solution may seem to be an appealing one, it would not be appealing to Descartes, or so I claim. It stands in too much tension with his view that there is no falsity in our God-given sensations. To see where the tension lies, it is helpful to briefly compare Descartes's view with that of a later Cartesian, Malebranche. Malebranche appears to hold the view that some commentators attribute to Descartes, the view that falsity in our sensations is immaterial because they are given to us not to discern the truth, but for the preservation of life. Understanding how their views differ will help us to see why this solution would not sit well with Descartes.

15. Malebranche on falsity in natural judgements

Malebranche's account of how vision works follows Descartes's closely.[111] Like Descartes, he notes the 'considerable defects' in our means of judging distance, and the consequent unreliability of all the judgements based on them.[112] Explaining why we see the moon as small even when we know it is not, he writes:

> although we might know for certain through reason that [the moon] is large and at a great distance, we cannot help but see it quite as near and small, because these *natural judgements of vision* occur in us, independently of us, and even in spite of us.[113]

What Malebranche here calls 'natural judgements' are clearly constructive judgements. For him, they are judgements made not by us, but by God. As far as we are concerned, they are sensations; but they are sensations corresponding to judgements that we would make if we had the requisite knowledge and inferential capacity.[114]

---

this idea and much can be explained about how the senses dispose us to judge incorrectly that the world is a certain way…' (op. cit. note 52, 19).

[111] For an extended discussion of Malebranche's account of spatial perception that compares it with Descartes's, see Simmons, op. cit. note 105.

[112] Nicolas Malebranche, *The Search After Truth*, tr. and ed. T. M. Lennon and P. J. Olscamp (Cambridge: Cambridge University Press, 1997), Book I, Part 9, 46. Hereafter cited as *Search*.

[113] *Search* I.7, 35, emphasis added.

[114] *Search* I.7, 34. Malebranche here notes that there are many errors that these natural judgements or compound sensations enable us to avoid.

Since we lack that knowledge and capacity, Malebranche thinks, God fashions our visual perceptions in and for us in accordance with the laws of optics and geometry and the laws of soul and body.[115]

Now the problem of error arises. The manifold errors in our perception of distance, shape and size illustrate Malebranche's claim that 'our eyes generally deceive us in everything they represent to us'.[116] But why has a benevolent God created a system that gives us so many false judgements-cum-sensations? Malebranche replies that the defects in our natural judgements of distance, size and shape are just what one would expect in a sensory system geared to the preservation of life rather than the discernment of truth. For example, our methods of estimating distance via changes in the shape of the eye and the visual angles 'are quite useless when the object is from five to six hundred paces away and are not reliable even when the object is closer'.[117] As a result,

> we know the motion and rest of objects better as they come closer
> to us, and we are unable to judge them through the senses when
> they seem no longer to have any relation, or to have almost no
> relation, to our bodies (as when they are five or six hundred
> paces away and are of insignificant size, or even nearer than this
> and smaller, or finally, when they are larger but further away).[118]

For Malebranche, this just goes to show that 'our eyes were not given us to judge the truth of things, but only to let us know which things might inconvenience us or be of some use to us'.[119] It is important for our survival to know about bodies that are near to us, and therefore in a position to help or harm us; it is not important for our survival 'to know the exact truth about things occurring in faraway places'.[120] So, Malebranche says, the defects of vision exemplify his general doctrine about the senses, that they 'inform us of things only in relation to the preservation of our bodies and not as they are in themselves'.[121]

For example, we see people walking towards us as getting closer but not as getting larger, though the images they project on the retina do get larger (cf. note 95 However, they are also the cause of many errors.

[115] *Search* I.9, 47.
[116] *Search* I.6, 25.
[117] *Search* I.9, 43.
[118] *Search* I.9, 46.
[119] *Search* I.6, 30.
[120] Ibid.
[121] Ibid.

Consonant with this general doctrine, Malebranche holds that all our sensory perceptions incorporate false natural judgements. Some of these, as we have seen, lead to false perceptions of the size, shape and distance of bodies. Others lead us to falsely perceive our own sensations as existing in bodies. Our sensations of whiteness, coldness and pain are simply modifications of our souls, modifications that cannot exist in an extended body. But thanks to in-built natural judgements, we perceive whiteness and coldness as being in snow, and pain as being in our fingers.[122] The natural judgements that make us thus project our sensations onto bodies occur 'in us independently of us and even in spite of us... in connection with the preservation of life'.[123] Pain must be felt in the finger so that we pull it away from the thorn, and colour must be sensed in objects so that we can distinguish them from one another.[124] The falsity of these natural judgements-cum-sensations accords with God's benevolence, since it simply reflects the fact that the senses aim at preservation, not truth. We willfully go wrong, though, in habitually making free judgements that match these natural judgements. In making these erroneous judgements, the soul

> blindly follows sensible impressions or the natural judgements of the senses...it is content, as it were, to spread itself onto the objects it considers by clothing them with what it has stripped from itself.[125]

To avoid these habitual errors, we must judge in accordance with reason, which is given to us to discover the truth, and not in accordance with the natural judgements of the senses, 'which never discover the truth and which were given only for the preservation of the body.'[126]

16. Descartes and Malebranche compared

How do Descartes's views compare with those of Malebranche? One obvious difference is that Descartes never suggests that the defects in our means of judging distance, and the consequent falsity of

[122] *Search* I.10, 52.
[123] *Search* I.11, 55.
[124] Ibid.
[125] *Search* I.12, 58. This memorable image was later borrowed by Hume (see *A Treatise of Human Nature*, I.3.14).
[126] *Search* I.12, 59.

judgements based on them, are designed to further our preservation. We have to make judgements about shape and size on the basis of judgements about distance, because information about distance is needed to try to reconstruct the layout of the three-dimensional objects responsible for projecting the two-dimensional image. Our manner of judging the distance of objects is unreliable because it is based on cues that are relatively insensitive to that distance, such as the shape of the eye and the size of the visual angle. So the falsity in constructive judgements is simply a consequence of the way the visual system is structured, and that is the end of the matter. Descartes gives no sign of adumbrating an explanation of visual error in terms of preservation of the kind that Malebranche gives.

Why does Descartes not adopt Malebranche's solution? After all, their views seem very similar. Malebranche takes the view that sensory perceptions aim at preservation from Descartes, and both thinkers warn of the error of using perceptions given for this purpose as guides for free judgements about the nature of bodies. However, there is a fundamental difference underlying these similarities. For Malebranche, the mistake we make in judging in accordance with our sensations-cum-natural judgements is that of affirming something false. Our sensory perceptions of size and shape illustrate the falsity of sensations particularly well, because they incorporate natural judgements of distance that are clearly false.[127] For Descartes, by contrast, the distinctive feature of what he calls 'the grasp of the senses' is not that it is false, but that it is naturally obscure and confused.[128] Sensory perceptions occurring at the second grade of sensation involve no judgement and contain no falsity. So the error we make in our habitual judgements is not that of affirming sensory perceptions that are false, but that of treating obscure and confused perceptions of bodies as guides for immediate judgements about their essences. Notice that Descartes does not say that sensory perceptions provide no information about external bodies, nor that they provide false information; rather, they provide information about the nature of external bodies, but in a form that

---

[127] Presumably this is one reason why Malebranche begins with them in his campaign to set us right by bringing us 'to a general distrust of all the senses' (*Search* I.6, 25). The falsity of natural judgements of distance can be used to prepare the way for his more controversial claims about the error of perceiving sensible qualities such as colour and heat in bodies.

[128] He writes, 'in many cases the grasp of the senses is very obscure and confused', AT VII 80, CSM II 55.

is obscure and confused.[129] For example, we might think of our sensory perception of heat in an external body as an obscure and confused perception of motions in its parts, or of a similar property that can be understood in mechanical terms.[130] On this picture, we perceive heat as located in the body because we are perceiving something that is actually in the body, rather than projecting our own sensation onto the body, as we do for Malebranche.[131] Though our sensory perception of heat is not false, its obscurity and confusion means that it does not clearly reveal the nature of its object.[132] That is why we are mistaken if we assume that we can read the true nature of bodies straight off our sensory perceptions of them – if we assume, for example, that heat as it exists in a body exactly resembles our sensory perception of heat.[133]

For Descartes, unlike Malebranche, our perceptions of distance, size and shape are atypical among sensory perceptions through being false, and through involving judgement. When we habitually

[129]   This point is stressed by Alison Simmons, in 'Are Cartesian Sensations Representational?', *Noûs* 33 (1999), 347–69, 350.

[130]   In *Principles* I.198–9, Descartes describes heat, colours and so on as nothing but certain arrangements or dispositions (*dispositiones*) in objects, depending on size, shape and motion (AT VIIIA 323, CSM I 285). We are accustomed to distinguish between mechanical properties per se and dispositions grounded in them, but Descartes shows little sign of being concerned with this difference.

[131]   Interpreting sensory perceptions as perceptions of features existing in bodies has the advantage of providing objects for them. Sensory perceptions are ideas, and all ideas are directed on objects. Indeed, according to the traditional model that Descartes inherits, ideas are objects existing in the mind. For further discussion, see my 'Clear and Distinct Perception' in J. Broughton and J. Carriero (eds), *A Companion to Descartes* (Oxford: Blackwell, 2008), 217–8 and John Carriero's very helpful 'Sensation and Knowledge of Body in Descartes' Meditations' in K. Detlefsen (ed.), *Descartes'* Meditations: *A Critical Guide* (Cambridge: Cambridge University Press, 2015), particularly 117–8.

[132]   This is the view I suggest in op. cit. note 131, 229. Gary Hatfield interprets the obscurity and confusion of sensory ideas in this way in 'Descartes on Sensory Representation, Objective Reality, and Material Falsity' in K. Detlefsen (ed.), op. cit. note 131, 141.

[133]   Malebranche and Descartes agree that we habitually mistake the purpose of sensory perceptions when we match our free judgements to them, but they differ over the nature of our mistake. For Malebranche, we mistakenly assume that sensory perceptions aim at truth. For Descartes, we mistakenly assume that sensory perceptions clearly reveal the nature of their objects (i.e., what they are perceptions of).

judge that the sun is small on the basis of how it looks, we erroneously assume that we can read the sun's size straight off our sensory perception of it. [134] But in this case, our sensory perception of the sun's size is not just obscure and confused, but false, because it reflects a false constructive judgement. This makes it difficult to think of our perception of the sun as small as simply an obscure and confused perception of its true size.

For Malebranche, then, the preservative function of sensory perceptions explains why they incorporate false judgements. For Descartes, by contrast, the preservative function of sensory perceptions explains why they present their objects obscurely and confusedly. This being so, explaining the falsity of visual perceptions of distance, size and shape in terms of the preservative function of the senses is not an obvious solution for him. Moreover, Descartes's view of sensation as a mode of perception that is obscure and confused, but not false, fits his conception of what follows from God's goodness. Since the faculty of sensation is part of our God-given nature, we should not expect to find falsity in our sensory perceptions. It is quite in order for our sensory perceptions to be obscure and confused, because this reflects the imperfection of our natures as composites of mind and body. Since we are embodied creatures which can be helped or harmed by the bodies surrounding us, information about those bodies needs to be provided in a format that makes relevant features salient and is easy to use for survival.[135] That is just what the senses provide. The falsity of sensory perceptions is no part of this story. But the constructive judgements involved in our perception of distance, size and shape seem to have a claim to be both natural and false. The fact that they are natural, that they are judgements we have a God-given propensity to make, creates pressure for them to be true. Hence these judgements are problematic for Descartes in a way they are not for Malebranche.

---

[134] In the Third Meditation, Descartes contrasts our visual perception of the sun's size with astronomers' calculations of its size to illustrate lack of resemblance between objects and sensory perceptions (AT VII 39, CSM II 27). The example is dialectically useful because it requires no controversial assumptions about the nature of sensible qualities.

[135] See Simmons, op. cit. note 129 for further discussion of the preservative role of the senses.

17. Conclusion

I have argued that Descartes's account of vision suggests that we are subject to a species of error that does not fit his solutions to the problems posed by errors of judgement and errors of nature. If this is right, then the errors of the senses he invokes in the opening paragraphs of the *Meditations*, errors in our perceptions of objects that are very small and very far away, are more problematic than he recognises. Here an obvious question arises: If that is so, why did Descartes himself not recognise it? The answer may lie in his differing concerns as a physiologist and as a philosopher. In the *Optics*, where his account of visual perception appears, he aims to explain how vision works in terms of a mechanism interacting with a mind, without making use of the Aristotelian notion of the transmission of a likeness. Judgement figures in his account because the two-dimensional image alone does not suffice to determine the size, shape, position of the objects that produced it. Information about distance must be acquired and incorporated by processes of inference and judgement. In the *Meditations*, by contrast, Descartes is concerned to combat the Aristotelian view that all the materials of thought come from the senses. He aims to show that the blueprint for our understanding of the underlying nature of the physical world comes from an idea of body that is innate in our minds. We perceive the physical world through our senses in an obscure and confused manner that is designed primarily to aid our preservation. Here his emphasis is on the error of assuming that sensory perceptions clearly reveal the essences of their objects, so that we can read the nature of the physical world straight off them. Our tendency to judge that bodies are exactly as they appear to our senses is not natural, but habitual, so it lacks the divine mandate of innate ideas. From the perspective of Descartes's plan of invoking the errors of the senses to help guide to us to a grasp of the innate ideas given by God to lead us to a true understanding of the nature of the world and of ourselves, false judgements of vision are easily overlooked.

Birkbeck College
s.patterson@bbk.ac.uk

Why Should We Read Spinoza?

SUSAN JAMES

Abstract

Historians of philosophy are well aware of the limitations of what Butterfield called 'Whig history': narratives of historical progress that culminate in an enlightened present. Yet many recent studies retain a somewhat teleological outlook. Why should this be so? To explain it, I propose, we need to take account of the emotional investments that guide our interest in the philosophical past, and the role they play in shaping what we understand as the history of philosophy. As far as I know, this problem is not currently much addressed. However, it is illuminatingly explored in the work of Spinoza (1632–77). Spinoza aspires to explain the psychological basis of our attachment to histories with a teleological flavour. At the same time, he insists that such histories are epistemologically flawed. To study the history of philosophy in a properly philosophical fashion we must overcome our Whiggish leanings.

The history of philosophy is like a city. Epochs of frenetic activity are followed by periods of stagnation; philosophical movements, like neighbourhoods, come in and out of fashion; and within them individual philosophers rise and fall. During the last few years, accompanied by a little restoration and town planning, Spinoza has become a more prominent feature of the philosophical cityscape. He appears in the equivalents of tourist guides, archival publications, architectural monographs and local fiction, and there is even a movement to make him a heritage site.

This change of sensibility is reflected in a great range of philosophical studies, which examine Spinoza and his work from many angles, interpreting him, for example, as a Cartesian, a contributor to the Jewish philosophical tradition, an Epicurean, a Stoic, or a Machiavellian. But alongside attempts to situate him within the *longue durée* of the history of philosophy, there is also a growing interest in bringing Spinoza's ideas to bear on contemporary philosophical concerns. His work is increasingly used to help illuminate and defend a range of positions, whether panpsychism, naturalism, toleration or democracy. Appealing to the work of a historical figure to lend lustre to a contemporary debate, and simultaneously enhancing the status of the figure by according them contemporary relevance, is of course a standard strategy within the history of philosophy, and it is easy to see how such a dynamic can strengthen or undermine an approach or viewpoint. But its status as a way of doing philosophy is harder to discern. What

doi:10.1017/S1358246116000266   ©The Royal Institute of Philosophy and the contributors 2016
Royal Institute of Philosophy Supplement **78** 2016   109

Susan James

gains do we make by bringing historical figures to bear on our own pre-occupations, and what philosophical motivations do we have for taking up this approach, which, in some of its manifestations, has been the object of stringent criticism? These questions can be addressed at many levels of generality. Rather than attempting a full exploration, my aim is a narrower one: I shall focus on a currently popular version of the approach I have mentioned, and consider how Spinoza himself might explain the fact that this approach continues to occupy a central place in contemporary history of philosophy.

Spinoza is therefore both the subject and the object of this enquiry, the object insofar as it reflects on one of the ways in which his philosophy is currently used, and the subject insofar as it offers an interpretation of an aspect of his own philosophical position. Merging these perspectives, I shall try to reconstruct what Spinoza would say about some of our attempts to use his work to illuminate our own problems, and about the approach to the history of philosophy that these attempts exemplify

1.

Even in its most analytical reaches, philosophy is a historical subject. It usually proceeds by criticising or embracing earlier philosophical claims, whether they are drawn from the last decade or the last millennium, and to this extent feeds upon its own past. Philosophers sometimes scan their history for the utterly alien or stimulatingly strange, but they more often turn to it for insight into positions to which they are already drawn. Those who adopt this approach look to their predecessors for anticipations of themselves, and their attention to the past is guided by their own preoccupations. In studies of Spinoza, for example, a renewed commitment to naturalism has prompted contemporary scholars to explore Spinoza's contribution to this general outlook. He is now often interpreted, in Don Garrett's words, as an exponent of 'the project of fully integrating the study and understanding of human beings, including the human mind, into the study and understanding of nature, so that human beings are not contrasted with nature but are instead understood as entities ultimately governed by the same general principles that govern all other things'.[1]

---

[1] Don Garrett, 'Representation and Consciousness in Spinoza's Naturalistic Theory of the Imagination' in C. Huenemann ed., *Interpreting Spinoza: Critical Essays* (Cambridge University Press, 2008).

Why Should We Read Spinoza?

To some extent, we are bound to read past philosophers in the light of our own philosophical culture, which in turn makes some features of their works apparent to us and others invisible. What we find is shaped by who we are. However, there are many ways in which our existing interests can guide interpretation, and a striking feature of much current history of philosophy is what I shall call its teleological flavour. Although it is rare for commentators to adopt a wholeheartedly teleological approach and explain particular historical events or processes by citing an end to which they contribute, we can detect a teleological flavour when the work of a past philosopher is assessed in the light of contemporary values and praised for anticipating them. We may, for instance, be invited to admire Spinoza for opening the way to modern naturalism. What makes his work worthwhile, so this interpretation implies, is that it was a step on the road towards a superior modern outlook.

Some commentators adopt this attitude with gusto. For example, Jonathan Bennett sets out, as he puts it, to 'get Spinoza's help in discovering philosophical truth',[2] and assesses his doctrines for their contribution to this goal. According to Bennett, some of Spinoza's positions, such as his adamant rejection of teleological explanation, offer worthy challenges to existing philosophical orthodoxies, but others do not. The final section of the *Ethics*, for instance, is 'an unmitigated and seemingly unmotivated disaster' (page 357). Or to take a more recent case, Jonathan Israel portrays Spinoza as the founder of a process of radical enlightenment, which he describes as issuing in 'an abstract package of values – toleration, personal freedom, democracy, equality racial and sexual, freedom of expression, sexual emancipations and the universal right to knowledge and "enlightenment".'[3] For both these authors, the value of studying Spinoza lies in his relevance to 'our' philosophy.

The tendency to focus on past doctrines or approaches because they are of contemporary interest, and the teleological tendency to assess them in the light of their contribution to the development of our own beliefs, are logically distinct. In principle, one might be interested in Spinoza's naturalism because one was oneself a naturalist, while denying that it played any significant role in the development of the forms of naturalism that are widespread today. In practice, however, the two often go together. Finding something of ourselves

[2] Jonathan Bennett, *A Study of Spinoza's Ethics* (Cambridge University Press, 1984), para. 9, page 35.
[3] Jonathan Israel, *Enlightenment Contested* (Oxford University Press, 2006), 11.

in Spinoza's philosophy slides easily into the teleologically-flavoured project of arguing or implying that what makes this aspect of his work significant is the fact that it anticipates our own philosophical commitments, and played some role, however indirect, in their development. Rather than merely noting resemblances, we tend to build them into narratives tinged with grandeur, in which our own era is represented as more insightful and better attuned to the truth than any of its predecessors.

Nevertheless, as historians are well aware, teleologically-flavoured interpretations are fraught with danger. Writing in 1931, Herbert Butterfield coined the term 'Whig history' to describe narratives that portray the past as marching towards the enlightened condition of democratic liberalism, and criticised them on several grounds.[4] Advocates of the Whig approach, he argued, assume that past figures or traditions shared our own conceptions of what is true and interesting, and therefore look to them for anticipations of their own philosophical problems; but in doing so, they run the risk of suppressing past attitudes or points of view that diverge from their own. Their tendency to homogenise history is in turn liable to distort it by excluding or overlooking unfamiliar ideas and constructing a factitious continuity between past and present. Reinforcing a rhetorical conception of philosophy as the study of age-old problems, it sounds a note of comforting steadiness, while at the same time introducing an overtone of tedium. It produces a history that is already playing fragments of our tune, waiting for us to harmonise them. Still worse, this approach can turn into an indirect exercise in self-congratulation, in which some of our ancestors are criticised for failing to get the point, while others are patted on the back for anticipating our beliefs. Bertrand Russell, for example, dismisses Spinoza's metaphysics as 'incompatible with modern logic and with scientific method' and consequently 'impossible to accept'.[5] Spinoza's failure to grasp what we know to be the truth deprives his metaphysics of any philosophical value.

A further and closely-related objection to Whig history is that, in cleaving to teleologically-flavoured interpretations, we assume that philosophy is a single unified enterprise and become insensitive to the ways it has changed over time. As well as inclining us to ignore alien doctrines, the habit of assessing the past in the light of our own convictions can blind us to unfamiliar conceptions of philosophy

[4] Herbert Butterfield, *The Whig Interpretation of History* (London: G. Bell, 1931).
[5] Bertrand Russell, *History of Western Philosophy* (London: George Allen and Unwin, 1946), 601.

itself. For example, when Russell rejects Spinoza's metaphysics, he sets aside the possibility that metaphysics as Spinoza understood it is not a primitive version of contemporary science and is consequently not answerable to scientific standards of assessment. By assuming that metaphysics is a proto-science, Russell closes off alternative conceptions of it and thus alternative conceptions of philosophy in general.

These limitations of Whig history have often been rehearsed and are widely acknowledged; so the fact that teleologically-flavoured interpretations of the past continue to be popular suggests that not all philosophers of our own era find the standard criticisms of Whiggery conclusive. Some of them presumably think that it is possible to take a teleologically-flavoured approach to the past while avoiding the abuses criticised by Butterfield and his successors. We can mine the history of philosophy for antecedents of our own convictions, and use past ideas productively, without assuming that the figures whose work we appropriate shared our philosophical outlooks, or that their ideas have come to fruition in our own. For example, one can focus on and learn from those features of Spinoza's work that anticipate contemporary naturalism, while allowing that certain aspects of his position are incompatible with naturalism as we understand it, and that it is an open question whether his position played a significant role in the emergence of its modern counterpart. We can simply select and concentrate on historical doctrines that we find relevant, and as long as we do not stray any further into Whig territory, no harm is done. On the contrary, philosophical thinking gains a depth and richness that takes it far beyond the insights of a single era.

This view regularly resurfaces in the historiographical literature.[6] If we avoid the explanatory errors identified by Butterfield, it demands, what is wrong with borrowing from the past in order to do philosophy in the present? Put like this, the answer seems to be 'nothing'; yet there remains something troubling about this reply. A sense of its incompleteness stems in part from the difficulty of putting it into practice. Philosophers whose interest in history is shaped by contemporary debates are liable to do more than merely select historical doctrines they favour and run with them. They also tend to assess these doctrines in the light of their own convictions, and to this extent adopt a Whiggish stance. If one studies Spinoza as a naturalist *avant la lettre*, for example, it is difficult to avoid

---

[6] See for example Eric Schliesser, 'Philosophic Prophecy' in M. Laerke, J. Smith and E. Schliesser eds, *Philosophy and its History* (Oxford, 2013), pp. 209–35.

appealing to our own understanding of naturalism to elucidate his position, and hard to refrain from congratulating or condemning him *sotto voce* for the modernity or backwardness of his insights.

This worry may in turn generate debate about when a teleological flavour becomes unpalatable. Is there anything wrong with assessing Spinoza's naturalism as, by our standards, wanting? Why should we not applaud him for gesturing towards a disenchanted nature? The boundary between acceptable and unacceptable teleological interpretations continues to be contested, and in order to reach agreement about it we would need a clearer sense of when a teleological approach becomes flawed. What makes it admissible to include Spinoza in a history of the development of naturalism, and in what circumstances does this do violence to the integrity of his philosophical position? One way to resolve this uncertainty would be to offer a clear account of what counts as an unacceptably teleological analysis, against which individual case studies could be tested. However, it is hard to imagine a single set of criteria that would command general assent. This is partly because philosophers turn to history to achieve many goals, and no single way of separating the acceptable from the unacceptable will answer to them all. But it is also for the overlapping reason that philosophers tend to be torn between two kinds of emotional investment in their past.

To understand the persistence of the debate between Whigs and their opponents, it is not enough to focus on the intellectual strengths and weaknesses of the stances we have been considering. Also at stake are two contrasting pleasures. On the one hand, there is the anthropological pleasure that historians of philosophy take in the strangeness of the philosophical past and its lack of relation to our own outlooks, an excitement in the discovery of ideas suppressed and paths not taken. On the other hand, there is the satisfaction of recognizing ourselves in earlier traditions, thus sustaining our sense of philosophical continuity and progress. These pleasures are not exclusive (we identify difference as a departure from continuity, and continuity as a departure from difference) and philosophers who engage with the past typically feel the pull of both. But while the anthropological pleasure acts as a brake on teleological interpretation by focusing our attention on rupture and untranslatability, the pleasure of recognition inclines us to view the past in a broadly teleological spirit. To satisfy it, we look to history for anticipations and affirmations of ourselves; and from there it is a short step to explanations and evaluations of the broadly teleological kind that we have so far been examining.

If this diagnosis is right, the debate between Whigs and their opponents has an emotional dimension that helps to keep it going. To commit firmly to one side or the other is to forego (or attempt to forego) a powerful intellectual pleasure. Historians who are convinced of the value of Whiggish interpretations may still suffer anthropological yearnings, just as those who are officially hostile to Whig approaches may find themselves drawn to interpretations with a teleological flavour. The pleasures that we seek in studying the past do not always line up with our explicit philosophical beliefs about the methods we ought to employ, and are not completely stilled by argument.

As far as I am aware, analytical historians of philosophy have not paid much attention to this aspect of philosophical practice. While many acknowledge that individual interpreters invest emotionally in the philosophers they study, wanting them, for example, to be morally or metaphysically admirable, the affective dimension of our relation to the past is not on the whole discussed. Perhaps this is because it is seen as a psychological phenomenon that lies beyond the bounds of properly philosophical investigation; but whatever the reason, explorations of this dimension of philosophising are largely absent from current debate. One may find this is a little surprising, the more so since there has recently been an increased recognition within analytical epistemology that humans are not very good at reasoning, and more the playthings of their passions than they know.[7] If this is view is right, should we not bring it to bear on our own practice as philosophers? Should we not try to get some critical distance on our researches by supplementing the back and forth of argument with an examination of the pleasures, anxieties and desires that are intertwined with our explicitly intellectual convictions?

There are many ways to reconnect with the emotional aspect of studying the history of philosophy, but an attractively reflexive route turns back to the history of philosophy itself, and specifically to past philosophers for whom affects lie at the heart of our thinking and activity. Here Spinoza's work offers an obvious starting point since, for him, all thinking is a manifestation of our striving for a satisfying and empowering way of life, and philosophising, like the rest of our thinking, expresses this orientation. Philosophy, we can say, is identified as an activity that gives us a certain kind of emotional satisfaction. Together with Spinoza's analysis of the operations of our affects, I shall suggest, this conception secretes an account of the desires and pleasures underlying teleological interpretative approaches to the history of philosophy, and an assessment of their role within philosophical enquiry.

---

[7] Daniel Kahneman, *Thinking Fast and Slow* (Allen Lane, 2011); Quassim Cassam, *Self Knowledge for Humans* (Oxford University Press, 2014).

It offers a hypothesis about the character and causes of our attachment to Whiggery, and opens up a fresh way to think about it.

2.

Spinoza's account of human affects is grounded on his view that, as long as an individual thing exists, it is exercising a power to maintain itself in existence. Things strive to persevere in their being by exercising their own power as opposed to being passively acted on by external things. Moreover, since this is as true of human beings as of anything else, all our activities, mental and physical, can be described at a highly abstract level as exercises of our power to maintain ourselves in existence in the face of our encounters with external things. In the human case, our disposition to preserve ourselves is manifested in our affects. Our experience of our fundamental striving takes the form of desires and appetites, and increases or decreases in our power present themselves as forms of joy and sadness. Whether we are walking down the street on autopilot or thinking through a logical proof, we are motivated by desires that are ultimately for empowerment, and are experiencing the emotional satisfactions and dissatisfactions that constitute our current power to actively maintain ourselves. This overarching disposition, which is constitutive of our human nature and does not have to be learned, shapes our sense both of ourselves and of other things. It sensitises us to our own vulnerabilities and strengths, for example through the experience pride or fear, and attunes us to the threats and opportunities that external things present, so that instead of perceiving the world in a neutral fashion, our basic orientation towards it is affective. We encounter frightening enemies rather than men with weapons, welcoming friends rather than people with open arms, and these affects in turn shape our conscious and unconscious desires. In all our relationships with external things, and all our reasoning and reflection, we use our existing power to find ways of engaging with the world that are emotionally satisfying and strengthen our capacity to take delight in our lives.

Since these general features of human nature are at work in everything we do, they underlie both our successful and our less successful efforts to empower ourselves. Much of the time, Spinoza argues, we strive to persevere in our being on the basis of a partial and confused understanding of ourselves and external things, with correspondingly limited effects. For example, we pursue short-term ends to our long-term detriment, or develop attachments to objects that make us more sad than joyful. But although this mode of striving is always with us and determines many features of our lives, we are to some extent able to offset its limitations by cultivating a fuller knowledge of the world, and a wiser practical sense of how to live in an empowering fashion. As Spinoza puts it, we can compensate for the deficiencies of what he calls imagining by developing what he describes as the capacity to reason or understand. Moreover, as we do so we exercise our own power and become increasingly active.

Empowering ourselves thus consists in cultivating ways of life that do justice to our existing knowledge of ourselves and our environment, and leave room for us to enhance both our knowledge and our capacity to live in the light of it. However, in the account of this unending project that Spinoza offers in his *Ethics*, he focuses on the importance of understanding ourselves. While our capacity to live in an empowering fashion is often blocked by our ignorance of the world around us, our greatest problems stem from lack of self-knowledge, which is in turn partly due to our own imaginative dispositions. Since our efforts to empower ourselves are habitually limited by psychological dispositions that beckon us down paths leading to sadness, one of our first tasks is to learn to compensate for them.

Among the most pervasive of these tendencies is a disposition to exaggerate our individual power and overestimate what we can achieve. To offset it, we need to acknowledge the extent to which we are individually dependent on external things for our wellbeing, and learn how to put this insight to work in our ways of life. Rather than struggling on our own, we need to strengthen our power to persevere in our being by joining forces with other people. However, as Spinoza goes on to argue, this project is attended by its own difficulties. To manage it successfully, we have to deal with a further ambivalent aspect of our psychology, deriving from the fact that our affects are primarily focused on those of other human beings. We experience other people as like us in the sense that they share our repertoire of affects. Just as we can respond to their emotions so they can respond to ours, and this mutual recognition is in turn reflected in our individual and collective efforts to enhance our power.

To some extent, Spinoza argues, the mere fact that we recognise other human beings as sharing our emotional constitution is enough to make us imitate their affects. Whereas we do not envy trees their height or lions their strength, we pity humans with whom we have no other connection and may desire things simply because other people want them.[8] Moreover, these affective

---

[8] Spinoza, *Ethics* in E. Curley ed., *The Collected Works of Spinoza* (Princeton University Press, 1985), E3p27.

dispositions tend to operate more strongly among collectivities whose members perceive themselves as having more than their mere humanity in common. In all its manifestations, however, the imitation of the affects is a two-edged sword. As the examples of pity and competitiveness indicate, it can move us to cooperate with one another, as when pitying someone motivates us to ameliorate their suffering; but can also lead us to compete, as when the imitation of desire produces excessive demand for a scarce good that many individuals try to get for themselves.

In Spinoza's analysis, the negative aspects of the imitation of the affects are uppermost; although 'men ... are so constituted by nature that they pity the unfortunate but envy the fortunate', they are nevertheless more prone to vengeance than to compassion.[9] The main reason is that our efforts to empower ourselves by developing co-operative and mutually beneficial ways of life are cross pressured by an impatient tendency to try to realise our desires by imposing them on others. 'Each of us', Spinoza claims, 'strives so far as he can that everyone should love what he loves and hate what he hates' ... 'Each of us wants the others to live according to his *ingenium* or temperament'.[10] In addition to being drawn to people with whom we already have things in common, we try to make other individuals into the kind of people to whom we can be drawn. This goal can be achieved by various means, including force, coercive threats and offers, flattery or persuasion; but Spinoza is particularly interested in the fact that our efforts to empower ourselves by these routes are often tinged with fantasy. We tend to project our desires onto others, representing them to ourselves as people who already share our *ingenium* or temperament and are already as we want them to be. Short-circuiting the difficulties of generating a co-operative ethos, we behave as though our own affects are already shared, and view other people through the lens of our own yearnings and aspirations.

Imagining therefore shapes our conception of the people around us and the opportunities for empowerment that they afford; but our tendency to make the world in our image can also lead us to a more ambitious form of anthropomorphising, in which we imagine quasi-human agents who mirror our desires. The most striking example of this phenomenon, in Spinoza's view, is our imaginative construction of powerful, anthropomorphic deities, whose affects are analogous to our own and who have our interests at heart. Here, our disposition to respond affectively to things that are like us, and thus to other

---

[9]   *Ethics*, IIIp32s.
[10]   *Ethics* 3p31c; 4p37s.

human beings, extends into fictional territory. We imagine that we have affective relationships with deities who are somewhat like us, and imbue non-human natural things with providential powers to respond to our needs. We come to think, as Spinoza puts it, 'that there is someone else who has prepared those means for our use' and that 'the gods direct all things for the use of men'.[11]

Fantasies of this kind may play a role in helping a community to live harmoniously. In some circumstances, for example, a shared belief in the existence of an anthropomorphic god may produce convergent desires that bind a group of individuals together, encouraging the positive aspects of affective imitation and restraining the negative ones. However, while Spinoza by no means underestimates the power of this phenomenon, and discusses it at length in his *Tractatus Politicus*, he remains convinced that the most effective basis of cooperation lies in understanding.[12] To create lasting and stable ways of life, we need to discover what we really have in common with those around us, and, on the basis of this knowledge, work out how to sustain mutually empowering ways of life. Moreover, this is a philosophical as well as a political project – a matter of extending our rational knowledge of ourselves and our environment and finding ways to live as this knowledge dictates. Taking account of our tendency to imitate one another's affects, and of the consequences of this disposition, our task is to use it to live together, not on the shaky basis of fantasy, but in ways that reflect our understanding and nurture the development of our active power.

In setting out this programme, Spinoza sometimes seems to invoke an idealised conception of philosophy as the preserve of wise individuals, who view the project of increasing our active power from on high. Since they have already achieved an exceptional level of insight into human nature, their problems lie not so much in extending their understanding as in exercising it while living amongst a less enlightened majority, bringing their knowledge to bear on the conflict and disorder of everyday politics and promoting a philosophically grounded way of life. In fact, however, Spinoza's view is more nuanced. In any individual, understanding is mixed with imagination, and the power to live as one's understanding dictates will be stronger and more resilient in some circumstances than in others. Although we may imitate other people's affects to better or worse effect, the disposition to project our desires is always with us and,

---

[11] *Ethics*, I App. [1].
[12] Spinoza, *Tractatus Politicus* in A.G. Wenham ed., *The Political Works* (Clarendon Press Oxford, 1958).

however wise we may become, continues to shape our relations with other people and things.

This being the case, historians of philosophy will remain liable to imitate one another's affects, and will be subject to the disposition to project their desires on to others. By acknowledging the part that this process plays in their study of their subject, we may be able to uncover some of the underlying pleasures and desires that draw them to specific modes of interpretation, and particularly to those with a teleological flavour. What, then, can Spinoza's discussion of our affective relations with things that we regard as like us reveal about the practice of the history of philosophy? In the first place, it suggests that this disposition will be at work in the relations between living historians, each of whom will try to achieve the satisfactions that empowerment brings by forming bonds with other whom they regard as like themselves. Those who are already teleologically inclined may, for example, try to empower themselves by joining forces, thus promoting a kind of factionalism that is a familiar feature of intellectual life. However, because individuals will also be liable to try to impose their desires on their colleagues, we should expect the relations between historians to be marked by dissent, and to give rise to conflicts that may become significantly disempowering. If Spinoza is right, competition will outweigh co-operation.

So far, we have a rather banal and pessimistic image of historical practice; but Spinoza's analysis also suggests that we should expect to find imitations of affect in the relations between living historians and the dead philosophers they study. Historians will try to satisfy their aspirations, whether for prestige, integrity or self-respect, by identifying with past philosophers who seem to them to share something of their outlook, adding lustre to their philosophical convictions by allying themselves, for example, with Plato, Confucius or Kant. More than this, however, the fact that dead philosophers cannot respond affectively to the living makes the past a particularly fertile field for projection. It provides historians with an arena, we might say, in which they can relieve the distinctively philosophical sense of lack that Novalis describes as a desire to be at home every-where, by finding themselves in their predecessors and aligning themselves with this or that tradition. Here, then, Spinoza's account of our imaginative disposition to project our desires onto other people and things illuminates the first of the two elements that characterise teleologically-flavoured approaches to the history of philosophy, namely the pleasure we take in focusing on aspects of the past with which we can identify, and the connected tendency to imaginatively obliterate the differences between past and present. Much as we may try to proceed in a cool, investigative spirit, imagination is liable to sweep us along, creating empowering similarities where none exist and heightening them wherever they are to be found. In short, when we study the history of philosophy, we try to consolidate our power and satisfaction by imagining the world as answering to our desire that others should be like us.

It remains to consider whether Spinoza's psychology can also account for the second element of teleologically-flavoured interpretations of the past – the fact that such interpretations construe historical processes as steps on the road to our own superior outlooks and values. Here again our disposition to make the world answer to our affects plays a crucial role. It is, Spinoza tells us, a deep fact about human beings that we think of ourselves as purposive creatures who formulate short- and long-term ends and assess states of affairs in relation to these goals. Furthermore, we unselfconsciously attribute this mode of operating to other kinds of things, taking it, for example, that other animals are designed to serve our purposes. Pressing this line of interpretation a stage further, we may conceive of them as created by an anthropomorphic deity who made them for our use. Thus represented, the world is our oyster, a domain in which our desires are legitimated by nature and by God, and in which we can confidently strive to empower ourselves.

Our disposition to impose our human ends on nature therefore plays a role in satisfying our affective needs, and our attachment to teleologically-flavoured interpretations of the past forms part of this broader pattern. As Spinoza implicitly acknowledges when he criticises philosophers who dream of a long-gone golden age, dwelling on the glories of a past way of life that we can no longer realise, and that puts our own in a bad light, is liable to be dispiriting. By contrast, we gain confidence and energy from interpretations of the past that harness it to the creation of our own power, by representing our achievements as rooted in a steady process of historical growth. On the one hand, past events are construed as conducive to our values; on the other hand, they do not rival or threaten our achievements, but instead reflect back our desire for supremacy.

3.

We have been tracing Spinoza's use of a strategy that he describes (implausibly) as a completely novel feature of his work: the attempt to *explain* the workings of the affects. Once we take account of the constellation of emotional habits that constitute the imitation of the affects, the persistence of teleologically-flavoured approaches to understanding the past should not in his view surprise us. We should recognise them as manifestations of a set of psychological dispositions that shapes much of our everyday grasp of the world. However, the fact that such approaches are to be expected does not mean that they are philosophically defensible, and we may also be curious to know what he thinks of them. Do they make a valuable contribution to the history of philosophy or should we eschew them as far as we can?

It is clear that Spinoza regards each of the two elements of a teleologically flavoured approach that we have distinguished – the tendency to focus on aspects of the past with which we can identify, and the tendency to regard these aspects as forming a process that culminates in our own outlook and way of life – as epistemologically flawed. Insofar as our explorations of the past are shaped by our disposition to imagine and heighten empowering affective relationships between ourselves and other things, they are not primarily responsive to the way things are. Striving to satisfy our desires, we are liable to arrive at distorted conceptions of historical events and processes. However, the disposition to misconstrue the past in this fashion is not ineluctable; we can learn to offset it by understanding the operations of our affects and learning how to identify our projections for what they are. We are not condemned to error by the very fact that we discern similarities and differences between ourselves and our historical predecessors, but rather by the way we do so, and part of the art of philosophising consists in training ourselves to be more cautious than we naturally are.

By contrast, the second element of teleologically-flavoured explanations goes with a deeper epistemological limitation. As we have seen, our affective dispositions incline us to view the past as adapted to our ends, and manifest themselves in a tendency to construct historical narratives in which our way of life provides the happy ending. But Spinoza is adamant that all teleologically-flavoured explanations are wanting. Since nature has no end, the way to understand natural events is not to posit goals to which they contribute, but to identify their antecedent causes. It is true that it can be helpful, in everyday contexts, to account for an event by appealing to its end, as when you tell me that you are turning on the tap because you want a drink; but shortcuts of this kind do not do justice to the complex pattern of causes from which particular events flow and in which their full explanation lies. Teleologically- flavoured explanation therefore rests on and perpetuates a radically misconceived view of the operations of natural things, including ourselves, and has no place in philosophy. In order to understand nature adequately, we must eschew such explanations, and if our histories of philosophy are to live up to the epistemological standard that philosophy sets, we must learn to do without them. Comforting as they may be, we must seek our pleasures elsewhere.

Thus conceived, philosophy is an extraordinarily demanding undertaking. The surest way to empower ourselves is to concentrate on finding out how nature is structured, how it impinges on us and how we respond to it, and in using this knowledge to build stably satisfying ways of life. We must learn to avoid the conflicts that arise from affective competition by discovering what we really have in common with other people and finding ways to satisfy our common needs. We must learn to recognise teleologically-flavoured explanations as partial and epistemologically misleading reconstructions of past events, and avoid them as far as possible. In part, then, philosophy is a matter acquiring knowledge, and requires a range of intellectual virtues such as ingenuity and dedication. But it also consists in developing the capacity to put this knowledge into practice and live as it dictates. Here a further range of epistemological virtues comes into play, of which the two most prominent are *animositas*, the determination to live as understanding dictates, and *generositas*, the disposition to do so by joining forces with others. Philosophers, as Spinoza conceives them, need to develop a particular *ingenium* or character; they must be willing to learn rather than rigidly committed to a particular outlook, and be gentle rather than aggressive, inclusive rather than exclusive, in their pursuit of understanding.

Being human, philosophers strive to empower themselves by imitating the affects of people they perceive as like them; but in doing so, they exercise their virtues. Rather than imposing their desires on others or competing with them for scarce goods, they are on the lookout for individuals who share their commitment to a philosophically-informed way of life. They employ the imitation of the affects to unite with people who share something of their temperament, and to encourage others to develop it. Moreover, once their understanding alerts them to the overarching limitations of teleological explanation, they will try to avoid interpreting their own philosophical past in a teleological fashion, and will search instead for the antecedent causes of historical events. Rather than viewing history as a prelude to their own achievements, Spinozist philosophers will study the past for insight into the continuing philosophical project of living in the light of our understanding.

There seem, then, to be two ways in which the study of the history of philosophy can further the philosophical project as Spinoza conceives of it. First and most straightforwardly, dead philosophers may teach us how nature operates. Spinoza, for example, is interested in the natural philosophy of his era, particularly the work of Bacon and Descartes, and is alert to earlier theories of the affects including those of the Stoics. These figures belong to a philosophical community that encompasses the dead as well as the living and is relatively indifferent to chronology. In addition, past philosophers may help their descendants to live in the light of the philosophical knowledge they possess by offering them models or images of empowering ways of life that they can use as guides. In some cases, these will be models of the good life; for example, images of the virtuous man as discussed by Aristotle, Cicero and Seneca are all present in Spinoza's work. As well as these forms of theoretical guidance, however, Spinoza is if anything more interested in seeking historical advice about the practical aspects of philosophy. His supreme exemplar of a philosophical life is that of Jesus Christ; and he clearly thinks that there are many other accounts of the lives of rulers and statesman from which we can draw lessons about the art of good government. The philosophical community, as he now begins to portray it, includes historians such as Tacitus, Livy and Josephus, statesmen such as Machiavelli, and rulers such as Alexander and Moses, whose actions or writings can inform our efforts to live in the light of our understanding.

Assessing the strategies and decisions of past legislators and sovereigns can therefore help us to learn to live together; but we also need to see how their actions contributed or failed to contribute to the security and longevity of political communities. One of Spinoza's most comprehensive historical investigations consequently focuses on the history of the ancient Hebrew commonwealth. By studying its laws and the decisions of its leaders, he contends, Dutch philosophers such as himself can identify the flaws that led to its downfall and, thereby enabling the Dutch Republic to avoid the same mistakes.

The view that Spinoza endorses therefore looks to the history of philosophy not as a source of self-congratulation or reassurance, but rather of inspiration. Living philosophers are committed to promoting a way of life in which they pool their insights and help one another to live as their shared understanding dictates; but part of this project involves drawing on the theoretical and practical insights that have come down to us in the works of philosophers, historians, prophets and rulers. Some of these figures were themselves engaged in the very practice of philosophy that Spinoza is advocating; they were philosophers in his sense of the term, and can help philosophers like him understand the demands of a philosophical life. Others were not. (Spinoza is emphatic, for example, that Moses was a prophet rather than a philosopher, and distinguishes the roles of philosophers and statesmen.) But the insights of these individuals can nevertheless contribute to philosophical understanding. For example, genuine prophecy can, in Spinoza's view, reveals moral truths. Equally, the political skills of rulers and statesmen can teach us how to live in the light of our knowledge, and until this knowledge is put into practice, the work of philosophy is only half done. Spinoza's conception of the community of the wise to which philosophers can turn for inspiration therefore extends more widely than we might nowadays expect. Where we tend to conceive of philosophy as a theoretical undertaking and view its history accordingly, he sees it as the collective project of learning to live as powerfully as possible in the light of a true understanding of nature. Philosophers should consequently turn to history for both theoretical and practical insight, and make what they can of the models that have come down to them.

Returning to one of the commentators from whom we began, we can now see that Spinoza would not have objected to Jonathan Bennett's efforts to mine the *Ethics* for philosophical insights, though he would have found Bennett's conception of philosophy radically incomplete. Where Bennett treats philosophy as a theoretical undertaking, Spinoza regards it as a practical one. Furthermore, Spinoza would have rejected the teleological flavour that characterises Bennett's work, and indeed much contemporary history of philosophy. As Spinoza's theory of the affects suggests, overcoming the tendency to think teleologically about the past is not easy. Nevertheless, in resisting it, we prevent ourselves from falling prey to an ultimately disempowering disposition to interpret nature in the light of our own purposive operations that is itself a manifestation of the incompleteness of our understanding. Interpreting the past in a teleological fashion is not blameworthy. It is an aspect of our striving to empower ourselves and answers to our affective needs. But it is not philosophy.

Birkbeck College, London
s.james@mail.bbk.ac.uk

Managing Expectations: Locke on the Material Mind and Moral Mediocrity

CATHERINE WILSON

Abstract

Locke's insistence on the limits of knowledge and the 'mediocrity' of our epistemological equipment is well understood; it is rightly seen as integrated with his causal theory of ideas and his theory of judgment. Less attention has been paid to the mediocrity theme as it arises in his theory of moral agency. Locke sees definite limits to human willpower. This is in keeping with post-Puritan theology with its new emphasis on divine mercy as opposed to divine justice and recrimination. It also reflects his view that human beings are (probably) essentially material machines.

In his *Essay Concerning Human Understanding* of 1689, John Locke declared that the human being is 'inconsiderable, mean, and impotent ... in all probability ... one of the lowest of all intellectual Beings' (IV. iii. 23).[1]

Locke hammered this point home throughout the book. We have no innate knowledge of theoretical or practical principles (Book I. i–iv). Our words are largely 'doubtful and uncertain in their signification,' which impairs communication and the representation of states of affairs (III. ix. 10–17). Where the acquisition of empirical knowledge is concerned, we are confined to 'a small part of the immense Universe,' and as to the other planets 'what sorts of Furniture and Inhabitants those Mansions contain in them, we cannot so much as guess (IV. iii. 24). Here on earth, we are limited to the perception of middle-sized objects; we can't see the subvisible corpuscles upon which everything depends (IV. iii. 25). Even if we could see them, we wouldn't be able to understand how configurations of primary qualities give rise to secondary and tertiary qualities (IV. iii. 25–6).

The limits theme in Locke has been well studied in connection with these issues. It is less a recapitulation of the theological view that our linguistic and epistemic capacities were destroyed in Adam's Fall, though it trades on it, than it is an attack on both

---

[1] Intertextual references: References are cited by book, chapter and section to *John Locke, An Essay Concerning Human Understanding*, ed. P. H. Nidditch, (Oxford, Clarendon, 1975). R = John Locke, *The Reasonableness of Christianity*, Volume VII in *The Works of John Locke*. 10 vols., 12th ed. (London: Tegg, Sharpe, et al. 1823).

doi:10.1017/S1358246116000357

scholastic metaphysics and the Cartesian ambition of explaining everything in corpuscularian terms and achieving practical mastery over nature. It is constructive as well as destructive. The key notion is 'mediocrity,' not depravity. Locke wants us to see things differently and to act differently, abandoning certain futile scientific pursuits along with nonreferential metaphysical discourse, and perhaps adopting a experimental-observational approach to medicine in place of the theoretical one suggested by Descartes.[2]

The other context in which Locke employs the feeble, fallible man theme, his moral philosophy, has not been as well studied. His chapter on 'Powers' presents us as strikingly powerless; and in *The Reasonableness of Christianity*, he comments on 'the frailty of our minds, and weakness of our constitutions; how liable [we are] to mistakes, how apt to go astray, and how easily to be turned out of the paths of virtue.' Our moral limitations, he says, are apparent to anyone from 'the testimony of his own conscience.' And if some saintly person 'feels not his own errours and passions always tempting, and often prevailing, against the strict rules of his duty; he need but look abroad into any stage of the world, to be convinced ... ' (R 112).

Had Locke been a more conventional philosopher, human mediocrity would not have presented him with the problem of reconciling anthropology with moral demandingness; he could have subscribed to the traditional scheme of fallen-man-but-with-God-given-free-will that had long served to reconcile inherent sinfulness with moral obligation. But Locke did not really believe in free will. On the contrary, he thought that human beings are essentially passional, hedonistic organised bodies. Our constitutions, in all their reactivity and impulsiveness, are given to us by God for our own benefit, but God at the same time requires from us behaviour in conformity with Christian moral principles.

Doubting the existence of an incorporeal soul and regarding the person as a material machine endowed with a bundle of powers, Locke decided to try, as he explained in his Epistle to the Reader of the *Essay*, the difficult task: 'to put Morality and Mechanism together' (I. iii. 14). He had to show why libertinism was not the inevitable

---

[2]   See Steven Shapin, 'Descartes the Doctor: Rationalism and its Therapies', *The British Journal for the History of Science* 33 (2000), 131–154. Locke's approach to medicine is studied by Kenneth Dewhurst, *John Locke, 1632–1704, Physician and Philosopher* (London: Wellcome Historical Medical Library, 1963), more recently by Jonathan Walmsley, 'Sydenham and the Development of Locke's Natural Philosophy', *British Journal for the History of Philosophy* 16 (2008), 65–83.

consequence of accepting mortalism and materialism. He had three distinct solutions to this problem, which also required him to present a new theory of the Resurrection as personality-restoration via memory-restoration. The first solution involved undercutting his own passional account by assigning the mind a power of suspension. A second, more satisfactory and interesting solution was to treat moral competence on analogy with physical skill, as a capability achieved through instruction and practice. The third solution was to face the mediocrity problem head on and to insist on divine forgiveness.

In the final analysis, Locke didn't paint a very convincing picture of moral responsibility. For, despite – indeed, because of – his suspicion that we are hedonistic machines, he needed the Christian revelation with its carrot-and-stick approach to defining and cultivating rectitude.[3] This commitment sat oddly, to the contemporary mind, with his metaphysically cautious and sociologically observant outlook. Nevertheless Locke's project of relating morality to nature and education as far as possible is impressive, and the more radical elements of his moral psychology, though they were evident to 18th century empiricists, have perhaps not been appreciated fully. Locke describes multiple instances of passional behaviour, striving for a descriptively adequate, realistic account of human cravings, ambivalence, and weakness. He was a mechanical philosopher who denied the will an autonomous role and who refused to assert that the faculty of reason is sovereign over feeling.

To explore the limits theme in Locke's moral philosophy and to argue for this interpretation of the morality-and-mechanism passage, I will first defend the claim that humans, in Locke's view are soulless corporeal machines (or at least that moral theory must assume that they are). Next, I draw attention to some of Locke's many passages on emotionality and impulsivity; and finally I comment on the forgiveness theme in his moral theology, a conceptual device that to some extent mediates between his naturalism and his moralism.

1. Locke's theory of the material soul

One of the many background assumptions Locke was challenging in the *Essay* was that an incorporeal, intrinsically immortal soul

---

[3]   On the conflict between empiricism and philosophy of religion, see Richard Ashcraft, 'Faith and Knowledge in Locke's Philosophy,' in *John Locke: Problems and Perspectives*, ed. John W. Yolton, (Cambridge: Cambridge University Press, 1969), 194–223.

endowed with a free will was a necessary condition of morally significant agency. He did not think our practices should rely on an experi-
ence-transcendent proposition, and, on his considered view, 'All the
great Ends of Morality and Religion, are well enough secured,
without philosophical Proofs of the Soul's Immateriality' (IV. iii. 6).

There is room for debate on the question what Locke had in mind
with his counterproposal that God might have superadded powers of
thought to matter 'suitably organised.' There is further room for
debate over whether he believed that that is what happened, and
that we are wholly material and mortal beings, or held, more cau-
tiously and circumspectly, that the existence of the separable
Cartesian soul was an unproved though possible, indeed probable
hypothesis.[4] Although his language sometimes indicates the latter –
Locke declares that it not his intention anywhere to 'in any way
lessen the belief of the Soul's Immateriality' (IV. iii. 6) – and
although there was apparently nothing to be gained by way of
public esteem and much to be lost in advancing the former thesis,
consideration of the *Essay* as a whole suggests that Locke, in
company with many physicians of the 17th century, suspected the
former to be true.

The attack on the Cartesian soul and the corresponding defense of
thinking matter is developed by employing the mediocrity argument.
According to Locke, 'The simple ideas we receive from sensation and
reflection are the boundaries of our thoughts; beyond which the
mind, whatever efforts it would make, is not able to advance one
jot; nor can it make any discoveries, when it would pry into the
nature and hidden causes of those ideas' (II. xxiii. 29). We have an
idea of the soul derived through experience as an immaterial thing
that thinks and that can 'excite motion in the body by willing or
thought' (but not bodies at a distance from it) (II. xxiii. 20–22), and
an idea of body derived through experience as involving 'the cohesion
of solid, and consequently separable parts, and a power of communi-
cating motion by impulse' (II. xxii. 17). Both ideas are 'obscure'.

---

[4]   On superadded powers see Margaret D. Wilson 'Superadded properties: the limits of mechanism in Locke.' *American Philosophical Quarterly* 16
(1979), 143–150; M. R. Ayers, 'Mechanism, Superaddition and the Proof of
God's Existence in Locke's *Essay*,' *Philosophical Review* 90 (1981), 210–51;
and Matthew Stuart, 'Locke on Superaddition and Mechanism, *British
Journal for the History of Philosophy* 6 (1998), 351–379. It is clear that
Locke is really departing from 'pure' mechanism, but this is not surprising
since there are no pure mechanists in early modern philosophy with the possible exception of Hobbes.

The idea of matter is obscure because cohesion is inexplicable, and so is the communication of motion. The idea of the soul is obscure because we can have no experience of things that do not impact on our senses. So, as far as proper epistemology, that is 'Contemplation of our own Ideas, without revelation,' is concerned, we cannot discover either that 'Omnipotency has given to Matter fitly disposed, a power to perceive and think' or that God has 'joined and fixed to Matter so disposed, a thinking immaterial Substance' (IV. iii. 6).[5]

In his lengthy correspondence with Stillingfleet over what was obviously a provocative remark, Locke refused to back down. He developed an argument that is not found in the *Essay*, though it is consistent with his view that nature is characterised by continuity and with his appeal to gravity as a superaddition.'[6] First, he argued that even in purely material systems such as the solar system, the 'bare essence' or 'natural powers' of matter are unable to account for planetary orbits. Next, he pointed out that 'the vegetable part of the creation is not doubted to be wholly material; and yet he that will look into it, will observe excellencies and operations in

---

[5] We have the *Ideas* of *Matter* and *Thinking*, but possibly shall never be able to know, whether Matter thinks, or no; it being impossible for us, by the contemplation of our own *Ideas*, without revelation, to discover, whether Omnipotency has given to Matter fitly disposed, a power to perceive and think, or else joined and fixed to Matter so disposed, a thinking immaterial Substance: It being equally easie, in respect of our Notions, to conceive, that GOD can, if he pleases, superadd to our *Idea* of Matter a Faculty of Thinking, as that he should superadd to it another Substance, with a Faculty of Thinking; since we know not wherein Thinking consists, nor to what sort of Substances the Almighty has been pleased to give that power, which cannot be in any created Being, but meerly by the good Pleasure and Bounty of the Creator.' ((IV. iii. 6). This mode of argumentation echoes that of Galileo. In his *Dialogue Concerning the Two Chief World Systems* of 1632. Simplicius observes that, insofar as God might have produce the celestial phenomena by any number of underlying systems, 'it would be excessive boldness for anyone to limit and restrict the Divine power and wisdom to some particular fancy of his own.' (tr. Stillman Drake, New York: Modern Library 2001), 538).

[6] 'For since we must allow he has annexed Effects to Motion, which we can no way conceive Motion able to produce, what Reason have we to conclude, that he could not order them as well to be produced in a Subject we cannot conceive capable of them, as well as in a Subject we cannot conceive the motion of Matter can any way operate upon?' (IV. iii. 6) Locke also held that ' All stones, metals, and minerals, are real vegetables that is, grow organically from proper seeds, as well as plants,' which requires superadded powers. *Works* III: 319.

Catherine Wilson

this part of matter, which he will not find contained in the essence of
matter in general, nor be able to conceive how they can be produced
by it.' Advancing to the animal world, we 'meet with yet greater perfections and properties, no ways explicable by the essence of matter
in general.' This indicates that the Creator superadded the 'qualities' of life, sense, and spontaneous motion, along with a power
of propagation, and so, the implication is, the addition of the property of thought is only the next step in 'the superinducement of
greater perfections and nobler qualities'.[7]

As well as professing ignorance as to the nature of substance, and as
to God's employment of His powers, and advancing the stepwise
argument just cited, Locke engages in constant sniping at the incorporeal Cartesian soul that is the repository of imprinted innate ideas
and whose essence it is to think. Their claim that the essence of the
soul is to think forced the Cartesians to embrace the conclusion that
the soul always thinks (on pain of the self's not existing), in the
womb, when asleep, when detached from the body (II. i. 9–19),
even if we are not always aware of ourselves as thinking those
thoughts. But thinking, says Locke, is an operation of the mind,
something we suppose 'it' can do, not an essential attribute (ibid.).
Why would God have created an incorporeal soul that produces
thoughts of which the subject is unaware, or that it immediately
forgets, along with the follies of dreams? A thinking mind of whose
thoughts we are unaware 'makes two persons of one man' (ibid.
19). Further,

They who make the soul a thinking thing, at this rate, will not
make it a much more noble being, than those do, whom they
condemn, for allowing it to be nothing but the subtilest parts
of matter. Characters drawn on dust, that the first breath of
wind effaces; or impressions made on a heap of atoms, or
animal spirits, are altogether as useful, and render the subject
as noble, as the thoughts of a soul that perish in thinking; that
once out of sight are gone for ever, and leave no memory of themselves behind them (II. i. 15).

Matter, he concludes, is not such useless stuff (ibid.).

There are however some passages in which Locke seems to acknowledge the existence, or at least the probable existence of incorporeal
spirits. For example, in *Some Thoughts Concerning Education*,
Locke argued that materialism is a tempting position but one

[7] Locke, *A Letter to Edward, Bishop of Worcester, The Works of John
Locke*, 10 vols., 12th edition (London: Tegg, Sharpe *et al*, 1823) IV: 461–2.

inadequate to explain all the phenomena, and that young gentlemen ought to be discouraged from adopting it. 'Matter being a thing, that all our Senses are constantly conversant with, it is so apt to possess the Mind, and exclude all other Beings, but Matter, that prejudice, grounded on such Principles, often leaves no room for the admittance of Spirits, or the allowing any such things as *immaterial Beings in rerum natura.*'[8]

Locke's concern here is however with atheism, not with the existence of other spiritual substances. Locke did believe in an incorporeal God, the necessary author of the many active powers he ascribed to material nature, and he believed himself to have given a good and novel argument for the existence of the 'eternal cogitative Being,' namely that 'It is impossible to conceive, that ever bare incogitative Matter should produce a thinking, intelligent Being, as that nothing should of it self produce Matter' (IV. x. 10). His references to other spirits, even in the context of his 'mediocrity' sentiments, appear exaggerated and ironic. 'How inconsiderable a rank the Spirits that inhabit our Bodies hold amongst those various and possibly innumerable, kinds of nobler Beings; and how far short they come of the Endowments and Perfections of Cherubims and Seraphims, and infinite sorts of Spirits above us, is what by a transient hint, in another place, I have offered to my Reader's Consideration.' (IV. x. 17). As he has already pointed out several times, 'having the Ideas of Spirits does not make us know, that any such Things do exist without us, or that there are any finite Spirits, or any other spiritual Beings but the Eternal GOD' (IV: xi. 12).[9]

Several other passages seem initially to pose apparent problems for ascribing materialism-with-powers to Locke. First, at (II. xxiii. 16) he says that the soul is a 'real being' and that 'I ... know, that there is some spiritual being within me, that sees and hears. This, I must be convinced, cannot be the action of bare insensible matter; nor ever could be, without an immaterial thinking being.' Second, at II. xxvii. 25, he says, 'I agree, the more probable opinion is, that this consciousness is annexed to, and the affection of one individual immaterial substance.' And third, in his discussion of personal identity, at II. xxvii. 15–23, he appears to take seriously the idea that souls

---

[8] Locke, *Some Thoughts Concerning Education* 3rd ed. (1695), ed. J. W. Yolton and J. S. Yolton, (Oxford: Clarendon, 1989), 246.
[9] Cf. IV. iii. 27: 'But that there are degrees of Spiritual Beings between us and the great GOD, who is there, that by his own search and ability can come to know?'

Catherine Wilson

can be detached from bodies in which they are or were ordinarily resident and attached to other bodies.

To the first point, all Locke appears to mean here is that neither matter nor thought could have come into the world in the absence of an original thinking being with creative powers. The 'real being' of the soul does not imply the reality of individual incorporeal cogitative substance, by contrast with the real existence of soul-functions. All we know is that 'we have in us something that thinks' (IV. ii. 6) – a 'spiritual being' – not what its metaphysical nature is, and we can safely take the reference to the 'immaterial thinking being' that is a condition of anything's seeing and hearing to be the Creator. To the second point, when Locke refers to the existence of the incorporeal soul as the more 'probable' opinion, I take it he is using 'probable' in the casuistic sense; it is the opinion accepted by most authorities. He cannot be using 'probable' in an evidentiary sense, insofar as he maintains that we have no positive evidence whatsoever for the existence of individual incorporeal cogitative substance. Finally, as for the supposition of 'detachable souls,' the aim of all the examples involving pigs and Socrates, cobblers and princes, is not to make it appear probable that souls can flit about, alighting in other bodies, but to show that what we consider relevant to identity is entirely experiential: the existence of first-person memories.

Perhaps, someone might insist, Locke genuinely has no preference for or against the hypothesis of the incorporeal soul? Perhaps thinking matter is merely a worst case scenario to be armed against? Given the evidence, text external as well as text internal, this is implausible. The criticism of Locke as a 'Hobbist' by John Edwards, the careful distinction Edwards made between Locke and Boyle, who was very much like Locke in his presentation of the corpuscularian hypothesis and his doctrine of qualities, but above theological suspicion, together with Locke's reception in the 18th century as the principal proponent of thinking matter as shown years ago by John Yolton[10] all confirm the seriousness of Locke's attraction to the hypothesis. If you truly regard theologically scandalous hypothesis A as no more likely than theologically safe hypothesis B, why strive to impress on your readers that the arguments and evidence for B are utterly lacking without correspondingly casting aspersions on A? Further, Locke's agenda for moral philosophy is premised on our being hedonistic, but not entirely unreasonable machines, as I now show.

[10] J. W. Yolton, *Thinking Matter: Materialism in Eighteenth-century Britain* (Minneapolis: University of Minnesota Press, 1984).

134

2. Locke's Depiction of Passional Man

We are, then, corporeal machines with superadded qualities and powers, including life, movement, reproduction, experience and thinking, and we find ourselves in the world endowed with a set of re-actions and mental habits that preserve our lives. Pain and pleasure, punishment and reward, are the basic elements of the human experi-ential economy.[11] 'God has so framed the constitutions of our minds and bodies,' says Locke in his early essay on the passions[12] 'that several things are apt to produce in both of them pleasure and pain, delight and trouble, by ways that we know not, but for ends suitable to His goodness and wisdom. Thus the smell of roses and the tasting of wine, light and liberty, the possession of power and the acquisition of knowledge please most men, and there are some things whose very being and existence delights others, as children and grandchildren.'[13]

The references to pleasure – to sensory pleasure and the pleasures of human relationships – establish Locke as something of a voluptu-ary, refusing both Christian aceticism and Stoic ideals of independ-ence and tranquillity. Here he follows Descartes, who insisted that perceptions, feelings, and emotions are all essentially good, and Hobbes who considered tranquillity a false and absurd ideal. Like the 'ideas' of the external world generated by the senses, and the 'ideas' of hunger and thirst generated by the bodily organs, feelings and emotions are 'ideas' produced by situations. According to Descartes's influential account, pleasure and pain and their prospects prompt actions, according to the designs of God, for the welfare of the living creature. Although the senses and our internal sensations can deceive us, they mostly do not, and we do well for the most part to trust them.[14] The same holds for the emotions. For Hobbes,

[11] Locke's hedonism was definitively established by von Leyden; see his Introduction to Locke's *Essays on the Law of Nature, Works* III: 70–72. Von Leyden comments on 'the inherent difficulty in the issue between Locke's hedonism and his belief in an absolute system of moral principles. Since he wished to retain both, he had on the one hand to avoid strong hedonistic expressions in his theory of the nature of the good, and on the other to show reserve in putting his case for natural law and the 'proper basis' of morality.'
[12] Locke, *Essays on the Law of Nature, Works* III: 326.
[13] Ibid., 265.
[14] 'I am ... taught by nature that various other bodies exist in the vicin-ity of my body, and that some of these are to be sought out and others avoided ... [T]he fact that some of the perceptions are agreeable to me while others are disagreeable makes it quite certain that my body, or rather my whole self, in so far as I am a combination of body and mind,

tranquillity belongs neither to death nor to life, for it is a denial of the 'vital motions' by which we live.[15] For both of Locke's predecessors, the passions sometimes need repression, not because tranquillity is a desirable state of the soul but rather because they can be dangerous to oneself or harmful to other people. For Locke, as for Hobbes and Spinoza, emotion-driven religious and political enthusiasms and the persecution manias of groups become the focus of concern.[16]

Locke agrees with Descartes: 'our All-Wise Maker, suitable to our constitution and frame, and knowing what it is that determines the Will, has put into man the uneasiness of hunger and thirst, and other natural desires, to move and determine their Wills, for the preservation of themselves and the continuation of their Species' (II. xxi. 34), thereby adding sexual desire to the list of beneficial human endowments. In his chapter on 'Powers,' in the *Essay* he evokes vividly the misery of needing and wanting things, and the individuality and specificity of our desires.

The ordinary necessities of our lives, fill a great part of them with the uneasiness of Hunger, Thirst, Heat. Cold, Weariness, with labour, and Sleepiness in their constant returns ... To which ... if we add the fantastical uneasiness, (as itch after Honour, Power, or Riches, etc.) which acquired habits, by Fashion, Example, and Education have settled in us, and a thousand other irregular desires ... we find, that a very little part of our life is ... vacant from these uneasinesses ... (II. xxi. 45).

---

can be affected by the various beneficial or harmful bodies which surround it.' Descartes, *Meditation VI* in *The Philosophical Writings of Descartes*, 2 vols., tr. J. Cottingham, R. Stoothoff and D. Murdoch (Cambridge: Cambridge University Press, 1985) II: 81. Cf. *The Passions of the Soul*, op. cit I: 141: 'As for desire, it is obvious that when it proceeds from true knowledge it cannot be bad, provided it is not excessive and that it is governed by this knowledge ... [I]if we had no body, I venture to say we could not go too far in abandoning ourselves to love and joy, or in avoiding hatred and sadness. But the bodily movements accompanying these passions may all be injurious to health when they are very violent; on the other hand, they may be beneficial to it when they are only moderate.'

[15] '[I]n the first place I put for a generall inclination of all mankind a perpetuall and restlesse desire of Power after power, that ceaseth only in death.' Thomas Hobbes, *Leviathan*, ed. Richard Tuck (Cambridge: Cambridge University Press, 1996), 70.

[16] See Susan James, 'Passion and Politics,' *Royal Institute of Philosophy Supplement* 52 (2003), 221–234.

Some wants and preferences of particular human beings – such as
food, drink, shelter, and liberty – are universal; others, such as ambition and lust, take forms that vary from culture to culture.

Locke appeals to the innocent pleasures and satisfactions of consuming Cheese, Lobsters, Apples, Plumbs, and Nuts. He also comments
on the painful deprivations that render people pathetic and desperate.
There is the drunkard, whose 'habitual Thirst' drives him to the tavern
despite his ability to see that 'his Health decays, his Estate wastes;
Discredit and Diseases', pursue him (II. xxi. 35); the bridegroom
driven to conjugal life by 'burning' (ibid. 34); and Rachel in the
Bible, who cries out 'give me Children, give me the thing desir'd or
I die.' For Locke, 'Life it self and all its Enjoyments, is a burden
cannot be born under the lasting and unremoved pressure of such an
uneasiness' (ibid. 32).'

In his 'Powers' chapter, Locke analyses liberty as a relationship
between a person's preferences and their environmental constraints.
A person has liberty not when his or her will is free, as the notion
of a free will is meaningless in his eyes, but when there are no constraints imposed by their situation or the laws of external nature on
what they prefer to do, or (Locke is not always clear on this point)
no constraints on what a person could do if they preferred to do
that thing (II. xxi. 8–12). A person also lacks liberty when there are
internal constraints that prevent them from doing what it is in their
long term interest to do, that is what they would (continuously)
prefer to do, absent the blocking feature. Lacking liberty is in fact a
fairly common occurrence. In the morning, the drunkard prefers
not to waste his estates and he is is free to resist a drink, but as
evening comes, the drinking motivation swamps that preference
and he cannot do otherwise than go down to the soaking club.

Locke refers in this connection to those 'extreme disturbances' that
can possess 'our whole mind.' 'Some ideas,' he says,

> like some motions to the body, are such as in certain circum-
> stances it cannot avoid, nor obtain their absence by the utmost
> effort it can use. A man on the rack is not at liberty to lay by
> the idea of pain, and divert himself with other contemplations:
> And sometimes a boisterous passion hurries our thoughts as a
> hurricane does our bodies, without leaving us the liberty of
> thinking on other things, which we would rather choose'
> (II. xxi. 12).

> ... [A]ny vehement pain of the body, the ungovernable passion of
> a man violently in love, or the impatient desire of revenge, keeps
> the will steady and intent; and the will, thus determined, never

Catherine Wilson

lets the understanding lay by the object, but all the thoughts of the mind and powers of the body are uninterruptedly employed that way, by the determination of the will, influenced by that topping uneasiness as long as it lasts (II. xxxi. 38).

For a woman who has lost a beloved child, its death 'rends from her Heart, the whole comfort of her Life, and gives her all the torment imaginable; use the Consolations of Reason in this case, and you were as good preach Ease to one on the Rack, and hope to allay by Rational Discourses, the Pain of his Joints tearing asunder' (II. xxxiii.13). The idea of the child and her lost enjoyment are so tightly associated that if time does not erode her memories she may 'carry an incurable Sorrow' to the grave.

Thus reason has no definite power over the emotions. The powers of self-control we associate with the will come and go; when, experientially, we regain control of ourselves in a moment of fury, or are able to resist some temptation, we feel and describe ourselves as 'free.' But freedom is not a metaphysical attribute that we possess in virtue of having a soul. Contrary to what Descartes said, it is not in the least comparable with God's will. 'Willing' implies desiring and preferring, and emotion-driven behaviour is not what takes over when reason loses its grip but the only real option. Consequently, moral motivation can only take the form of appetite; it is on all fours with hunger and thirst: 'Let a man be never so well perswaded of the advantages of virtue ... yet till he hungers and thirsts after righteousness, till he feels an uneasiness in the want of it, his will will not be determin'd to any action in pursuit of this confessed greater good' (II. xxi. 35).

Having analysed human freedom in terms of preferences and obstacles, and voiced the view that human beings are neither free nor determined but sometimes able to direct their thoughts and actions, at other times utterly undone and overwhelmed by them, Locke, in the first edition of the *Essay*, declared that 'Good, therefore, the greater good, is that alone which determines the will.' It is widely believed that he changed his mind in response to criticism, but close analysis shows that he changed only his wording, which was misleading, but not his underlying view.[17] His original argument in First Edition of the *Essay*, II. xxi. 28–45, ran as follows

Pleasure and pain, whether of mind and body, are produced by the operation of bodies on us.

[17] For the contrary view, see Jack D. Davidson, 'Locke's Finely Spun Liberty,' *Canadian Journal of Philosophy* 33 (2003), 203–227, esp. 204–6.

Happiness is pleasure, Misery is pain.

Whatever produces or contributes to Happiness is what we call Good.

Whatever produces or is conducive to Misery we call Evil.

The will is determined by what best pleases it.

'Good, therefore, the greater good, is that alone which determines the will.'

If we were able to look on happiness (pleasure) and our misery (pain) with indifference, he comments, we would not be free but miserable and enslaved. Someone who does not respond to hedonic incentives and ahedonic disincentives, in other words, must be in the grip of some pathology. But if the Good is, ultimately, pleasure, isn't this to say that our liberty is not diminished in having no freedom to be indifferent to pleasure? How is this view tenable?.

Locke's original answer to this question was that 'good' and 'evil' do just reflect preferences; every evil is somebody's good and vice versa. Some people are attracted by study and knowledge, some by hawking and hunting; some go in for luxury and debauchery, others for sobriety and riches. Some people prefer wine to the preservation of their eyesight. In the second edition of the *Essay*, where the chapter on Powers was greatly expanded, Locke apologised to his readers for his apparent error in agreeing with the received view that the will always pursues, is always determined by, the greater Good (II. xxi. 35). He had obviously realised that his subjectivism was unacceptable. So he introduced a notion of the 'true (greater) good' as opposed to the apparent. Locke continued to hold that everyone simply pursues what looks best to him or her, and if there were no 'Prospect beyond the Grave and if "all Concerns of Man terminated in this Life", the diversity of preferences would be beyond criticism' (II. xxi. 54). However, what produces the most pleasure and least pain over the very long term is compliance with God's commands as far as possible. The 'true good' is accordingly 'what produces the most pleasure and least pain' for the individual over the long term. Nobody pursues the true good, however, unless they actually develop a hunger for it.

The emendation to his theory of motivation was accordingly essentially verbal. Locke no longer speaks of the greater good as attracting and so determining the will as a Platonist who believed that the soul of man years for the Good, the True and the Beautiful might. Rather he emphasises the push from 'uneasiness' – the desire to escape from conditions of want and deprivation. The 'uneasiness' account does not however replace the 'greater good' account. It was already there in the first edition, where he had observed that there are in us 'a great many uneasinesses always solliciting and ready to determine the will...' When possessed by the pain of deprivation, we cannot attend to any pleasure in prospect 'a little of it extinguishes all our Pleasures ... [w]e desire to be rid of the present Evil, which we are apt to think nothing absent can equal' (II. xxi. 41). Motivation remains personal and subjective. The true good remains what it was – happiness or pleasure – either the greater happiness and pleasure that result in terrestrial life by moderating desires, or the happiness and pleasure that attend obedience to divine commands in the next world.[18]

As observed earlier, Locke's chapter on Powers turns out to be largely about powerlessness. We can't understand power metaphysically, but there is empirical reality to being in a locked room, or longing for a child we can't conceive, or being overcome by rage or by some addiction. Locke presents the reader with a distinctly mediocre moral agent. Because the mind is not metaphysically distinct from the body, or the will from desire, it would seem that there are no *a priori* generalisations to be made about what lies within 'our' power. For different individuals, in different cases, what lies within their power is different.

The moralist in Locke could not accept his anthropological conclusions. Shifting into the admonitory and moralistic mode, he declares that we are not entitled to appeal to our own frailty, as our excuse. 'Nor let any one say he cannot govern his passions, nor hinder them from breaking out, and carrying him into action; for what he can do before a prince, or a great man, he can do alone, or in the presence of God, if he will' (II. xxi. 53). The same lecture is delivered at II. xxi. 71, where Locke startlingly asserts that 'the satisfaction of any

---

[18] Von Leyden quotes an unpublished note on volition that reads as follows: 'Voluntas: That which has very much confounded men about the will and its determination has been the confounding of the notion of moral rectitude and giving it the name of moral good. The pleasure that a man takes in any action or expects as a consequence of it is indeed a good in the self able and proper to move the will. But the moral rectitude of it considered barely in itself is not good or evil nor any way moves the will, but as pleasure and pain either accompanies the action itself or is looked on to be a consequence of it. Which is evident from the punishments and rewards which God has annexed to moral rectitude or pravity as proper motives to the will, which would be needless if moral rectitude were in itself good and moral pravity evil. J. L.' *Works* III: 72.

particular *desire* can be suspended from determining the *will* to any subservient action, till we have maturely examin'd, whether the particular apparent good ... makes a part of our real Happiness, or be consistent or inconsistent with it.'

The suggestion that any passion or impulse whatsoever can be repressed on the spot is frankly inconsistent with everything else Locke has been arguing in his chapter, as several commentators have noted. He would have done better to remind his readers that they are thinking matter as well as emotional matter and that their passions are not entirely ungovernable, and are in fact more governable than they may suppose.

3. Mediocrity and Education

Locke's view of the person as an arena of competing powers, emotional and rational, situated in the midst of a complex, poorly-understood, unpredictable universe, and as highly vulnerable to psychological and moral upset recommended to him a solution that seems not to have occurred to Descartes, Spinoza or Hobbes, namely the education of the young. Where Descartes and Spinoza remain focussed on self-improvement, and Hobbes on social organisation, Locke, in keeping with his lifelong interest in children and childhood, sees early intervention into the structure of human mental machinery as critical. In this connection as well, he thinks materialistically and rejects the posit of an essentially rational soul. In his essay *On the Conduct of the Understanding*, he develops numerous parallel between physical and mental education. He argues that as the bodily deportment of a gentleman, the legs of a dancing master, and the fingers of a musician, which are no different in their original construction from those of the ploughman, can only be developed through long practice, so mental qualities including wit, poetic talent, and reasoning are advanced by practice and encouragement.[19] Skill in mathematics is like skill in writing, painting, dancing or fencing.[20] We are not born reasonable but only potentially so, and we become reasonable through 'Use and Exercise' of our mental faculties. Further, education should not overstress the educatee: 'The mind by being engag'd in a Talk beyond its Strength, like the Body, strain'd by lifting at a Weight too heavy

---

[19]   Locke, *The Conduct of the Understanding*, ed. J. Yolton (Bristol: Thoemmes, 1996), §4.
[20]   Ibid. §6.

Catherine Wilson

often has its force broken.'[21] Finally, the 'variety of Distempers in Mens Minds is as great as those in their Bodies...'[22].

The constant references to legs and limbs in the *Conduct* speak only to the parallelism, not to the identity of mind and body. They do however invite the reader to regard human rationality in a robustly physical light. Moral education meanwhile serves to replace destructive or useless forms of uneasiness with more constructive ones. It aims at creating an appetite for the long term good and to make the pupil or oneself 'uneasy in the want of it, or in the fear of losing it...' (II. xxi. 53). Religious instruction, Locke thought, including instruction in the Christian duties and their rewards and penalties serves as input to the human machine that can modify the character of young persons. Even the Stoic philosophy found in Cicero can have this beneficial effect.[23]

At times, these remodelling efforts seem to be carried too far in Locke's imagination. He thought not only that children could be conditioned out of their baseless fears, such as fear of frogs, by a kind of cognitive behavioural therapy, but that they needed to be hardened against pain and discomfort by being made to experience them. 'Since the great Foundation of Fear in Children is Pain,' he observes in *Some Thoughts on Education*, the way to harden, and fortifie Children against Fear and Danger, is to accustom them to suffer Pain. This 'tis possible will be thought,' he admits, 'by kind Parents, a very unnatural thing towards their Children....'[24] Although his good friend Molyneux offered no comment on this passage, Molyneux professed himself 'shock'd' by Locke's view – 'all that in your whole book I stick at' – that the educator ought never to give into children's desires.[25] In his treatise, Locke had stated 'a child should never be suffer'd to have what he craves, or so much as speaks for, much less if he cries for it.'[26] Only in this way can children be taught to 'stifle their desires and to practice modesty and temperance'. Molyneux seems to agree that one should ignore children's complaints of hunger, but he thinks Locke

[21] Ibid. §27.
[22] Ibid. §37.
[23] Locke, Letter to Carey Mordaunt, September/October 1697 no. 2320 in *Locke: Selected Correspondence* ed. Mark Goldie (Oxford: Oxford University Press, 2002), 253.
[24] Locke, *Some Thoughts Concerning Education*, ed. Yolton and Yolton, 178.
[25] Molyneux to Locke, August 12, 1693, in *Some Familiar Letters Between Mr. Locke, and Several of His Friends, Works* IX: 318.
[26] Locke, *Some Thoughts*, 164.

goes overboard in applying his stifling to 'wants of fancy and affect-
ation.' Why may they not choose for themselves 'harmless things, and
plays or sports?' In response, Locke says that he is not against children's recreation. They are however apt to covet trips, 'fine cloaths,
and playthings.' Desires of this sort 'being indulged when they are
little, grows up with age, and with that enlarges it self to things of
greater consequence. And has ruin'd more families than one on the
world. This should be supressed in its very first rise.'[27]

This evident harshness and insistence on training in 'stifling'
seems to contrast with the more sympathetic attitudes towards tears
and neediness that Locke evinces in the *Essay*. This is consistent
with his view that children are highly plastic, whereas adults are comparatively rigid. Once the critical age is past, the machine, with all its
skills and associative habits is fully formed, and change is difficult.
Recognising the power of desires in adult life, Locke clearly thinks
it best to begin early in learning self-control. His apparent severity
on the subject of children's desires and vulnerabilities is consistent
with his overall picture: human appetitiveness shows up already in
childhood. The conflict between the demands of morality and the
God-given constitution of human emotional and appetitive machinery is accordingly mitigated by the susceptibility of the machinery to
teaching.

4. Mediocrity and Forgiveness

The comparative rigidity of the adult mind leaves a residual problem
of moral accountability. What about persons who have not received a
Christian education, such as the infanticidal and cannibalistic
Caribbeans described with evident horror in Book I, or those
whose fully-formed emotional dispositions or cravings leave them
vulnerable to rages and regrettable actions? Human emotionality
and its sequelae can obtain divine forgiveness in Locke's theology.
As our frame and constitution, and so the mechanisms that determine
the human will, are established by the Creator, it would be morally
and rationally unacceptable to be punished for every disobedient
action or omission to which we are impelled. In his treatment of
such persons, Locke reflects the softer theological mood of his contemporaries, the liberal Puritans and Anglicans, including Richard
Baxter, Gilbert Burnet, and Isaac Barrow who see divine knowledge
and power as manifest in the understanding and mercy of God rather

---

27 Locke to Molyneux, August 23, 169, *Familiar Letters*, 324.

than in God's piercing vision when it comes to the detection of hidden sins and the force and scope of his wrath.[28]

In the *Essay* as well as in *The Reasonableness of Christianity*, Locke makes this point clearly. The person whose rational self-control has forsaken them under intolerable pressure will receive divine mercy.

> But if any extreme disturbance (as sometimes it happens) possesses our whole mind, as when the pain of the rack, an impetuous uneasiness, as of love, anger, or any other violent passion, running away with us, allows us not the liberty of thought, and we are not masters enough of our own minds to consider thoroughly and examine fairly; God, who knows our frailty, pities our weakness, and requires of us no more than we are able to do, and sees what was and what was not in our power, will judge as a kind and merciful father (II. xxi. 53).

One cannot morally require, from a given human being, what their machine, by reason of its constitution and its experiences, cannot produce by way of prudent or correct behaviour. There is no point in trying to reason with a woman who has lost a beloved child or with the drunkard or the person in a jealous rage. In such cases, while the law or society must punish the crimes that result, God, who sees into the heart, may forgive

God, Locke says, 'did not expect ... a perfect obedience, void of slips and falls: he knew our make, and the weakness of our constitution too well, and was sent with a supply for that defect' (R 112). The Redeemer was sent to give mankind a second chance at eternal life after the first was botched, and God gives second chances to some persons who have blotted their copy-books. 'God will require of every man, "according to what a man hath, and not according to what he hath not." He will not expect the improvement of ten talents, where he gave but one; nor require any one should believe a

---

[28]   R. S. Crane argued in an influential essay that the introduction of a new sentimentalism in moral theory – the dominant framework of 18th century philosophy – with its constant references to sympathy, benevolence, and even pity, was stimulated by the theology of the 'Latitude-Men.' See 'Suggestions Towards a Genealogy of the 'Man of Feeling,' *English Literary History* 1 (1934), 205–230. Anticipating the doctrines of Hutcheson, Hume and Smith, Barrow refers in one of his sermons to 'that general sympathy which naturally intercedes between all men since we can neither see, nor hear, nor imagine another's grief without being afflicted ourselves.' Isaac Barrow, Sermon XXIX: 'Of a Peaceable Temper and Carriage', *Works of Dr. Isaac Barrow*, 2 vols., ed. T.S Hughes (London: A. J. Valpy, 1831) II: 287.

promise of which he has never heard' (R 132). The pagans and savages are not condemned to hell, despite their highly uncharitable behaviour.

Locke points out that his account of personal identity is 'forensic;' i.e., is meant to provide a relevant and useful criterion of responsibility in creatures subject to the law. (III. xxvii. 26). However, it emerges that the human law is not entirely capable of recognising persons. Agency depends on what we ought to remember, not simply on what we do remember, and that is a transcendental notion. Only God can ascertain what we ought to remember, given who we are and what the context of some actions of our body's was, and only God, it seems, can ascertain whether we could have exerted ourselves to avoid doing wrong on some occasion. 'Humane Judicatures' must punish the disorderly drunkard because the man, that is to say his body, committed a crime, but God may excuse him insofar as 'no one shall be made to answer for what he knows nothing of' (II. xxvii. 22).

5. Conclusions

The mediocrity of human beings is something of a cliché in Western philosophy. The notion that human beings are intermediate between angel and beast, sharing in the intellectual powers of angels but also the bodily functions and passions of beasts, can be traced back to Augustine and Neoplatonism. Locke made something new of the mediocrity figure. First, he instituted a sharp, double-pronged attack on both the certainty of Cartesian metaphysics and the realisability of the Cartesian ambition to explain all phenomena mechanically and to become 'masters and possessors of nature.' Second, he used the mediocrity figure to show the way to improving practical philosophy by understanding human psychology in a realistic, rather than in an idealistic or artificially exaggerated fashion. For Locke, human moral mediocrity is not the manifestation of an inherent metaphysical sinfulness permeating the human soul that can be expelled, momentarily or permanently by an act of divine grace. Rather it is an inevitability arising from the God-given powers of the human constitution and their liability to becoming unbalanced.

How well did Locke succeed in his project of making Morality consistent with Mechanism? By mechanism, Locke did not mean either atheism or, for that matter, deism. Judging by his professed horror at the brutality of warfare and the practices of savages involving women and children, Locke's moral ideals relate to the protection of the weak, a value he finds exclusively in Christian religious teaching. The

Catherine Wilson

implicit distinction between the morally desirable and the merely desired requires a transcendental source in God's commands, although the motive to obey them can only be a strictly prudential desire for eternal happiness over eternal misery. In the absence of God's ability to reward and punish obedience and disobedience, and his commitment to doing so, all human motivation would be properly governed by a combination of appetite and mundane prudence.

Locke thought his argument for an incorporeal Creator of matter and the many and varied powers of life and thought conclusive and irrefutable. He considered and rejected the position of Spinozists who conceded the necessary existence of an eternal cogitative being but considered it to be material, as well as that of the Epicurean atheists who thought that particles of matter can produce cogitation on their own (IV. x. 5–15). He did not, however, have an argument to show that the eternal cogitative being has an ongoing interest in the affairs of human individuals. Nothing in our experience or demonstrable *a priori* indicates that this is the case. And his discussion of Revelation and miracles in Book IV, Chs 16 and 18, needed to establish the unique warrant of Christian morality and its linkage with punishment and reward, is basically unconvincing.

The upshot is that there are fractures in Locke's moral philosophy that other philosophers, even those who shared his mechanistic view of the passions, avoided. Descartes put God out of the business of enforcing morality, avoiding having to address the question why God creates emotional, fallible beings and sends many of them to hell, and Spinoza explicitly dispensed with salvation and retribution in the usual senses. Instead of faulting Locke for having to introduce supernatural elements to explain normativity and to encourage obedience, his achievement can be recognised. Whilst remaining to some extent (though not enough to satisfy his critics) within a Christian framework, Locke made the passions and the gratification of desire prominent in his image of human life, propounded radical ideas about the power of education, insisted on divine understanding and mercy as constituents of divine justice, and adopted a highly tolerant, individualistic stance with respect to the pleasures and worldly goods.

University of York
catherine.wilson@york.ac.uk

Hume's 'Manifest Contradictions'

P. J. E. KAIL

Abstract
This paper examines Hume's 'Title Principle' (TP) and its role in a response to one of the 'manifest contradictions' he identifies in the conclusion to Book I of A Treatise on Human Nature. This 'contradiction' is a tension between two 'equally natural and necessary' principles of the imagination, our causal inferences and our propensity to believe in the continued and distinct existence of objects. The problem is that the consistent application of causal reason undercuts any grounds with have for the belief in continued and distinct existence, and yet that belief is as 'natural and necessary' as our propensity to infer effects from causes. The TP appears to offer a way to resolve this 'contradiction'. It states

Where reason is lively, and mixes itself with some propensity, it ought to be assented to. Where it does not, it never can have any title to operate upon us.' (T 1.4.7.11; SBN 270)

In brief, if it can be shown that the causal inferences that undermine the belief in external world are not 'lively' nor mixed with some propensity' then we have grounds for think that they have no normative authority (they have no 'title to operate on us). This is in part a response to another 'manifest contradiction', namely the apparently self-undermining nature of reason. In this paper I examine the nature and grounds of the TP and its relation to these 'manifest contradictions'.

1.

In the complex and dramatic dialectic of *A Treatise of Human Nature* T 1.4.7 'Conclusion of this book' Hume asks how we could possibly retain the 'glorious title' of 'philosophers' when 'we ... knowingly embrace a manifest contradiction' (T 1.4.7.4; SBN 266).[1] The contradiction to which he refers is not a formal one, but an opposition between two 'equally natural and necessary' principles of the human imagination. The first principle is our propensity to reason from causes to effects, a principle of the imagination in virtue of being grounded in the associative or 'natural relation' of cause and effect. The second principle, which is more difficult to characterize with

---

[1]   Norton and Norton (eds) *A Treatise of Human Nature* (New York: Oxford University Press, 2000), following the convention of book, part, section and paragraph numbers. Page references to *A Treatise of Human Nature* ed. L. A. Selby-Bigge, revised by P. H. Nidditch (2nd ed., Oxford: Clarendon, 1978) (SBN).

doi:10.1017/S1358246116000278   © The Royal Institute of Philosophy and the contributors 2016
Royal Institute of Philosophy Supplement **78** 2016   147

any brevity, is the propensity which 'convinces us of the continu'd existence of external objects'. The 'contradiction' lies in the fact that causal reason – a natural and necessary propensity – apparently dictates the conclusion that there are no external objects, and yet the belief in external objects is equally natural and necessary. It 'is not possible for us to reason justly and regularly from causes and effects, and at the same time believe the continu'd existence of matter' (T 1.4.7.4; SBN 266). If we reason properly, the external world must vanish.

This is not the only 'manifest contradiction' Hume identifies in his conclusion. Part IV of Book I of the *Treatise* opens with a section entitled 'Of scepticism with regard to reason', a scepticism to which he returns in the conclusion. 'Of scepticism with regard to reason' presents a seemingly radical argument that the normative demands of reason are such that their consistent application would lead to 'a total extinction of belief and evidence' (T 1.4.1.6; SBN 182). When Hume first presents this argument he tells us that that, fortunately, that such arguments have no doxastic effect: it is 'happy ... that nature breaks the force of all sceptical arguments in time, and keeps them from having any considerable influence on the understanding' (T 1.2.1.12; SBN 187). However, when he revisits the topic he states that although 'refin'd reflections have little or no influence upon us ... we do not, and cannot establish it for a rule, that they ought not to have any influence; which implies a manifest contradiction' (T 1.4.7.7; SBN 268). The contradiction, it seems, is that although reflection has no doxastic effect of belief we cannot say that it should not.

In what follows I shall examine these manifest contradictions and how they might be resolved. But it might seem that Hume's only answer to these manifest contradictions is, as it were, to go with the natural flow. The Humean predicament is one where reason makes an epistemic mockery of our doxastic life, though fortunately our beliefs are psychological immune to this mockery. 'Nature is obstinate', Hume writes, 'and will not quit the field, however strongly attack'd by reason; and at the same time reason is so clear in the point, that there is no possibility of disguising her' (T 1.4.2.52; SBN 215). And this might seem precisely what Hume says when the first of the manifest contradictions is alluded to in the first *Enquiry*. The reasoning which leads us to make the distinction between primary and secondary qualities renders it impossible to believe in external objects except in the sense of 'a certain unknown, inexplicable *something*, as the cause of our perceptions; a notion so imperfect, that no sceptic will think it worth while to attend against it.' (EHU 12.16; SBN 115) In a footnote, attributing these arguments to Berkeley, Hume responds by declaring them 'merely sceptical' and that they

> admit of no answer and produce no conviction. Their only effect is to cause that momentary amazement and irresolution and confusion, which is the result of scepticism (EHU 12.16; SBN 115n)

Reason dictates a sceptical conclusion, one that admits of no answer, but thankfully belief does not follow, and so no conviction is produced.

On the face of it, this general line of response seems unsatisfactory. We are still left with a negative epistemic evaluation of belief, in external objects in the first case, and belief more generally in the case of scepticism with regard to reason. So although philosophers are carried along with the tide of nature, they must do so with an air of ironic detachment.[2] But although this is the image of the Humean predicament outside of the circle of Hume scholarship, it is not one embraced by everyone within it. Hume's conclusion, and its relation to scepticism, has been the subject of a great deal of discussion in the last 20 years or so. One particular claim Hume makes in 'Conclusion of this book' is relevant to the manifest contradictions and has been dubbed by Don Garrett the 'Title Principle' (TP). It runs as follows:

> Where reason is lively, and mixes itself with some propensity, it ought to be assented to. Where it does not, it never can have any title to operate upon us.' (T 1.4.7.11; SBN 270)

On the face of it, the Title Principle is a normative one, telling us when and when not, reason should command assent and Garrett has deployed it in resolving the manifest contradictions. My interest in it began when I pointed out that Hume's claim that sceptical arguments about the external world are such as to 'admit of no answer but produce no conviction' can be read in the light of the TP. Putting aside the expression 'mixes itself with some propensity' for the time being, the TP connects the normative authority of reason to its 'liveliness' and its lack of normative authority when there is a lack of liveliness. Liveliness is the property that distinguishes the attitude of belief or conviction from mere conception. The fact that the arguments 'produce no conviction' means that such arguments have no 'title to operate on us'. We are permitted to ignore the 'merely sceptical arguments' and not simply because the conclusion is

---

[2]   See e.g. Broughton, J. 'Hume's Naturalism and His Skepticism' in Radcliffe (ed.) *A Companion to Hume* (Oxford: Basil Blackwell, 2008).

psychologically impossible for us. We are not *required* to follow the conclusions of such arguments.

In what follows I revisit and develop this earlier claim of mine. I shall begin by discussing the Title Principle and distinguish my reading of its nature and grounds from Garrett's. I shall then apply that reading to the manifest contradictions.

2.

The TP runs as follows

> Where reason is lively, and mixes itself with some propensity, it ought to be assented to. Where it does not, it never can have any title to operate upon us. (T 1.4.7.11; SBN 270)

What does Hume mean by 'reason', by 'lively' and by 'mixes itself with some propensity'? We shall begin with reason.

Hume's treatment of reason in the *Treatise* is oriented around a conception of reason as a psychological faculty that operates upon the mind's contents (ideas) and is concerned with the relations in which such contents stand. 'All kinds of reasoning', writes Hume, 'consists in nothing but a comparison, and a discovery of those relations ... which two or more objects bear to each other' (T 1.3.2.2; SBN 73). There are two classes of relation over which reasons ranges, one the object of *demonstrative* reason, the other the object of *probable* reason.[3] The first, constant relations, are relations that supervene on the intrinsic character of the ideas compared – they 'depend entirely on the ideas' (T 1.3.1.1; SBN 69) – and are a distant ancestor of what we would now call analytic relations. Inconstant relations are relations that change without any change in the intrinsic character of the ideas compared, and the most significant relation, and the object of probable reason, is that of *causation*. For the rest of this discussion, I shall be focussing on probable reason alone.

Causation is central because it is the only relation that 'can be trac'd beyond our senses, and informs us of existences which we do not see or feel' (T 1.3.2.3; SBN 74). That is, it is the only relation that can ground any inference from what we presently observe to what we do not. But although I have talked of probable reason as a 'faculty' that discovers this relation, such faculty talk is not left undischarged. For Hume uses the principles of association, and in particular the

---

[3] Not all relations are discovered by reason. Degree in quality, for example, is discovered by intuition, relations of space by perception.

associative relation of cause and effect, to explain the *inferences* we draw from cause and effect. Experience of (but not necessarily experiences *that*) objects standing in the relation of cause and effect impact upon the mind and leave the habits of inference which constitute the basic mechanism of probable reason. Probable reason as an inferential faculty is a 'mechanical tendency' (EHU 5.22; SBN 55), and 'nothing but a wonderful and unintelligible instinct in our souls, which carries us along a certain train of ideas, and endows them with particular qualities, according to their particular situations and relations' (T 1.4.16.9; SBN 179).

This 'mechanical tendency' of drawing such inferences is something that Hume terms probable reason and, what's more, a tendency that is tied to epistemic success. The mechanism is geared to causal relations and allows us to 'discover the real existence ... of objects' (T 1.3.2.2; SBN 73). Causation 'informs us of existences and objects' (T 1.3.2.3; SBN 74), and 'brings us acquainted with such existences' (T 1.3.2.13; SBN 108). Inferences in line with causal relations are 'just': causation is the only relation 'on which we can found a just inference from one object to another' (T 1.3.6.7; SBN 89).

Those used to seeing Hume as sceptic about probable reason or 'induction' might be surprised to see both that he discusses reason in terms that are redolent of epistemic success and that he uses terms like 'just' in connection with such inferences. However, the scholarly consensus is that Hume does treat probable reason as having positive epistemic value, though quite how that is to be understood remains a matter of controversy. I align myself to those take a consequentialist approach, namely that the justness of probable reason is connected to its being a faculty productive of true belief. To put it another way, at least part of the positive epistemic status of probable reason must owe itself to its (presumed) *reliability*.[4] Our 'reason must be consider'd a kind of cause, of which truth is the natural effect' (T 1.4.4.1; SBN 180) and his discussion of it is

---

[4] See, for example, L. Loeb 'Inductive Inference in Hume's Philosophy' in Radcliffe (ed.) *A Companion to Hume* (Oxford: Basil Blackwell, 2008). and H. Beebee *Hume on Causation* (London: Routledge, 2006). The most sophisticated and articulated statement of the view is Schmitt *Hume's Epistemology in the Treatise: A Veritistic Interpretation* (Oxford: Oxford University Press, 2014). I hereby reject the view I offered in Kail, P. J. E. *Projection and Realism in Hume's Philosophy* (Oxford: Clarendon Press, 2007).

often accompanied by factives like 'informs', 'discover' and 'brings us acquainted with'. Here, he writes, is a

> pre-established harmony between the course of nature and the succession of our ideas. ... Had not the presence of an object instantly excited the idea of those objects, commonly conjoined with it, all our knowledge must have been limited to the narrow sphere of memory and senses (EHU 12.2; SBN 54)

Our inferential mechanism is responsive to the course of nature in that our inferential dispositions are acquired through experiences of the manifestations of its regularities. Such a mechanism may be presumed reliable but not infallible. We can check first-order inferences and to that end Hume offers a series of rules 'by which to judge of causes and effects' (T 1.3.15). There is obviously much more that could said here,[5] and we shall presently come to another norm of correction, but let us now turn to 'liveliness'.

I mentioned above that liveliness is the mark of conviction and belief and I shall understand the liveliness of reason to consist its being productive of belief. The liveliness of belief involves the transference of the liveliness possessed by a present impression or memory to the idea constituting the content of belief. Indeed, Hume ties his account of inference to this transference of vivacity. He allows that there are cases of 'hypothetical' reasoning (i.e. moving from mere idea to idea) but his discussion of reasoning tends to be tied to the transference of vivacity from an impression or a memory. Although 'the mind in its reasonings from causes or effects, carries its view beyond those objects, which it sees or remembers, it must never lose sight of them entirely, nor reason merely upon its ideas, without some mixture of impressions, or at least ideas of the memory, which are equivalent to impressions' (T 1.3.4.1; SBN 82). If I merely conceive an idea of cause C I may, by association, come to have the idea of its effect E but that idea won't constitute belief since there is no source of vivacity. If, however, I experience C – in impression or memory – the liveliness of the impression is transferred up the associational track to the idea.

At first blush, reason would not be lively just in cases when there is no transference of vivacity, cases where the mind does 'lose sight of it objects'. To explore this, let us return to T 1.4.1, 'Of scepticism with regard to reason'. The discussion of 'Of scepticism with regard to

---

[5]   For a very extensive discussion, see Schmitt *Hume's Epistemology in the Treatise: A Veritistic Interpretation* (Oxford: Oxford University Press, 2014).

reason' begins with a statement of the presumptive reliability of reason on the one hand, and its fallibility on the other. Our 'reason must be consider'd a kind of cause, of which truth is the natural effect; but such-a-one as by the irruption of other causes, and by the inconstancy of our mental powers, may frequently prevented' (T 1.4.1.1; SBN 180). Our first-order inferences are 'sometimes just and sometimes erroneous' (T 1.4.1.9; SBN 184), the former being the result of appropriate causes, the latter determined by other 'contrary' causes, either from interference or by some psychological slackness on our part. Our memory of such errors issues in a demand that we arrive at a new judgment that is the combination of the first-order judgment and the memory of the erroneous judgment, one that has a lower degree of probability than the original judgment. 'We must...in every reasoning form a new judgment, as a check or controul on our first judgment or belief'. (T 1.4.1.1; SBN 180) This demand, however, iterates: the second judgment is liable to the same 'check or controul', and each new judgment has a lesser degree of probability than its predecessor. The first casualty of the demand is knowledge in that it degenerates into probability' (T 1.4.1.1; SBN 180). From a state of being certain, both doxastically and epistemically, that p, reflection on fallibility introduces grounds to be less certain that p. But that is not the end of the matter, given the iterative character of the demand. Eventually, we arrive at a judgment that gives no credence to the truth of p that was the content of the original judgment.

> When I reflect on the natural fallibility of my judgement, I have less confidence in my opinions ... and when I proceed still farther, to turn the scrutiny against every successive estimation I make of my faculties, all the rules of logic require a continual diminution, and at last a total extinction of belief and evidence. (T 1.4.1.6; SBN 182)

We shall return to the epistemic implications of this argument presently, but right now let us concentrate on the 'total extinction of belief', since we are considering non-lively reason. A key point Hume makes in this section is that we are not doxastically responsive to such iterative exercises. They are too remote from the original impression- and memory-based sources of vivacity (which he calls 'original evidence' (T 1.4.1.9; SBN 184)). The 'conviction, which arises from a subtle reasoning, diminishes in proportion to the efforts, which the imagination makes to enter into the reasoning', (T 1.4.1.11; SBN 186) and when 'the mind reaches not its objects with easiness and facility, the same principles have not the same effect as in a more natural conception of ideas' (T 1.4.1.10; SBN 185).

This gives us a working conception of non-lively reason: inferences are that comply with 'all the rules of logic' but which do not have any doxastic effect. Hume reiterates the upshot of this argument in 'Conclusion to this Book', stating that 'the understanding, when it acts alone, and according to its most general principles, entirely subverts itself, and leaves not the lowest degree of evidence in any proposition, either in philosophy or common life' (T 1.4.7.1; SBN 267). Here, however, Hume is not as sanguine as he was earlier about the implications of this observation. One could choose to reject 'refin'd or elaborate reasoning' but to do so would 'cut off entirely all science and philosophy' (T 1.4.7.7; SBN 268). However, such reasoning leads to a total destruction of evidence, and although 'refin'd reflections have little or no influence upon us...we do not, and cannot establish it for a rule, that they ought not to have any influence' (*op. cit.*). Now, to be somewhat brief and dogmatic, I shall take the term 'evidence' to be some positive epistemic property (rather a merely doxastic one[6]) and so refined reasoning destroys the positive epistemic standing of any belief. Furthermore, we cannot simply ignore the demand to proportion our belief to considered evidence: 'we do not, and cannot establish it for a rule, that they ought not to have any influence'.

At this point of 'Conclusion to this book' crisis looms: even the consolation that sceptical arguments have few or no doxastic consequences seems to disappear. He writes that although he stated that 'reflections very refin'd and metaphysical have little or no influence upon us' (T 1.4.7.8: SBN 266), from his 'present feeling and experience' the '*intense* view of these manifold contradictions and imperfections in human reason has so wrought upon me, and heated my brain, that I am ready to reject all belief and reasoning'. Noting that this 'deplorable condition' is dispelled by leaving the study and returning to company and relaxation, his reflections prompt a question: Why should he engage in subtle and refined reasoning at all? Why ought he 'torture [his] brain with subtilites [sic.] and sophistries' and why he must make 'so painful an application' when he has 'no tolerable prospect of arriving by its means at truth and certainty' (T 1.4.7.10; SBN 270)? 'Under what obligation do I lie of making such an abuse of time? And what end can it serve either for the service of mankind, or for my own private interest?' (T 1.4.7.10;

---

[6]   For this kind of reading see D. Owen *Hume's Reason* (Oxford: Oxford University Press, 1999) and what I take to be well-placed criticism see K. Meeker *Hume's Radical Scepticism and the Fate of Naturalized Epistemology* (London: Palgrave, 2013).

SBN 270) He resolves never to be 'led a wandering into search dreary solitudes, and rough passages' through which he hitherto been and will only strive against his natural propensities when he has a 'good reason'.

This sentiment – which expresses what Hume calls his 'spleen and indolence' – leads to his statement of the TP. At this juncture we should consider the last aspect of the TP, that of 'mixes with some propensity'. One question Hume in the vicinity is what constitutes a good reason to strive against inclination, and it seems that propensity here is some independent motivation to pursue refined reasoning and Hume mentions 'curiosity' and 'ambition' (T 1.4.7.1.13; SBN 271), when he is 'naturally *inclin'd*' (T 1.4.7.12; SBN 270) and that in not pursuing philosophy he would be 'the loser in the point of pleasure' (T 1.4.7.12; SBN 271). This might seem to us either rather odd or trivial. Surely the exercise of reason is *always* in the service of some motivational propensity, be it the importance attached to determining whether p, our curiosity in determining whether p or the pleasure of knowledge. However, if we think about the intellectual context in which Hume was working we can see this as a response to those who hold that the exercise of reason is of non-natural value, a value that is independent of humdrum practical concern. Perhaps the most explicit articulation of this is to be found in the philosophy of Nicolas Malebranche, a thinker with whom Hume was particularly exercised. Like many philosophers of the time, Malebranche held that the traditional doctrine that man is made in the image of God is best captured in the terms that we resemble Him with respect to our reason. Our *virtue* consists in the extent to which we resemble God and the properly virtuous person will exercise reason even against his natural inclinations. In the unconditional pursuit of truth and reason the devout, secluded from ordinary commerce can 'sacrifice his peace of mind for the sake of Truth, and his pleasures for the sake of Order ... He can, in a word, earn merit or demerit'.[7] Both here and in the conclusion to Book II of the *Treatise* 'Of curiosity and the love of truth' Hume is bring the pursuit of truth through reason down to earth. For Malebranche there is an independent demand to be 'led a wandering into search dreary solitudes, and rough passages', and is this, as I have argued at length elsewhere, one of Hume's targets in 'Conclusion to this book'.[8]

[7] Nicolas Malebranche, *Treatise on Ethics*, trans. C Walton (Dordrecht, Kluwer, 1993), 48.
[8] See my 'Hume's Ethical Conclusion' in Frasca-Spada & Kail (eds) *Impressions of Hume* (Oxford: Clarendon Press, 2005).

As I read it, 'mixes with some propensity' provides only a motivation to pursue reasoning. However that aspect of the TP has no *epistemic* bearing: it is not the case that what motivates one to reason determines the standing of reason's products. It cannot determine the conditions under which reason does or does not have a title to operate upon us. So we are left with the question of just why non-lively reason has no title to operate upon us.

It seems to me that the best way to understand this idea is as follows, though I cannot claim any direct textual smoking guns. The sceptical argument, recall, began with the presumption of the reliability of the faculty. Our first-order judgments are the product of reason, which we must think of as a kind of cause, of which truth is the natural effect in virtue of its being a mechanism that is responsive to causal relations. It is (presumptively) reliable, though not infallible, and it is presumptive responsiveness that allows for its normativity, relative to an interest in truth (one form of 'propensity' with which reason is mixed). But iterated use of the faculty appears to undermine the presumptive epistemic standing of its deliverances by delivering a conclusion that no belief so produced has any positive epistemic standing. If it is the case that reflection provides a reason that undermines the presumption of reliability it also at the same time undercuts the normative authority, relative to an interest in truth, of reflection. For it undermines the idea that its deployment in cases of reflections leads to the truth, and so undercuts the grounds for the demand it should be followed. So there is no reason to pursue reason to its self-undermining conclusion. The absence of such a reason means that we are permitted to ignore the conclusions of higher-order reasoning, i.e. those instances that are non-lively. This reading also explains why Hume tells us why a 'true sceptic is diffident of his philosophical doubts' (T 1.4.7.14; SBN 273) and why he suggests that one 'can find no error in the foregoing arguments'. (T 1.4.1.8; SBN 184) With respect to the first, Hume is sceptical about the compellingness of the sceptical argument given that it seems self-undermining but at the same time, and with respect to the second point, the norms governing reflection do seem to require iteration. The sceptic's response is the same inasmuch as the argument appears to leave us with no reason to pursue reason in that direction. This is not equivalent to rejecting all reflective reasoning. To do so, recall, would 'cut off entirely all science and philosophy' (T 1.4.7.7; SBN 268). For it remains true that reflective reasoning itself can be lively in the relevant sense. It is rather that very refined reason that is disconnected from liveliness has no title to operate on us.

3.

With this understanding of the TP, let us consider the second of Hume's 'manifest contradictions'. Hume describes how causal reasoning threatens our belief in the external world in T 1.4.4, 'Of the modern philosophy'. By 'modern philosophy' Hume means the distinction between primary and secondary qualities. Whereas primary qualities are supposed qualities of matter, modern philosophy maintains that 'colours, sounds, tastes, smells, head and cold...[are] nothing but impressions in the mind, deriv'd from the operations of external objects, and without any resemblance to the qualities of the objects' (T 1.4.4.3; SBN 226).[9] Hume finds only one argument in favour of the distinction 'satisfactory', one that is a variant on the Argument from Conflicting Appearances. X appears F under circumstance C, but appears F* under circumstances C*. It is assumed that there is no change in X. The fact of conflicting appearances, however, is insufficient to draw the distinction. It allows to infer that not all appearances F (F-impressions) are caused by resembling quality F. But with presumption that like causes have like effects, we conclude that none is caused by F, and that all instances of F are properties of impressions. However, Hume thinks that this line of reasoning 'rather than explaining the operations of external objects by its means, we utterly annihilate all these objects, and reduce ourselves to the opinions of most extravagant scepticism, concerning them' (T1.4.4.6; SBN 227–8). For once these qualities are excluded from body no content can be given to an external object. The upshot of this is that

> ... there is a direct and total opposition betwixt our reason and our senses; or more properly speaking, betwixt those conclusions we form from cause and effect, and those that perswade us of the continu'd and independent existence of body. When we reason from cause and effect, we conclude that neither colour, sound, taste, nor smell have a continu'd and independent existence. When we exclude these sensible qualities there remains nothing in the universe, which has such an existence. (T 1.4.4.15; SBN 231)

Hume presents a variant of this argument in the first *Enquiry*, which he claims comes from the 'most profound philosophy' of

---

[9]   Hume is often mistakenly accused of misunderstanding Locke on this issue. This, however, is itself a mistake. See my *Projection and Realism in Hume's Philosophy* (Oxford: Clarendon Press, 2007), chapter 7, section 2.1.

P.J.E. Kail

Berkeley.[10] Hume's presentation here does indeed have a more Irish flavour inasmuch as explicit reference is made of the impossibility of abstracting secondary qualities from primary qualities. In this case Hume doesn't explicitly discuss considerations of causation that drive the distinction in the first place, but takes the distinction as given and derives from it the mind-dependency of objects. His conclusion is that this objection represents our usual assumption of the continued existence of external objects as

> ... contrary to reason; at least, if it be a principle of reason, that all sensible qualities are in the mind, not in the object. Bereave matter of all its intelligible qualities, both primary and secondary, you in a manner annihilate it, and leave only a certain unknown, inexplicable *something*, as the cause of our perceptions; a notion so imperfect, that no sceptic will think it worth while to attend against it. (EHU 12.16; SBN 115, emphasis original)

Now, I have omitted the detail from both versions of the argument and I shall make no comment on their soundness. The main point is the causal reasoning leads to distinction, and the distinction to annihilation and this is what generates the 'manifest contradiction'. I shall call this combination of concerns the 'Annihilation Argument'.

Before we discuss the Annihilation Argument directly, it should be first noted that Hume is at best equivocal over whether the primary/secondary quality distinction is a sound one. This is significant inasmuch as the manifest contradiction is adduced from the distinction, and yet Hume seems at the very least ambivalent about that distinction. He says in the *Treatise* that the annihilation consequence is a 'very decisive' objection *to* the system of modern philosophy. That system that 'pretends to be free' from the 'defect' of stemming from principles of nature that are 'neither universal nor unavoidable in human nature', and in this section Hume claims to be examining 'this pretension' (T 1.4.4.2; SBN 226). We shall return to this point presently. Note too in the *Enquiry* presentation there is some initial distancing from the argument when he says 'if it be a principle of reason' that we should conclude that the distinction is sound. In 'Of the Standard of Taste', Hume says of the 'famous doctrine' that it is

---

[10]   J. Hakkarainen misleads somewhat when he labels this *argument* 'profound' (in 'Hume's Scepticism and Realism', *British Journal for the History of Philosophy* 20(2): 286. Hume doesn't call the argument profound, he instead calls Berkeley's philosophy profound.

158

'supposed to be fully proved in modern times' (EMPL p.166n) and in a letter he refers to the distinction as a 'paradox'.[11]

Still, such Hume's apparent distancing himself from the distinction does not itself get us very far in avoiding the 'manifest contradiction'. For, recall, Hume tells us of a conflict between two 'equally natural and necessary' principles of the human imagination. For Janet Broughton the choice here is a stark one. She writes that 'to avoid "contradiction" we would have to give up drawing causal inferences, or we would have to give up our commonsense belief in the existence of external world'.[12] But this is a false dilemma: the TP allows us to distinguish between instances of causal inferences to which we ought to assent and instances that have no title to operate upon us, i.e. those non-lively instances. So we need to see whether such inferences are of the non-lively variety.

Alas, however, it cannot be said that the evidence points one way or the other. The best piece of evidence that such reasoning violates the TP is the remark from the *Enquiry* about the arguments being such to 'admit of no answer and produce no conviction' (EHU 12.16; SBN 115n), but this obviously has to be treated with caution since the *Enquiry* and the *Treatise* are rather different texts. So let us take a closer look at Hume's language in 'Of the modern philosophy'. Hume tells us there the conflicting appearance argument is 'satisfactory' (T 1.4.4.3; SBN 226) and, what's more, a further conclusion can be drawn from it that 'is likewise as satisfactory as can be possibly be imagined' (T 1.4.4.3; SBN 226) That conclusion is that impressions have non-resembling causes. The expression 'likewise as satisfactory as can be possibly imagined' seems difficult to read as anything other than a lively instance of reason.

As things progress the argument is couched in terms that are a little more equivocal. He says that the distinction '*seem*[s] to follow by an easy consequence' (T 1.4.4.5; SBN 227, my emphasis). The next stage of the argument in 'Of modern philosophy' concerns the impossibility of conceiving extension without either colour or sensations of touch, both of which are secondary qualities. Hume certainly writes that 'will appear entirely conclusive to everyone that comprehends it', but, on the other hand, 'it may seem abstruse and intricate to the

---

[11]   Letter to Hugh Blair, July 1762, reprinted in P.B. Wood 'David Hume on Thomas Reid's An Inquiry into the Human Mind, on the Principles of Common Sense: A New Letter to Hugh Blair from July 1762', *Mind* 95 (1986) 411–16.

[12]   J. Broughton 'Hume's Naturalism and His Skepticism' in Radcliffe (ed.) *A Companion to Hume* (Oxford: Basil Blackwell, 2008): 431.

P.J.E. Kail

generality of readers' (T 1.4.4.10; SBN 229). But this is hardly decisive in favour of the relevant instances of reasoning being the non-lively sort. There are, it seems to me, only two other considerations that could be said to lend support to such reasoning violating the TP, though neither is particularly strong. The first is that the distinction between primary and secondary qualities itself difficult to believe. Thus so 'strong is the prejudice for the distinct continu'd existence of [secondary qualities], that when the contrary opinion is advanc'd by modern philosophers, people imagine that they can almost refute it from their feeling and experience, and that their very senses contradict this philosophy' (T 1.4.2.13; SBN 192). However, this does not directly tell against the arguments for the distinction being themselves instances of lively reasoning. The second would be to point out that Hume seems to be implying that the doctrine of modern philosophy is a principle is not amongst those which are 'neither universal nor unavoidable in human nature'. Recall we noted above that Hume is examining the 'pretension' that the doctrine is such a principle and argues that it is a decisive objection to the system that it 'annihilates' the external world. So then the doctrine is not an instance of a principle that is 'neither universal nor unavoidable in human nature'. But there are a number of problems with this move. First, if that is the implicit conclusion of 'Of the modern philosophy', why then does Hume talk about a conflict between two 'equally natural and necessary' principles of the human imagination in 'Conclusion of this book'? For it seems the doctrine of modern philosophy implicated is implicated in the 'manifest contradiction' and so is 'natural and necessary'. One might try to avoid this in the following way. Hume is implicitly distinguishing between instances of reasoning that are natural and necessary and those that are not in 'Of the modern philosophy' and it is only when we get to the TP that that distinction is properly drawn. There may be some mileage in this suggestion, but it doesn't itself show that the reasoning in the Annihilation Argument is non-lively and so we are still at a loss.

For the moment, it seems to me, that an appeal to the TP to solve the first of Hume's manifest contradictions remains an open option but the textual support is not very strong.

St. Peter's College, Oxford
peter.kail@philosophy.ox.ac.uk

Kant's Third *Critique*: The Project of Unification

SEBASTIAN GARDNER

Abstract

This paper offers a synoptic view of Kant's *Critique of the Power of Judgement* and its reception by the German Idealists. I begin by sketching Kant's conception of how its several parts fit together, and emphasize the way in which the specifically moral motivation of Kant's project of unification of Freedom and Nature distances it from our contemporary philosophical concerns. For the German Idealists, by contrast, the *CPJ*'s conception of the opposition of Freedom and Nature as defining the overarching task of philosophy provides a warrant and basis for bold speculative programmes. The German Idealist development therefore presupposes Kant's failure in the *CPJ* to resolve the problem of the relation of Freedom and Nature. What is fundamentally at issue in the argument between Kant and his successors is the question of the correct conception of philosophical systematicity and in this context I reconstruct Kant's defence of his claim to philosophical finality.

It is fair to say that the third and last of Kant's critiques, the *Critique of the Power of Judgement* (*CPJ*), does not hold the same importance for us as its predecessors. The *Critique of Pure Reason* addresses what are still central concerns of epistemology, metaphysics, and philosophy of mind. The *Critique of Practical Reason*, paired with the *Groundwork*, articulates a position that every contemporary moral (and political) philosopher regards as worth engaging with and that some regard as deeply right about fundamental matters. The Third *Critique* is not in the same league. The difficulties begin when we try to say what it is a critique of. If the title is to be believed, the subject is *Urteilskraft*, the power of judgement, but judgement as such is discussed only in the Introduction and is in any case for us a topic in philosophical logic, which is certainly not Kant's concern here, while the notion of a 'power' or 'faculty' of judgement does not resonate with our concerns. Only one of the topics treated in the book, the aesthetic, has a relatively firm (though hardly central) place on our contemporary philosophical agenda, and the bulk of the attention paid to the Third *Critique* is accordingly directed at the first of its two parts, the 'Critique of Aesthetic Judgement', which is standardly taken in isolation from its surroundings. The second part, the 'Critique of Teleological Judgement', centres on a problem that is widely supposed to have

doi:10.1017/S1358246116000254

been overtaken by Darwin, while the other bits and pieces contained in the work – a few brief sections on the methodology and presuppositions of the natural sciences, some passages on the philosophy of history, a lengthy restatement of Kant's moral theology, and a rather strange new account of what defines human cognition – all of these do not obviously belong to a single train of thought. All in all, then, it can seem that the Third *Critique* is something of a dog's dinner, and that, once Kant's aesthetics have been liberated from their textual cage and the remainder of the work has been picked over, its interest is exhausted.

There is, I think, not much to be gained by directly contesting this assessment of what the Third *Critique* has to offer philosophical enquiry of the present day. The worthwhile issue to pursue is instead how and why Kant conceived the work as an integral whole. The first half of my discussion provides accordingly an overview of how its parts are integrated. The second half is devoted to its reception by the German Idealists. This is not a change of subject, for as I hope to show, their critical appraisal raises a deep and difficult question about what, in Kant's terms, constitutes an integral whole of philosophical knowledge. Since this paper is in the nature of a synopsis, the issues on which I touch receive only extremely sketchy treatment, though I try to give a sense of their great complexity.[1] Although my discussion is not designed to save the philosophical interest of the *Critique of the Power of Judgement* by showing that its problems are those that form our contemporary agenda, it does not follow that its interest is 'merely' historical: the present case is one in which the history of philosophy best serves philosophical interest by displaying its object's historical distance, showing us a road not taken, or more accurately, a road once taken but later abandoned and now hard to reimagine, but which, when reimagined, opens up a world of possibilities.[2]

[1]   The complexities are explored in the following recent works, selected because they to a greater or lesser extent address the *Critique of the Power of Judgement* as a whole: Henry Allison, *Kant's Theory of Taste: A Reading of the Critique of Aesthetic Judgment* (Cambridge: Cambridge University Press, 2001), Hannah Ginsborg, *The Normativity of Nature: Essays on Kant's* Critique of Judgement (Oxford: Oxford University Press, 2015), Paul Guyer, *Kant's System of Nature and Freedom: Selected Essays* (Cambridge: Cambridge University Press, 2005), Angelica Nuzzo, *Kant and the Unity of Reason* (Lafayette: Purdue University Press, 2004), Robert Wicks, *Routledge Philosophy Guidebook to Kant on Judgement* (London: Routledge, 2006), and Rachel Zuckert, *Kant on Beauty and Biology: An Interpretation of the* Critique of Judgment (Cambridge: Cambridge University Press, 2007).
[2]   Yitzhak Y. Melamed puts the point well in 'Charitable Interpretations and the Political Domestrication of Spinoza, or, Benedict in the Land of

1. Kant's aims in the Third *Critique*: the project of unification

If we want to know what in Kant's eyes holds all of its disparate topics together and makes the Third *Critique* more than a collection of appendices to his Critical system, then we need to look at the Introduction to the work, where we find Kant explaining its unitary project in different ways.

The Introduction is an exercise in *architectonic*, which Kant defines as the 'art of system', *die Kunst der Systeme*, where 'system' means an intellectual structure that employs Ideas to transform an aggregate of common cognitions into scientific knowledge, *Wissenschaft*, a genuine unity.[3] The key to the architectonic of the *CPJ*, as set forth in the Introduction, is not the concept of judgement as such but the idea that the *faculty* of judgement, which *intermediates* between our other two conceptual faculties, reason and understanding, has a subterranean connection with the *hedonic* faculty, the faculty of pleasure and unpleasure, which intermediates between our theoretical and practical powers. The connections are shown in the map of our faculties with which Kant concludes the Introduction:[4]

All the faculties of the mind	Faculty of cognition	*A priori* principles	Application to
Faculty of cognition	Understanding	Lawfulness	Nature
Feeling of pleasure and displeasure	Power of judgment	Purposiveness	Art
Faculty of desire	Reason	Final end	Freedom

Secular Imagination', in M. Lærke, J.E.H. Smith, and E. Schliesser (eds), *Philosophy and Its History: Aims and Methods in the Study of Early Modern Philosophy* (Oxford: Oxford University Press, 2013), 258–277: 'We should engage in the study of good past philosophers, *not in spite, but because* of the fact that frequently past philosophers argue for views that are significantly different from ours' (274).

   [3]   *Critique of Pure Reason* (henceforth *CPR*), A832–835/B860–863; see also A13/B27. Determination of form by an Idea is what distinguishes architectonic from merely 'technical' unity.

   [4]   *Critique of the Power of Judgement* (henceforth *CPJ*, followed by the Akademie Ausgabe pagination), ed. P. Guyer, trans. P. Guyer and E. Matthews (Cambridge: Cambridge University Press, 2000), Introduction, Sect. IX, 5:198.

Sebastian Gardner

The guiding idea, then, is that the triadic division of the mind as a whole, the left-hand column, is reproduced *within* its first term, the faculty of cognition, yielding the second column, each member of which determines, according to its own *a priori* principle, a specific range of objects. 'Art', the middle term of the last column, refers not just to fine art but primarily to 'nature as art', that is, nature regarded as a *technique*, i.e. considered teleologically. The importance of this will emerge shortly.

A crucial part of Kant's story is that judgement divides into two classes, what he calls 'determinant' and 'reflective' judgement, distinguished by the way in which they connect particulars and universals.[5] Determinant judgement subsumes a particular encountered in cognition under a concept which is *already given*. Reflective judgement *seeks out* for particulars a concept which is not already given, that is, it seeks to form *new* concepts. Determinant judgements, theoretical and practical, have already been dealt with in the earlier *Critiques*. Explicating reflective judgement is the new task, and Kant tells us that the concept-seeking function of judgement is associated with the concept of end or purpose, *Zweck*; some reflective judgements employ this concept explicitly, predicating it of their objects, and those that do not nonetheless presuppose it in their background. Kant's claim is that, armed with this apparatus, we can substantiate this model of our rational powers, and the main body of the Third *Critique* is an attempt to supply the detail and fill it out.

It is safe to say that the architectonic project is unlikely to grab us, and while we may look with favour and interest on Kant's endeavour to extend his account of how experience is conceptualized – the new theory of reflective judgement – it may reasonably be doubted that it strictly requires Kant's architectonic surroundings. But Kant has another way of explaining the task of the Third *Critique*, which makes it seem considerably more inviting. Kant focusses on the needs of the moral agent, who has (he now concedes) been left adrift by the two earlier *Critiques*, in so far as each of these has merely sought to account for its *own* domain, without *coordinating* them. The first *Critique* established that practical reason's legislation over the 'domain' (*Gebiet*) of Freedom, and theoretical reason's legislation over Nature, cannot conflict, even though their 'territory'

---

[5]   The new conception of reflective judgement is needed in order to give substance to the idea that judgement constitutes a distinctive faculty of its own; without it, Kant would have little reason to add anything to the brief remarks on the power of judgement in the *Critique of Pure Reason* (A132–136/B171–175).

(*Boden*) is the same, namely objects of possible experience; and the second *Critique* showed what use can be made of the concept of Freedom, once it has been rendered unproblematic. But this separation has not been followed up by any reunification. Here is the famous paragraph stating the problem:

> Now although there is an incalculable gulf [eine unübersehbare Kluft] fixed between the domain of the concept of nature, as the sensible, and the domain of the concept of freedom, as the supersensible, so that from the former to the latter (thus by means of the theoretical use of reason) no transition is possible, just as if there were so many different worlds, the first of which can have no influence on the second: yet the latter *should* have an influence on the former [...] Thus there must still be a ground of the *unity* of the supersensible that grounds nature with that which the concept of freedom contains practically, the concept of which, even if it does not suffice for cognition of it either theoretically or practically, and thus has no proper domain of its own [kein eigentümliches Gebiet hat], nevertheless makes possible the transition from the manner of thinking [Übergang von der Denkungsart] in accordance with the principles of the one to that in accordance with the principles of the other.[6]

Now this talk of unifying Freedom and Nature brings to mind a very familiar task, the problem of understanding the relation of the mental to the physical and of normativity to nature. What one makes of those dualities – whether one affirms the reality of mind and normativity, and if so in what form – is decisive for the particular form of naturalism, if any, that one regards as defensible. This might seem to make the *Critique of the Power of Judgement* a book for our times, but there are deep differences between Kant's conception of the task of unification, and the tasks that occupy us, which once again set the Third *Critique* at a historical distance.

First, Kant denies that a unification of the physical and the mental, of the kind we consider necessary if substance dualism is to be avoided, is possible: the first *Critique* argues that transcendental idealism, which interrelates the physical and the mental systematically at the level of our representations of each and denies them any further knowable essence, provides the only coherent account of the mind-body relation; on Kant's view, it is only if we mistake inner and outer appearances for *things in themselves* that we will attempt to determine their underlying metaphysical relation.

[6]   *CPJ*, Introduction, Sect. II, 5:175–176.

Second, and even more importantly, Kant's task of unification has the specific presupposition that 'Freedom' has at its core what Kant calls *pure practical reason*, that is, the moral law. If practical reason were exclusively empirical, then its integration with theoretical reason would present no problem: practical reason would already be integrated with nature, since its job would simply be to steer action in accordance with the inclinations that nature has given us.

There is scope for different interpretations of the exact problem to which Kant is drawing attention in this passage, but from what he says later in the main body of the text, it would appear that he is concerned with the success conditions of the *worldly* moral enterprise. In order to act morally, I need to believe that my actions *qua moral* stand a chance of success, and no reassurance on this front is supplied by my long experience of getting my body to move when I want it to, and of succeeding in a reasonable number of morally indifferent tasks. These successes tell me only that I *qua natural creature* fit well enough into the natural world. Whether I also do so as a *moral being* is another matter.

This problem of a need for moral reassurance differs from the one that Kant addressed in the Dialectic of the second *Critique*, and which he claimed to solve by means of the theological postulates. There, the problem concerned the *non-identity of morality and happiness*, which threatened to check moral willing at its root: the worry was that, if to form a dutiful will is to renounce the hope of, to declare oneself indifferent to, happiness, then the demands of morality are nonsensical for creatures like us, who have compound rational-and-sensible natures. Here in the Third *Critique* the problem is that, even if I am reassured by Kant's moral theology that morality and happiness harmonize ultimately, outside the natural world if not within it, still I have no reason to think that the world is going to prove *receptive* to my moral purposes – that it is the *sort* of world in which it makes sense to act morally. The problem may express itself in concrete worries about the seeming futility of striving for, say, a just society in face of global capitalism, but ultimately it consists in a hiatus at the intersection of theoretical and practical reason: the problem is that *no content* has yet been given to the thought that the natural world – the world that we *know* – and the moral world – the world that we *will* – are the *same world*. Still less do we have grounds for thinking of them as *congruent*. Of course we can frame thoughts in which elements from each world are adjoined – I can think that this empirical object is something that I have borrowed and thus ought to return –

and these thoughts can effectively determine me to act, but *how* all this is possible is left a mystery.[7]

In sum, then, because Kant's specific problem of unifying Freedom and Nature presupposes his identification of Freedom with morality conceived as pure practical reason, and because Kant's resolution of this problem is not going to help with the mind-body problem that we have resumed from the early moderns, it continues to seem that there is little reason to expect the Third *Critique* to engage with our concerns. And if we turn to the detail of its argument, we find this suspicion largely confirmed.

The argument of the *CPJ* starts with Kant's analysis of judgements of taste, which is guided by the assumption that these must be differentiated sharply from moral judgements on the one side and judgements of the mere 'agreeable' on the other. As Kant's analysis unfolds, we learn that aesthetic response arises from a special configuration of our ordinary cognitive faculties, and it is demonstrated that beautiful objects manifest the *transcendental fact* that nature is mind-congenial in a way that goes beyond the conformity of nature to our understanding argued in the first *Critique*: we do not *prescribe* to the rose its specific form, on account of which its bare disinterested apprehension brings pleasure; the rose did not *need* to give pleasure, in order to be knowable, but it does so nevertheless; what it does for us is an epistemological supererogation. This deepens the sense in which mind and nature cohere – it exposes another, deeper level at which our *theoretical* power and nature are fitted to one another – but it is not enough to effect a rapprochement of Freedom and Nature. For that, Kant needs to show that, despite the sharp distinction of aesthetic from moral judgements, there is a point where the two come together. And so Kant extends his analysis in an attempt to show that the 'rightness' to which judgements of beauty lay claim – the rose's normative halo, its 'calling for' pleasure to be taken in it, and *our* calling, in our judgement, for others to take pleasure in it – can be accounted for only if we have in view, albeit in a very indefinite and indirect way, the moral good. As Kant puts it, the beautiful is a 'symbol of morality', and taste is a power of estimating the way in which moral ideas have been rendered sensible.

Kant's theory of the sublime, the junior partner of his theory of beauty, reaches the same general result – insight into the moral meaningfulness of aesthetic response – through a more circuitous route,

---

[7] An analogy may be drawn with the problem of the Transcendental Deduction concerning how appearance can be conformable to the categories.

Sebastian Gardner

and in a way that supplements the moral vision of beauty. With beauty, the moral good as it were shines through the natural object: the rose is at one with its morally purposive ground. In the case of the sublime – the towering mountain and the raging storm – the face that nature displays is indifferent or hostile. But because this extinction of our empirical significance (the mountain and storm brushing us aside as mere perishable specks) induces awareness of our essential transcendence of nature (no mere natural phenomenon can touch what we *essentially* are), the sublime teaches that the counter-purposivity found at the *surface* of Nature is in the service of an underlying moral purposiveness. The harsh lesson of sublime nature is that we can, after all, consider ourselves imperishable, but only on the condition that we are *prepared* to sacrifice our natural existence, should the moral law demand it. The sublime thus reveals our moral fitness, while the beautiful reassures us that, if we are morally adequate, then no actual and uncompensated sacrifice will be required of us.[8]

The second half of the work, the Critique of Teleological Judgement, begins afresh, with another class of distinctive forms encountered in nature, natural organisms, and argues that these demand for their explanation (and even their identification) the concept of a whole which determines its parts. Here the reflective power of judgement is manifested: because the plant or animal exhibits a form that made no sense in mechanistic terms, we had to go looking for a concept under which to bring it. To conceive an object as a living, organized being, Kant argues, is to think of the *concept* of the whole as *producing* its parts; and since the production by concepts of objects which satisfy those concepts counts for us as purposive rational agency, Kant tells us that natural organisms must be conceived as 'natural ends'. This then sets a double problem, since teleological judgement, though it is judgement *of* the very same objects that we think via the categories and in accordance with the mechanical principle of causality, is not licensed by the *Critique of Pure Reason*, in fact it appears to stand in *competition* with the mechanical forms of explanation that the earlier *Critique* showed to be strictly necessary.

Kant's solution is to admit teleology on the basis of a strictly *regulative* construal of its status. This allows him to present teleological judgement as (first) the result of conjoining our need to understand organic form in nature with the form of our faculty of reason, which hankers after wholes or totalities – thereby accounting for

---

[8] Jointly comprising an analogue in the rational ethical sphere of the testing of Abraham.

the basis of teleological judgements of nature; and (second) as having merely 'as if' force, that is, as entailing nothing whatever regarding the intrinsic constitution of objects, but instead as instructing us how we do best to think about them – thereby eliminating the threat of conflict with mechanism. Once again, then, Kant has enlarged the scope of *theoretical* reason, but more needs to be provided if the teleologically enriched theoretical picture of Nature is to be joined up with Freedom: on that front no gain has yet been made, since Kant rejects the argument from design, which would allow nature to be regarded as invested with God's rational will.[9] This last crucial step is taken by allowing our reason to take its natural course (something which in the first *Critique* is shown to lead to illusion, but to which there can be no objection here, where reason is not pretending to be able to make constitutive pronouncements concerning the objects composing supersensible reality: it understands its business to be merely the satisfaction of its own needs). Reason reasons: If certain natural objects are conceived as realizing the concept of purpose, then we must (as in every field of rational knowledge) form the concept of a *system* of purposes, and systematicity demands a highest unifying point. For this we require something *within* nature which can be thought of as the final purpose *of* nature – and to that extent as something which is *also outside* nature. And the only candidate here is, of course, humanity – not as a bare natural species, *homo sapiens*, but as bearing its own purpose within itself, the unconditionally valuable good will, which *cannot* be a means to any further end. So we arrive by a long discursive route at the same point as the *Critique of Aesthetic Judgement*: a vision of Nature as our moral home.

What I have just given is, to repeat, only a very curtailed and selective sketch of the territory covered in the Third *Critique*, but it is enough to bring out the way in which the culminating point of both of its halves, the point where they *converge*, as distinct from merely exhibiting parallels, is provided by morality. To say this is not to say that there is nothing in Kant's aesthetic theory or his theory of teleology that can stand on its own two feet: the point is just that, to the extent that we have in view Kant's project of unification, the moral element is essential – it is what binds the parts of the text together. It follows that since – or to the extent that – we can no

---

[9]   In a more profound sense than Hume. Kant's claim is not just that the inference to an Author of Nature is not inductively secure: it is that the concept of a natural end, which we apply to organisms, is distinct from that of an artefact.

longer countenance according the same sort of philosophical authority to moral consciousness as Kant requires, the construal of the work
as a would-be integral whole cannot grip us.[10]

2. 'Almost unfathomable insight': the German Idealist reception of the Third *Critique*

I want to now talk about the early reception of the work. The motive
here is not to turn away from philosophical to merely historical
matters, but to use the history of philosophy as a way of approaching
the Third *Critique* on something closer to its own terms. And the
first, salient historical fact to fix on is that the *CPJ* exerted its greatest
influence by a long chalk in the immediate Kantian aftermath, on the
German Idealists, who regarded it as the most important of the three
Critiques – not of course in a sense that would imply its independence
from the others, but in so far as they took it to *set the agenda* for what
philosophy after Kant should do, or put another way, which for them
came to the same thing, what should be *done with* Kant's philosophy.

Schelling and Hegel pay tribute to it in writings from early to late.
Schelling's *Of the I as Principle of Philosophy* ranks the Critique of
Teleological Judgment alongside the Transcendental Deduction of
the first *Critique*:

> [W]hoever has read his deduction of the categories and his cri-
> tique of the teleological power of judgment in the spirit in
> which everything he ever wrote must be read, sees the depth
> of his meaning and insight, which seems almost unfathomable
> [... Kant presented the ultimate substratum of all being and
> all identity] in a manner which appears possible only in a
> genius who, rushing ahead of himself, as it were, can *descend*
> the steps from the highest point, whereas others can ascend
> only step by step.[11]

---

[10]   Even if the need for some sort of reassurance of morality's purposiveness is acknowledged, it will not be agreed that the *CPJ*'s transcendentalism
is the right way to meet it. See Paul Abela, 'Kant, Naturalism, and the Reach
of Practical Reason', in S. Gardner and M. Grist (eds), *The Transcendental
Turn* (Oxford: Oxford University Press, 2015), esp. 67–73.

[11]   F. W. J. Schelling, *Of the I as Principle of Philosophy, or On the
Unconditional in Human Knowledge* (1795), in *The Unconditional in
Human Knowledge: Four Early Essays 1794–1796*, trans. and ed. F. Marti
(Lewisburg: Bucknell University Press, 1980), 120n.

Schelling is of course implying that whoever has grasped this unfathomable depth of insight, will acknowledge that his own Fichtean Spinozism is present in Kant himself. Similarly, in his Munich lectures on the history of modern philosophy from the 1830s Schelling describes it as 'Kant's deepest work, which, if he could have begun with it as he finished with it, would have probably given his whole philosophy another direction'.[12] Hegel's early *Faith and Knowledge* (1802) describes the critique of teleological judgement as 'the most interesting point of the Kantian system',[13] and in the essay on ancient skepticism from the same year, he says that in the *CPJ* the mere 'philosophy of understanding' has been elevated above itself and displays the Idea of reason: 'The effective presence of this Idea is already visible in the outward scaffolding of its parts [of Kant's philosophy]; but it also emerges more explicitly at the culminating points of its syntheses, especially in the *Critique of Judgement*.'[14] In §55 of the *Encyclopaedia Logic* (1817) Hegel again singles out the Third *Critique* as approximating more closely than anywhere else in Kant to the Idea, indeed as the *only* place in which 'the Kantian philosophy rises to the speculative height':

> The outstanding merit of the *Critique of Judgement* is that Kant has expressed in it the notion and even the thought *of the Idea*. The notion of an *intuitive understanding*, of *inner* purposiveness, etc., is the *universal* concurrently thought of as *concrete* in itself. It is only in these notions that Kant's philosophy shows itself to be speculative.[15]

In the late *Lectures on the History of Philosophy* Hegel again attributes its 'special importance' to the fact that it responds to a philosophical demand that Kant had failed to recognize in his previous works.[16]

[12] F. W. J. Schelling, *On the History of Modern Philosophy* (1833–34/1836–37), ed. and trans. A. Bowie (Cambridge: Cambridge University Press, 1994), 173.
[13] G. W. F. Hegel, *Faith and Knowledge* (1802), trans. W. Cerf and H. S. Harris (Albany, NY: SUNY Press, 1977), 79.
[14] G. W. F. Hegel, 'On the Relationship of Skepticism to Philosophy' (1802), in G. di Giovanni and H. S. Harris (eds), *Between Kant and Hegel: Texts in the Development of Post-Kantian Idealism* (Indianapolis: Hackett, 2000), 352.
[15] G. W. F. Hegel, *The Encyclopaedia Logic* (1817), trans. T. F. Geraets, W. A. Suchting and H. S. Harris (Indianapolis: Hackett, 1991). §55(c), 102.
[16] G. W. F. Hegel, *Lectures on the History of Philosophy, Vol. 3: Medieval and Modern Philosophy*, trans. E. S. Haldane and F. H. Simson (Lincoln: University of Nebraska Press, 1995), 464: 'There is still left for

Sebastian Gardner

It is worth noting, in connection with what I have said about the way in which the moral dependence of the Third *Critique* makes it alien to our concerns, that although the German Idealists did *not* accept Kant's accounts of moral knowledge, moral psychology, or human freedom, they were in no doubt (first) that Freedom represents the correct 'master concept' for general axiological purposes and (second) that the comprehensive task of philosophy must be defined at the *outset* in terms of the opposition of Freedom to Nature. (How that opposition is to be viewed at the end of the day – whether as a necessary starting point which has been overcome, or as sustained on some all-comprehending condition that explains its metaphysical necessity – is a separate matter.)

Now there are two questions concerning the German Idealists' reception of the Third *Critique* that I want to discuss. I said they took the *CPJ* to set an agenda, and as the quotations make very clear, not as saying the last word. So the question is: What in their eyes is wrong with or missing from the *CPJ*, such that it points up the need for further philosophical work? The second question follows on: If further work is needed, can it be done on the basis of anything contained within the *CPJ* itself?

We can begin to answer the first question by looking at the two major works in the post-Kantian period that constitute extended responses to the Third *Critique*, Schiller's *Letters on Aesthetic Education* (1794–95) and Herder's *Kalligone* (1800). Schiller is pro-Kant, with reservations, and Herder virulently anti-Kantian. But they agree on one thing: that human personality stands in need of a wholeness which is not on the cards if Freedom and Nature can only be unified only in the way and to the degree that the *Critique of the Power of Judgement* allows. Schiller argues accordingly that the aesthetic has the power to *fuse* Freedom and the Nature within us. His strategy is to use the intermediate position accorded by Kant to aesthetic judgement to, so to speak, 'get behind the back' of our theoretical and practical powers, in order to *remould* them: where Kant thinks of the aesthetic only as *bridging* theoretical and practical reason, a supervening late-comer that can react back on our theoretical and practical powers only in very limited ways, Schiller thinks of it as a superior standpoint with the power to

---

us to consider the third side in Kant's philosophy, the Critique of the Faculty of Judgment, in which the demand for the concrete comes in, the demand that the Idea of unity spoken of before should be established not as a Beyond, but as present; and this side is of special importance.'

condition them at their foundation.[17] Herder's argument is that the gross inadequacies of Kant's aesthetics – its incongruity with the manifest character of the experience of beauty – are just what is to be expected from an intellectualist philosophy that splits reason from sense at root.[18] For Herder, Kantianism is a lost cause – it cannot be enriched and repaired in the way Schiller proposes, and we must take a quite different approach; we must retrieve a rich, unitary concept of Nature which will avoid Kant's dualistic dead-end. Such an appreciation of Nature is exactly what Kant's merely subjective aesthetic of mental play stands in the way of, and Herder proceeds to give a painstaking account of how Kant has falsified aesthetic reality for the sake of scholastic philosophical abstractions.[19]

Herder's *Kalligone* plays no direct role in the development of German Idealism, but the axiological sensibility to which it gives expression is entirely characteristic of the age, and Schiller may be viewed as laying down a first, incomplete rough version of the German Idealist programme and as having projected the main lines of development that would carry post-Kantianism beyond Fichte's relatively conservative early reconstruction of the Critical philosophy.

The Third *Critique* was intended, among other things, as a criticism of the hyperbolic life-expectations of *Sturm und Drang*, as a vindication of the constraints of reason and a call for self-discipline.[20] In the eyes of many of its contemporary readers, however, Kant's acknowledgement of the existence of a rift between Freedom and Nature merely highlighted a desideratum which the work could not itself satisfy, and the truly important question which it raised was whether Kant's admission of incompleteness, and his failure to repair it, amounted to the Critical system's self-condemnation or whether, as Schiller believed, the trajectory that Kant had begun to follow in the *CPJ* could be extended to a full solution.

---

[17] See in particular Letters XVIII–XXII: *On the Aesthetic Education of Man: In a Series of Letters* (1793–95), trans. E. Wilkinson and L. Willoughby (Oxford: Clarendon, 1982), 122–159.

[18] See Herder's assault on the core claims of Kant's Analytic of the Beautiful in Part I, Ch. 5, of *Kalligone* (in *Werke*, ed. G. Arnold *et al*, Vol. 8 of *Schriften zu Literatur und Philosophie 1792–1800*, ed. Hans Dietrich Irmscher (Frankfurt am Main: Deutscher Klassiker Verlag, 1998), 725–746).

[19] Herder's positive antagonism towards the *CPJ* reflects the thoroughly metaphysical character of his naturalism, and contrasts with the indifference to its concerns warranted by a purely scientific naturalism.

[20] See John Zammito, *The Genesis of Kant's* Critique of Judgment (Chicago: University of Chicago Press, 1992).

Closely associated with this demand for theoretical and axiological wholeness in the human being was the complaint that Kant fails in the *CPJ* to satisfy his *own* formal conditions for philosophical finality. In Fichte's late lectures we find a precise formulation of this objection:

> The way his decisive and only truly meaningful works, the three critiques, come before us, Kant has made three starts. In the *Critique of Pure Reason*, his absolute (x) is *sensible experience* [... In the *Critique of Practical Reason*] we get the second absolute, a moral world = z [... With the] introduction of the moral world as the one world in itself, the empirical world is lost, as revenge for the fact that the latter had initially excluded the moral world. And so the *Critique of the Power of Judgement* appears, and in its Introduction, the most important part of this very important book, we find the confession that the sensible and supersensible worlds must come together in a common but wholly unknown root, which would be the third absolute = y. I say *a third* absolute, separate from the other two and self-sufficient, despite the fact that it is supposed to be the connection of both other terms; and I do not thereby treat Kant unjustly. Because if this y is inscrutable [unerforschlich], then while it may indeed always contain the *connection*, I at least can neither comprehend it as such, nor collaterally conceive the two terms as originating from it [ich wenigstens kann es als solchen nicht durchdringen, und die beiden Nebenglieder, als aus ihm hervorgehend, nicht mittelbar begreifen]. If I am to grasp it, I must grasp it immediately as absolute, and I remain trapped forever, now as before, in the (for me and my understanding) three absolutes. Therefore, with this final decisive addition to his system, Kant did not in any way improve that which we owe to him, he only generously admitted and disclosed it himself.[21]

Fichte concludes: Kant first 'factically discovered the distinction between the sensible and supersensible worlds and then added to his absolute the additional inexplicable quality of linking the two worlds'.[22]

Now this passage is highly revealing of what is at issue in the argument between Kant and his successors, and it repays close attention.

---

[21]   J. G. Fichte, *The Science of Knowing: J. G. Fichte's 1804 Lectures on the Wissenschaftslehre*, trans. Wayne Wright (Albany, NY: SUNY Press, 2005), 31–32.
[22]   Ibid., 44.

Fichte assumes three things: that each of Kant's *Critiques* must be taken as presenting an 'absolute'; that whatever is posited as absolute must be 'grasped', indeed 'grasped immediately'; and that Kant's invocation of a third term, 'y', to connect Freedom and Nature, fails because *y*, as theorized by Kant, is not equipped to be their 'root' and provide their 'origin'.

The first two will be unhesitatingly rejected by Kant, who will retort that Critical philosophy is not in the business of grasping absolutes. The third however is not so easily dismissed. Even if Fichte is too quick to assert that 'y' needs to be grasped as an absolute, he is right that it needs to have some independent identity if it is to be effective in its connecting role, and that if this role is to be fulfilled *rationally* then its occupant must show the *intelligibility* of the connection; if it does not – if 'y' is inscrutable, if it cannot be comprehended in its role – then it means nothing to assert that it 'contains' the connection of *x* and *z*. Now Kant may reply that all of this work is indeed done in the *CPJ*, which provides an account of what judgement amounts to as a power of its own, with a principle of its own, and of how the world may be conceived as an interconnected domain of Freedom and Nature, namely as a system of purposes. Yet Fichte can still reasonably object that interposing *y*, even if it displays thematic continuity with *x* and *z*, fails to improve our situation: if our knowledge of *y* is *on a level* with our knowledge of *x* and *z* – if *y* is similarly un-self-grounding – then we have merely added complexity, for we now need to understand how all *three* hold themselves together. Fichte's point is therefore that postulating *y* would bring a gain only if it stood *behind* Freedom and Nature, grounding them at a *deeper* level – which is certainly not what Kant is either prepared or able to claim regarding judgement, taste, and teleological judgement of nature. For even if the concept of purposiveness is shown in the *CPJ* to stand in some sense at the summit of our cognition,[23] the way that it comes to be established in that position – namely as an afterthought, once the theories of theoretical and practical cognition have been completed – means that it lacks both (i) the epistemic primitiveness and self-sufficiency, and (ii) the capacity to generate the terms subordinate to it, required for the Kantian 'system' to count as anything more than a patchwork. Kant may have shown that *y* is *continuous* with *x* and *z* but not that it is their 'root' and 'origin'.

---

[23]   The 'highest formal unity that alone rests on concepts of reason is the *purposive* unity of things' (*CPR*, A686/B714).

Sebastian Gardner

In the background to Fichte's complaint is the notorious 'single first principle' issue that dominated discussion of Kant's epistemology in the first phase of its reception, centred on the contention that the Kantian system's lack of such a principle rendered it vulnerable to skeptical attack and incapable of meeting the skeptical challenge to human knowledge in general. The two debates are not straightforwardly the same, because in the present context we are not concerned with finding a principle that will resist skeptical doubt, but nor are they dissociated.[24] And in both contexts Kant appears to have contributed to the difficulty in which he finds himself by virtue of a claim that he makes in the first *Critique* concerning the meaning of systematicity:

> If we survey the cognitions of our understanding in their entire range, then we find that what reason quite uniquely prescribes and seeks to bring concerning it is the *systematic* in cognition, i.e., its interconnection based on one principle [Zusammenhang aus einem Princip]. This unity of reason always presupposes an idea, namely of the form of a whole of cognition, which precedes the determinate cognition of the parts and contains the conditions for determining *a priori* the place of each part and its relation to the others. Accordingly, this idea postulates complete unity of the understanding's cognition, through which this cognition comes to be not merely a contingent aggregate but a system interconnected in accordance with necessary laws. One cannot properly say that this idea is the concept of an object, but only that of the thoroughgoing unity of these concepts, insofar as the idea serves the understanding as a rule.[25]

If Kant is held to this statement, then the expectation of finding in the *CPJ* a grounding, superordinate principle may seem reasonable, and Fichte's disappointment with Kant justified. And yet, if this is so, then it is puzzling that Kant failed to see the problem. It is true that he spells out in the Introduction a principle, the *a priori* principle of judgement concerning nature's purposiveness,[26] which might in a thin and somewhat forced sense be said to overarch Freedom and

---

[24]   That Fichte does not, in the passage quoted, invoke the threat of skepticism, does not mean that he regards the issues as properly separate. See Paul Franks' magisterial account in *All or Nothing: Systematicity, Transcendental Arguments, and Skepticism in German Idealism* (Cambridge, MA: Harvard University Press, 2005).

[25]   A645/B673.

[26]   *CPJ*, Introduction, Sect. IV, 5:180–181.

Nature, but it is not a source of 'necessary laws' for either, and this can hardly have escaped Kant's notice. This should lead us to ask if the Third *Critique* is perhaps aiming to satisfy the conception of systematicity laid down in the *Critique of Pure Reason* in some less direct, more oblique and qualified way.

As every reader discovers, the cumulative effect of the text of the *CPJ* is that of a kind of echo chamber, in which structures on one side of a distinction are found to reappear, in inverted form, on the other, setting up a complex system of internal correspondences. These correspondences are not inferential relations or relations of explanation, at any rate not in the first instance. At the same time, the text gives an impression of conceptual *movement*, of pieces drawing together and converging on unity, but because this final point is never achieved, the movement is never completed; and because what sets them in motion is not force of deduction but elective affinity, the movement has a spontaneous character, as if the various domains were arranging themselves of their own accord and yet at the same time in accordance with reason.[27] Here is an example, from Section VIII of the Introduction:

> In an object given in experience purposiveness can be represented either on a merely subjective ground, as a correspondence of its form in its *apprehension* (*apprehensio*) prior to any concept with the faculties of cognition, in order to unite the intuition with concepts for a cognition in general, or on an objective ground, as a correspondence of its form with the possibility of the thing itself, in accordance with a concept of it which precedes and contains the ground of this form. We have seen that the representation of the first sort of purposiveness rests on the immediate pleasure in the form of the object in mere reflection on it; thus the representation of the second kind of purposiveness, since it relates the form of the object not to the cognitive faculties of the subject in the apprehension of it but to a determinate cognition of the object under a given concept, has nothing to do with a feeling of pleasure in things but rather with the understanding in judging them.[28]

Here Kant is spelling out the kinship and differentiation of aesthetics and the teleology. Both involve representing an object as purposive,

---

[27] Explicitly dynamic images of systematicity are associated with, on the one hand, the task of infinite approximation of the German Romantics, and on the other, Hegel's Concept. My suggestion is that the image is also to be found implicit in Kant.

[28] *CPJ*, Introduction, Sect. VIII, 5:192.

Sebastian Gardner

the former on a *subjective*, the latter on an *objective* ground. The subjective ground is a *correspondence of the form* of the object with the faculties of cognition, established independently of any concept. The objective ground is a *correspondence of the form* of the object with the concept that provides its ground. The former involves form *as apprehended*, the latter form *as conceptualized*. So the former manifests itself sensibly in *feeling*, the latter intellectually in a judgement of the *understanding*; – though the terms of *that* distinction too are mutually implicating, since the feeling which is distinctive of aesthetic experience rests on an activity of judgement, and it is only because the mind has a 'feel for' purposive form, as taste shows, that nature can be taken up teleologically. Aesthetics and teleology are therefore each the inversion of the other. Taste *feels* the purposivity which teleology *thinks*. Teleology refers to the object's *own* possibility; taste indexes the possibility of its figuring as an object *for us*.

Numerous other passages of this sort, where architectonic pressures drive the argument, may be cited.[29] Kant has been derided for his obsession with architectonic, but it can hardly be doubted that he regards it as a serious matter. The reason for its prominence in the *CPJ*, which is greater than elsewhere, is that there Kant is elevating it from being merely the *means* by which one eventually arrives at a system – 'art' in the sense of *techne*, production of an object – to being what *constitutes* systematicity. This does not mean Kant has abandoned the conception of philosophical systematicity described in the *Critique of Pure Reason* and to which Fichte appeals in his criticism of the *CPJ*. For Kant the bare *idea* of a philosophical system is simple enough, and adequately expressed by the 'one principle' formula, but this is only because it is *indeterminate*, and it is only when it has been made determinate that we can be said to know what philosophical systematicity consists in; and because rendering it determinate is a matter of knowing how it is to be *realized*, architectonic is constitutive of systematicity.[30] *Within* the sub-systems which

---

[29]   For example, Kant's interweaving of purposiveness and aesthetic pleasure in Section VII of the Introduction, 5:188–192, or the argument in Section II of the First Introduction, 20:201–205, that, since judgement is a faculty of cognition located between understanding and reason, and these have their *a priori* principles, judgement too should be thought to have one.
[30]   The first paragraph of the original (First) Introduction to the *CPJ* explains that philosophy as 'the *system* of rational cognition through concepts' is to be approached *via* the critique of pure reason, which 'outlines and examines the very idea of it in the first place' – implying that it is for critique to determine to what extent, and in what form, the idea of a

form the *parts* of the system of philosophy, the foundations of empirical knowledge and the metaphysics of morals, the search for 'interconnection based on one principle' has a straightforward methodological significance, leading to the principles of apperception and autonomy, but in application to the system of philosophy *as a whole*, in the singular context of unifying Nature and Freedom, it must be understood as requiring something different, namely an exposition of the *inter-relatedness* of its sub-systems and the thematic unity of those unifying relations. This exposition of course involves, but it also goes beyond, logical connection in a strict deductive sense, and the extra-logical formal affinities and structural correspondences of sub-systems are philosophically probative, for the fact that the results of philosophical enquiry in different domains display common patterns, appearing as variations on a theme (namely purposiveness), assures us that we have got things right, and allows us to regard the system we construct as holding itself up from the inside.[31]

This might seem to imply that Kant is offering a quasi-aesthetic satisfaction, architectonic harmony, in place of philosophical understanding, running him implausibly close to the *Frühromantiker*. But in fact we can understand how the architectonic conception of systematicity serves strictly philosophical purposes, and even that Kant has an argument for why it is the *only* kind of philosophical systematicity available to the human intellect.

Going back to the original paragraph affirming the 'incalculable gulf' between Freedom and Nature, we should note that Kant confines the aim of the task of unification to *facilitating the transition* from the one to the other (thinking in accordance with the principles of the one to those of the other). This is something different from *cognizing their connection* and it shows immediately how far he is from sharing Fichte's view of the problem. Also notable is that Kant

---

philosophical system can be realized (*CPJ*, 20:195; see also *CPR*, A13/B27). In the *CPR* Kant asserts that for its execution (realization: *Ausführung*) the idea 'needs a *schema*' incorporating a manifold (A833/B861), and that architectonic must *begin* 'only at the point where the general root of our cognitive power divides' into the rational and empirical.

[31] See *CPJ*, §68, 5:381: 'Every science is of itself a system; and it is not enough that in it we build in accordance with principles and thus proceed technically; rather, in it, as a freestanding building, we must also work architectonically, and treat it not like an addition and as a part of another building, but as a whole by itself, although afterwards we can construct a transition from this building to the other or vice versa.'

talks in one breath of facilitating the transition, and of positing an *object* that would rationalize it, suggesting he regards the distinction that we ordinarily draw between *cognizing* an object, and being able to *do* something, as a vanishing distinction in the rarefied context at hand. Exactly the same is signalled in the passage from the first *Critique* where Kant said that the idea which 'postulates complete unity of the understanding's cognition' cannot properly be said to be 'the concept of an object' but rather 'serves the understanding as a rule'.

This notion – that at the outer limit of transcendental reflection ideas of the supersensible are equivalent to rules for transitions between domains of cognition or sub-systems of philosophy – is one that evidently appealed to certain philosophers in Kant's wake, such as Peirce, who were interested in a basal fusion of theory and practice and proposed that concepts in general be regarded as speci-fying procedures and modes of operation. That Kant himself is so far advanced in pragmatism as to recommend a reduction of this sort may be doubted, and if we look further into the *CPJ* we can understand how he manages to keep objective reference in play along-side his conception of ideas as having essentially regulative signifi-cance, and without admitting knowledge of the noumenal.

The other suggestion I made was that Kant can rationalize his con-ception of systematicity by referring to the distinctive character of the human intellect. In two remarkable sections of the Dialectic of Teleological Judgement, §§76–77,[32] Kant describes the differences between our *discursive* mode of cognition, and another, *non*-discur-sive mode of cognition which we cannot know to exist, but of which we can at least form a concept, and which he calls an *intuitive intellect*. In §77 he explains that the non-discursive cognition of this intuitive intellect would proceed *from the universal to the particular*:

> [W]e can also conceive of an understanding which, since it is not discursive like ours but is intuitive, goes from the *synthetically universal* (of the intuition of a whole as such) to the particular, i.e., from the whole to the parts.[33]

Human cognition is not like this: our *a priori* concepts do not contain knowledge of any particulars (they are not intuitions), and all of our determinate concepts of really existing things have to be built up out

---

[32]   Picked out by Hegel in the earlier quotation as approximating to 'the Idea'.

[33]   *CPJ*, §77, 5:407.

of sensible intuitions of particulars. God's knowledge may be top-down, but ours is bottom-up:

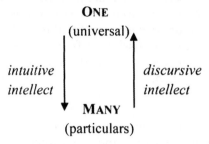

That is why we need *reflective* judgement: it provides the ladder allowing us to climb up from the Many to the One.[34]

When all of this is appreciated – when we see that our cognition travels logically in the opposite direction from that of an intuitive intellect – it becomes clear that the conception of final philosophical systematicity as knowledge of a whole *out of which* its parts can be determined, cannot in principle be satisfied. At the very point where we would achieve knowledge of this whole, our mode of cognition would cease to be discursive, and we as knowers would be extinguished. What we may think nevertheless is that this idea of a prior whole, though unrealizable by our cognition, has *regulative* value, in so far as it furnishes an imaginary focal point towards which we steer our cognition. And so long as we appreciate that its status is merely regulative, we avoid transcendental illusion. What may also be claimed, compensating for the lesson in humility, is that we can regard our discursive representation, as it gains in systematicity, as *tracking the reality* given to an intuitive intellect:[35] our progress towards an ever

---

[34]   And more specifically why we need teleological judgement. See the conclusion of §70, 5:388, which explains how teleological judgement makes up for our ignorance of a 'single principle'. Discussion of the single principle issue is resumed in §78: 'it follows that the unification of the two principles cannot rest on a ground for the *explanation* (explication) of the possibility of a product in accordance with given laws for the determining power of judgment, but only on a ground for the *elucidation* (exposition) of this for the reflecting power of judgment. – For to explain means to derive from a principle, which one must therefore cognize distinctly and be able to provide' (5:412).

[35]   This move involves a further element, not yet mentioned: Kant argues in *CPJ*, §76, 5:403–404, that what has the value of *Seyn-Sollen* for the human intellect, what *should* be the case, has being, *Seyn*, for the intuitive intellect. More detailed discussion of the themes in this section may be found in my 'German Idealism, Classical Pragmatism, and Kant's Third

more determinate, tightly coherent conceptualization of appearance is a continual approximation, within the idiom of human cognition, to the things in themselves which are present to God's creative intellect.[36] The cognitive maximum possible for human cognition according to Kant has therefore two aspects. On the one hand it presupposes what Kant calls, in his discussion of freedom in the *Groundwork*, a *comprehension of incomprehensibility*, the sphere of the incomprehensible being the domain of the intuitive intellect *as cognized* by the intuitive intellect. This absolute limitation is reflected in the necessity of our employing concepts that, the critique of reason shows, cannot be taken to determine any object and can serve only as formal rules. But at the same time, the projected totality of human cognition available in principle at the end of enquiry may be regarded as an *indirect* presentation of the intuitive intellect's whole of reality. The concept of such an oblique, analogical cognition is developed within the *CPJ*, under the heading of symbolic presentation, *symbolische Darstellung*, the type of relation which holds between the beautiful and the morally Good.[37] The conclusion to which discussion of Fichte's complaint leads is therefore that Kant does indeed fail to supply a single principle from which the parts of the system of philosophy might be derived, but that this seeming shortfall is rationalized by §§76–77, which also explains why the concept of purpose should emerge as the key to the unification of Freedom and Nature: it stands in for the 'synthetically universal' intuition of a whole available to the intuitive but not the human intellect. In a sense, then, though it is not one that Fichte will accept, the 'absolute' that he finds missing from the *CPJ* can after all be found in it: it is present in a *negative* form, as the account of human cognition given in §§76–77.

Kant's exposition of the idea of an intuitive intellect in §77 leads directly to the other question I raised, concerning the extent to which the Third *Critique* may provide resources for the more ambitious philosophical task which the German Idealists took it to set (and thereby promote its own surpassing).

Critique', in Gabriele Gava and Robert Stern (eds), *Pragmatism, Kant, and Transcendental Philosophy* (London: Routledge, 2016).

[36] The image needed here is complex but coherent: human cognition and the intuitive intellect comprise two heterogeneous non-intersecting dimensions, but as we move in a certain direction along the one that is ours, the content of our cognition, the order of objects that it represents, becomes increasingly isomorphic with that of the intuitive intellect.

[37] *CPJ*, §59, 351–352.

Fichte did not consider it to do so. Fichte returns to the themes of the first two *Critiques* – the self and moral consciousness – in order to close the gap between Freedom and Nature. But the crucial, decisive move to the more radical form of post-Kantianism, absolute idealism, taken by Schelling, *does* draw on the *CPJ*. One should hesitate before saying that Schelling's absolute idealism strictly *depends* on his critical appropriation of the *CPJ*, because there are so many forces at work in Schelling, but it is certainly one major element.

Schelling's claim is that Kant has in the *CPJ* all of the materials required to take the step to a stronger form of idealism, and that it is arbitrary to hold back. His argument is best seen by looking at a passage (from the First Introduction) which allows us to pinpoint where, as Schelling sees it, Kant's idealism properly passes over into his own idealistic Spinozism:[38]

> Now it is clear that the reflecting power of judgment, given its nature, could not undertake to *classify* the whole of nature according to its empirical differences if it did not presuppose that nature itself *specifies* its transcendental laws [die Natur *spezifiziere* selbst ihre transzendentale Gesetze] in accordance with some sort of principle. Now this principle can be none other than that of the suitability for the capacity of the power of judgment itself for finding in the immeasurable multiplicity of things in accordance with possible empirical laws sufficient kinship among them to enable them to be brought under empirical concepts (classes) and these in turn under more general laws (higher genera) and thus for an empirical system of nature to be reached [...] The special principle of the power of judgment is thus: *Nature specifies its general laws into empirical ones, in accordance with the form of a logical system, in behalf of the power of judgment* [Das eigentümliche Prinzip der Urteilskraft ist also: *die Natur spezifiziert ihre allgemeine Gesetze zu empirischen, gemäß der Form eines logischen Systems, zum Behuf der Urteilskraft.*].[39]

Here Kant is arguing – and this is yet another piece in his puzzle, not yet mentioned – that in order for us to be able to form empirical concepts at all, experience needs to exhibit the type of regularity that will allow us to formulate concepts of natural kinds and laws of nature.

---

[38]   To be clear, Schelling does not discuss this passage: I am extrapolating from what he does say about Kant's teleology in the Introduction to his *Ideas for a Philosophy of Nature* (1797, 2nd & revised edn. 1803), trans. Errol E. Harris and P. Heath (Cambridge: CUP, 1988), 30–42.

[39]   *CPJ*, First Introduction, Sect. V; 20:215–216.

Sebastian Gardner

This regularity cannot be proven, or its ground known; so all that can be done is to assume, as a *subjective* and merely *regulative* matter, that (as Kant puts it) nature 'specifies itself' in accordance with the principle that *it is to be possible for us to have knowledge of it*. In ignorance of what may *in fact* determine nature's self-specification, we project this principle 'up' the order of cognition, as it were demanding of the intuitive intellect that it produce objects in accordance with our cognition.

Schelling regards Kant's reasoning to the conclusion that nature must specify itself as sound, but his subjective construal of the conclusion as incoherent. If we must (as a matter of transcendental necessity) think of nature as self-specifying, rather than simply as subject to our legislation (as throughout the first *Critique*), then we cannot, having granted it this autonomy, take it away again by identifying its principle with a mere subjective necessity of *ours*. In attempting to save his Copernican principle that our mode of cognition must be ultimately determining of its objects, Kant takes back with one hand what he gives with the other: he cancels his own insight that by consistently following through the Copernican programme we are brought to a point where subjective idealism must yield to realism, or rather, to objective idealism. When this is recognized, what comes into view is Schelling's Spinozistic view of Nature:

> As long as we only know the totality of objects as the sum total of all being, this totality is a mere *world*, that is, a mere product for us [...] Insofar as we regard the totality of objects not merely as a product, but at the same time necessarily as productive, it becomes *Nature* for us, and this *identity of the product and the productivity*, and this alone, is implied by the idea of Nature, even in the ordinary use of language. Nature as a mere *product* (*natura naturata*) we call Nature as *object* (with this alone all empiricism deals). *Nature as productivity* (*natura naturans*) we call *Nature as subject* (with this alone all theory deals).[40]

The 'theory' referred to here is Schelling's *Naturphilosophie* or 'speculative physics', which views nature in its productivity as an organic whole, reducing the difference of organic and inorganic nature to a relative distinction within nature *qua* product.[41]

---

[40] Schelling, *Introduction to the Outline of a System of the Philosophy of Nature* (1799), §6, in *First Outline of a System of the Philosophy of Nature* (1799), trans. K. R. Peterson (Albany, NY: SUNY Press, 2004), 202.

[41] Ibid., 227, 232.

Now one might accept that the *CPJ creates space* for absolute ideal-ism, while also thinking that more reassurance is needed before it would make sense to embrace it. So is there any reason for thinking that this move is necessary? Here we can go back to Fichte's criticism and state his point in a slightly different way. Kant is committed, we have seen, to multiple worlds or sub-systems of rational cognition, the inter-relations of which are to be elucidated *from within* the stand-point of each, without stepping outside them. (So we try to work out, from *within* Nature and *within* Freedom, how the gulf between them might be bridged.) This part-to-whole model fits empirical knowl-edge and it is what Kant's conception of the human intellect implies. But even if Kant can show the sub-systems to be not only consistent with one another but also convergent in the way his archi-tectonic claims, what his multi-systemic model omits and cannot account for, arguably, is the antecedently given transcendental, meta-fact of our contemporaneous occupation of multiple worlds or sub-systems – the fact, which announces itself when we find it puz-zling that we are able to move from the one to the other, that at the very outset we can *take ourselves* to occupy multiple domains. If this problem is to have a solution, so it may be argued, then Kant's commitment to confining philosophical reason within the perspec-tives of each world or sub-system must be surrendered, and this means laying claim, as absolute idealism does, to the perspective of the whole.

Whether absolute idealism fulfills its promise to preserve Kant's differentiation of reason into its specific forms, while holding them in unity, is, of course, another story. What I have tried to do is just to give a glimpse into the perspective from which the Third *Critique* displays, as Schelling put it, a 'depth of meaning and insight which seems almost unfathomable'.

University College London
sebastian.gardner@ucl.ac.uk

Why Hegel Now (Again) – and in What Form?

ROBERT STERN

Abstract

This paper considers the prospects for the current revival of interest in Hegel, and the direction it might take. Looking back to Richard J. Bernstein's paper from 1977, on 'Why Hegel Now?', it contrasts his optimistic assessment of a rapprochement between Hegel and analytic philosophy with Sebastian Gardner's more pessimistic view, where Gardner argues that Hegel's idealist account of value makes any such rapprochement impossible. The paper explores Hegel's account of value further, arguing for a middle way between these extremes of optimism and pessimism, proposing an Aristotelian reading which is more metaphysical than Bernstein recognizes, but not as at odds with thinking in current analytic philosophy as Gardner suggests, as it finds a counterpart in the work of Philippa Foot, Michael Thompson, Rosalind Hursthouse and others.

1. Introduction

The aim of this paper is to consider the relation between Hegel and the recent history of analytic philosophy, and what we should think about the prospects for genuine convergence and co-operation between these two traditions. On the one hand, writing in the 1970s but continuing to hold the same today, Richard J. Bernstein has offered what might be called *the optimistic view*, which sees hope for ever greater rapprochement, as analytic philosophy itself takes an increasingly Hegelian turn. On the other hand, more recently Sebastian Gardner has argued strongly for the *pessimistic view*, that there are fundamental differences in approach between analytic philosophy and German Idealism generally, including Hegel, and that various attempts by prominent so-called 'analytic Hegelians' to connect the two are misconceived: what we are faced with, in fact, is an 'either/or'. His claim, in particular, is that while analytic philosophy is predominantly naturalistic, the sort of 'soft naturalism' that has been attributed to Hegel is a delusion both interpretatively and philosophically, and once this is seen through, the contrast between the two positions remains stark. My own suggestion (typically for an Hegelian, perhaps) is to try to steer between the two options of optimism and pessimism: that is, Gardner is right to

doi:10.1017/S1358246116000345 © The Royal Institute of Philosophy and the contributors 2016

warn against facile optimism here, but on the other hand, there is a way of taking Hegel's idealism which while it does not fit the position of 'soft naturalism' Gardner criticizes, is nonetheless close enough to naturalism to provide some bridge between Hegel and analytic philosophy, but not in the way that Bernstein identifies.

2. Optimism: Bernstein

In a well-known article from 1977, Richard J. Bernstein posed the question: 'Why Hegel Now?'. The article starts as follows:

> During the past decade there has been an explosion of interest in Hegel. One can barely keep up with the new editions, translations, commentaries, and articles that have been appearing throughout the world. The reasons for this burst of scholarly activity vary in different cultural milieus, but the question is especially perplexing in the context of Anglo-American philosophy. If there is one philosopher who had been thought to be dead and buried, who embodied all the vices of the wrong way of philosophizing, who seemed to have been killed off by abuse and ridicule, it was Hegel.[1]

A similar question might be posed today regarding Anglo-American philosophy, insofar as there has been a continuation in the 'explosion of interest', with even more editions, translation, commentaries and articles appearing since Bernstein wrote. And not only has the burst of scholarly energy grown, but so too has the attempt to *employ* Hegel in a constructive way within contemporary philosophical thinking, to treat Hegel as a valuable aid in moving philosophy forward.

In his article, Bernstein not only gives reasons for why the Hegel revival of the 70s happened, but also give reasons for why it was set to continue and grow – and thus he presents what might be called the optimistic view, that Hegelian thinking and Anglo-American 'analytic' philosophy are set for greater and greater rapprochement. It is enlightening to consider both aspects of his discussion.

In offering reasons for the 70s revival, he starts by quoting some comments by Walter Kaufmann,[2] who proposed the following as his reason for the revival in interest in Hegel in the 70s: 'Hegel is

---

[1]   Richard J. Bernstein, 'Why Hegel Now?', *The Review of Metaphysics* 31 (1977), 29.

[2]   Walter Kaufmann, 'Coming to Terms With Hegel', *Times Literary Supplement*, January 2nd 1976, 13.

immensely interesting'; 'he provides a striking alternative to all kinds of positivism and to the mainstream of Anglo-American philosophy'; there is student interest in his work; and '[t]he explosion of interest in Marx'. Bernstein objects to this, that 'this "explanation" doesn't really explain, or at best merely scratches the surface',[3] as it needs to be explained why people *find* Hegel 'immensely interesting' now, why people are seeking an alternative to positivism, why students are interested in him; and while there may be some connection between Marx and Hegel, a concern with Marx was not part of the mainstream current of Anglo-American philosophy, so this cannot explain the preoccupation with Hegel there either.

Bernstein argues instead that a proper explanation needs to focus on what really grounds any true revival, namely 'the realization that there is a basic affinity between the problems that are in the foreground of current philosophical discussion and those with which the relevant philosopher was struggling',[4] a realization that he then sets out to clarify. He starts by putting Hegel in a familiar trajectory from Hume to Kant, as the positivist revival of the former came to be replaced by the conceptual turn associated with the latter – but where he then quotes Wilfrid Sellars as remarking '...now that philosophy has gone "back to Kant" for the second time, can a Hegelian "trip" be far behind?'.[5] Tellingly, he illustrates this claim by reference to 'contemporary philosophy of science', which he insists 'is more than a subspeciality of philosophy', but is instead 'the locus of some of the most exciting and controversial epistemological and metaphysical disputes'[6] – where of course Bernstein is writing in the shadow of the upheaval in the field caused by Thomas Kuhn's *The Structure of Scientific Revolutions*, which was published in 1962. Taking philosophy of science as central, Bernstein lists the following themes which he thinks point in an Hegelian direction. First, various distinctions taken for granted by 'early logical positivists and empiricists' concerning the nature of science have been put into doubt, such as the distinctions between observation and theory, historical and philosophical issues, and science as knowledge and science as activity. Second, the criteria for scientific verification, falsification or confirmation cannot be abstracted from historical context. Third,

---

[3]   Bernstein, 'Why Hegel Now?', 35. Wilfrid Sellars, 'The Double-Knowledge Approach to the Mind-Body Problem' *New Scholasticism* 45 (1971), 270.
[4]   Bernstein, 'Why Hegel Now?', 38.
[5]   Op. cit.
[6]   Op. cit.

Robert Stern

scientific change involves anomalies and the clash of paradigms and theories. Fourth, traditional conceptions of rationality do not apply to science as a rational activity. And fifth, science takes place in a social context.

Bernstein therefore sees a close connection between developments in contemporary philosophy of science, and thus (because of the latter's disciplinary centrality) contemporary epistemology, and a transition from Kant to Hegel. For, while Kant had moved beyond empiricism in recognizing the theory-ladenness of observation, his account of the concepts with which we structure experience was static and ahistorical, while also seeming to leave us in a sceptical problem concerning our knowledge of 'things in themselves'. Hegel, by contrast, gives an account of the historical development of our thinking in terms of dialectical clashes between conceptual schemes, but also shows why the sceptical problem does not arise, as the thought of a world somehow outside or prior to such schemes is not intelligible; they are not merely 'alternative conceptual frameworks' giving us different views of a world independent of them, as there is no such world. In adopting such a view, Bernstein claims, there is a clear affinity between Richard Rorty and Hegel, referencing Rorty's article with the telling title 'The World Well Lost',[7] thus underlining the remarkable way that philosophy in the 70s and Hegel's own thinking had come to converge, in a way that explains the latter's current significance and revival within 'philosophy of science, and analytic epistemology'.[8]

Having mentioned these two fields of analytic philosophy, Bernstein then adds a third, which is 'the theory of action', where he thinks contemporary philosophers have come to see that '[i]n attempting to account for what is distinctive about human action (or at least some types of human action), it is necessary to examine the ways in which actions themselves are constituted by rules, practices, and institutions', where this naturally again leads to Hegel, for '[f]ew philosophers have equaled Hegel in the passion with which he argued that the character and dynamics of human action must be understood within the context of intersubjective interactions'.[9]

Overall, then, Bernstein both explains the reasons why the 70s revival in interest in Hegel had a solid intellectual basis in the direction taken by analytic philosophy at that time, and also why he thinks

[7] Op. cit. 41. Richard Rorty, 'The World Well Lost' *Journal of Philosophy* 69 (1972), 649–665.
[8] Bernstein, 'Why Hegel Now?, 42.
[9] Op. cit. 43.

it is set to continue. And in later writings,[10] he suggests that this early optimism was indeed born out, pointing in particular to those doughty so-called 'Pittsburgh Hegelians' John McDowell and Robert Brandom, where both have analytic credentials, and combine this with a serious interest in, and commitment to, Hegel. In this context, Bernstein does not mention philosophy of science as such a bridge (perhaps because the centrality to this discipline to philosophy has somewhat dropped away since the heyday of the 70s), but turns to pragmatism instead, with Sellars again as a key figure. In this context, then, the interpreters of Hegel who have in turn influenced McDowell and Brandom, such as Robert Pippin and Terry Pinkard, are seen as helping push Hegel scholarship in the right direction, and taking Hegel in a way that ensured such connections would flourish.

3. Pessimism: Gardner

In marked contrast to this kind of upbeat and positive story, however, Sebastian Gardner has recently[11] poured a good deal of cold water on this way of viewing the relation between Hegel and contemporary analytic philosophy, and has suggested that we should view them as radically different alternatives instead; to assimilate them, it is argued, does no favours to the intellectual strengths of either side, and just produces an unstable and bland compromise of positions that should really be kept apart. In this respect, then, Gardner's approach represents a striking contrast to Bernstein's, and offers a blast against the perhaps rather smug assimilationism of much recent Hegel scholarship, and its hopes of 'domesticating Hegel'.

At the centre of Gardner's view is his claim that the outlook of contemporary analytic philosophy is essentially *naturalistic*, whereas that of idealism in general, including Hegel's idealism, is not – where for

[10] See for example Richard J Bernstein, 'McDowell's Domesticated Hegelianism', in N. H. Smith (ed.), *Reading McDowell: On 'Mind and World'* (London: Routledge, 2002), 9–24, and *The Pragmatic Turn* (Cambridge: Polity Press, 2010), 95–105.
[11] See 'The Limits of Naturalism and the Metaphysics of German Idealism', in E. Hammer (ed.), *German Idealism: Contemporary Perspectives* (London and New York: Routledge, 2007), 19–49. For an equally pessimistic voice, on related grounds, see Frederick C. Beiser, 'Introduction: The Puzzling Hegel Renaissance', in F. C. Beiser (ed.), *The Cambridge Companion to Hegel and Nineteenth-Century Philosophy* (Cambridge: Cambridge University Press, 2008), 1–14.

him, the fundamental division comes over questions concerning *value*, and is thus a matter of axiology, which again he puts at the heart of the debate, and of the development of German Idealism itself.[12] Now of course, to say exactly what naturalism is, is notoriously hard to do in any uncontentious way, as are defining its precise parameters: is it a metaphysical, a methodological or a disciplinary claim – so does it concern what there is; how we go about investigating what there is; or how the natural sciences stand in connection to other disciplines? In setting up his argument, Gardner doesn't quite say, but instead takes his lead from a 1919 paper by the Kant translator and scholar Norman Kemp Smith, who defines naturalism as the view that 'man is a being whose capacities, even in their highest activities, are intelligible only as exercised *exclusively in subordination* to the specific requirements of his *terrestrial* environment' – where Kemp Smith then goes on to contrast this to idealism, with its 'supreme concern to show that the aesthetic and spiritual values have a more than merely human significance', so that man is measured 'against standards for which [his natural environment] cannot account'.[13]

[12] This focus on value is also central to Gardner's treatment of German Idealism in his paper 'From Kant to Post-Kantian Idealism I: German Idealism', *Proceedings of the Aristotelian Society*, supplementary volume, 76 (2002), 211–28. In this paper, Gardner argues that the theme of value also shows how German idealism and German romanticism can be seen to connect to one another in important ways, where he characterizes the latter position as follows: 'German romanticism... insists on regarding value as in some sense an object of experience, and our relation to this object as teleological, i.e. such that the subject who enjoys consciousness of this object necessarily finds itself endowed with purposiveness by virtue of this relation... Value conceived as manifested in this objectual mode allows itself to be conceived more readily in a straightforwardly realist manner than value conceived in a strictly practical mode, and this satisfaction of the natural realism of pre-philosophical consciousness, in conjunction with the teleological dimension, is plausibly a ground for regarding the romantic world-view as of enduring philosophical importance' (op. cit. 221–2).

[13] Norman Kemp Smith, 'The Present Situation in Philosophy' *The Philosophical Review* 29 (1920) 25; cited Gardner, 'The Limits of Naturalism', 21. Cf. also Kemp Smith, 'The Present Situation', page 6, where he characterizes naturalism as 'frankly revolutionary', in trying 'to trace moral distinctions to social conventions adopted for their beneficial consequences in forwarding the secular welfare of the individual and of society'; and page 18: 'Naturalism has to treat human values as merely relative'; and page 20: '[for naturalism] should we attempt to consider moral or spiritual values in abstraction from the complex contingencies in which alone they

As Gardner sets things up, therefore, the crucial issue concerns the nature of *value*, and whether values are absolute and unconditioned and hence independent of our particular human needs, interests and 'terrestrial' concerns, or whether they fundamentally rest on the latter.

Now, Gardner argues, viewed clear-headedly there is no way to bring these two views together, and indeed that seems right, if we put them in a standard Euthyphro format:

> Naturalism: What has value is fixed by what we as humans determine ourselves by, in the light of our prior interests and concerns
>
> Idealism: We determine ourselves by what has value, which things have prior to our interests and concerns.

However, Gardner thinks this contrast has been blurred by the rise of so-called 'soft naturalism', which wants to combine elements of both views, but ends up with an unstable and incoherent compromise, which cannot really fend off the challenge of hard naturalism. For, in trying to find a place for values within nature as conceived by the sciences, in the end it can only do so by introducing a 'perspectival' element into its account of those values, but which then makes them less than real from the standpoint of the hard naturalist; a move to fully non-naturalistic idealism is therefore required if the hard naturalist is to be properly countered:

> The reflexive move – the reference back to the reality of such-and-such to *our* concepts, *our* practices, taken on their own – thus misses the point: the hard naturalist will reasonably reply that it is not in doubt that our concepts and practices weigh with *us*, but that the whole issue concerns what it *means*, in the *overall* scheme of things, for something to be a practice of ours. What are *we*, the hard naturalist asks, such that the fact of a representational practice's being ours is supposed to raise its status, not merely in the trivial sense of its having status in *our* eyes, but in the sense of its ranking alongside the hard reality of natural science. The metaphysical significance of the soft naturalist's use of the first person plural has to be *shown*, not merely asserted.[14]

---

are know to is, they lose all definiteness and meaning. They are so many forms of adaptation, and are as specific as the environment that prescribes and defines them'

[14]   Gardner 'The Limits of Naturalism', 34.

Robert Stern

Now, once hard naturalism and idealism emerge as the only (and competing) options, and once it is accepted that analytic philosophy must gravitate to the former pole, Bernstein's more optimistic scenario looks too rosy, and to have been bought at the price of confusion. For, what made the convergence of analytic philosophy and idealism seem plausible, was the claim that the latter is less metaphysically rebarbative than it may once have seemed, where so-called 'metaphysical' readings have been replaced by the sort of socialized and historicized form of idealism that Bernstein so admires, often dubbed 'non-metaphysical'.[15] But, Gardner argues, if Idealism it to hold on to the axiological commitments that are so distinctive of it, and if it can only do so by standing up properly against hard naturalism, then it must go beyond any such non-metaphysical view, and must instead ground the values it champions in a clearly anti-naturalist commitment to something *beyond* the human perspective, namely the perspective of absolute spirit – at which point, the hope of any rapprochement with analytic philosophy has been well and truly lost.[16] Thus, pointing to texts in which Hegel appears to robustly set *Geist* prior to and outside nature, Gardner argues that this is no accident, but precisely what one would expect, given the realism about value that he and the other Idealists wanted to maintain, a realism that cannot be maintained by 'soft naturalism' and thus by 'non-metaphysical' readings of the idealist position.

[15]   Cf. also 'German Idealism', 212–3: 'There is also, among some of German idealism's defenders, a tendency to suppose that the best reconstruction of German idealism will be one that brings it into line with (and thereby shows it to be formative in the creation of) the post-metaphysical, broadly naturalistic climate which appears to be the legacy of both Anglophone and continental European philosophy of the last two centuries. This orientation is visible in some of the most striking recent work on Hegel'.

[16]   Cf. also 'German Idealism', 213: 'The thesis that German idealism is value-driven, as I wish to understand it, comes into conflict with this post-metaphysical tendency, for reasons that will emerge'. Cf. also 228: 'Third, it should be emphasised that the axiological reading entails a metaphysical, ontologically committed interpretation of German idealism: if German idealist metaphysics seeks to accommodate the axiological demand articulated in German romanticism, then a non-metaphysical, ontologically deflationary construal of German idealism, even if it were to make complete sense of the internal machinery of the German idealist systems, omits their prime mover and final end'. In this paper, Gardner uses Fichte's conception of positing as an example of the kind of 'inflationary' view that he thinks is required.

Why Hegel Now (Again) – and in What Form?

Now, in citing Norman Kemp Smith, Gardner is right to see him as speaking for a kind of orthodoxy within the British idealist tradition of which Kemp Smith was a part.[17] And certainly many other members of this group would have shared Kemp Smith's view of idealism and its relation to the question of value. To take just one further example, from James Seth:

> That metaphysics [of ethics] may be either naturalistic or idealistic. On the one hand, the law of human life may be reduced to terms of natural law, the moral ideal may be resolved into the reality of nature. Or, on the other hand, the ultimate measure of human conduct and character may be found in a spiritual order which transcends the natural; the moral ideal may be found to express a divine Reality to which the real world of nature would, in itself, give no clue... Thus an adequate interpretation of morality compels us to predicate an ultimate and absolute moral Reality, a supreme Ground of goodness as well as of truth; and the moral idealism which we have maintained against empirical realism in ethics brings us in the end to a moral realism, to a conviction of the reality of the moral ideal.[18]

And a view of this sort also finds defenders among more contemporary authors who take similar views in arguing against naturalism and in favour of theism, based on the objectivity of value. For example, John Cottingham has written recently:

> What does it mean, however, to say that God is the source of goodness? To begin with, it evidently implies a firm denial of relativism. If goodness derives from an objective being that exists independently of us, then this rules out pragmatic and relativistic conceptions according to which the good is simply what works for us, or what is currently approved in our culture circle; nor can the good be something we can create or invent

[17] Cf. 'The Present Situation of Philosophy', where Kemp Smith remarks that he is 'speaking as a convinced idealist' (p. 6).

[18] James Seth, *A Study of Ethical Principles* (New York: Charles Scribner's, 1905), 359–60 and 425. For other examples, see: J. R. Illingworth, *Personality Human and Divine* (London: Macmillan 1902), 110–11; Hastings Rashall, *The Theory of Good and Evil* (Oxford: Oxford University Press, 1907), II, 212; A. S. Pringle-Pattison, *The Idea of God* (Oxford: Oxford University Press, 1916), 42; W. R. Sorley, *Moral Values and the Idea of God* (Cambridge: Cambridge University Press, 1918), 352–3; A. E. Taylor, *Does God Exist?* (London: Macmillan, 1945), 92–3.

by our own choices or acts of will, in the way Friedrich Nietzsche envisaged... But in addition to underwriting *objectivity* and *non-relativity*, the idea of a divine source of goodness also implies a certain kind of *authority*. This connects with the notion (by no means confined to theists) that beauty and goodness exert some kind of normative pull on us. Beauty is *to be admired*, goodness is *to be pursued*. These values in a certain sense constrain us, whether we like it or not.[19]

Thus, if we also put Hegel in this tradition as Gardner suggests we should, with its clear anti-naturalism, Gardner's pessimism would seem to be fully justified: The reconciliationist agenda so hoped for by Bernstein, and championed by McDowell, Brandom, Pippin, Pinkard and many others must therefore be abandoned, and all such hopes dashed upon the rocks.

4. Qualified optimism?

While recognizing that there is considerable force to Gardner's concerns, I now want to put forward the case for a more optimistic position – but based on different grounds from those offered by Bernstein, and which Gardner's critique undermines. The position I will put forward is a kind of metaphysical view, but not so radically anti-naturalist as the conception of spirit or Geist that Gardner takes to be central to the axiology of idealism; but nonetheless I hope this view still allows for a defense of the absoluteness of value which he claims to be central to the idealistic outlook.

We can start by following Gardner and accepting his focus on the issue of value as being fundamental. As we have seen, Gardner then objects to the approach of soft naturalist and non-metaphysical readers of Hegel, like Terry Pinkard, who take Geist conceived of in a 'deflationary' sense as bringing normativity into the world; but this then is said to be vulnerable to the challenge that the kind of value and normativity in question is too perspectival – and hence a stronger and more metaphysical notion of Geist is needed, which will break any possible link with naturalism. Gardner thus quotes Pinkard as treating Geist as 'us' *qua* historically located human beings,[20] and then challenges this approach as giving the values

[19] John Cottingham, *Philosophy of Religion: Towards a More Humane Approach* (Cambridge University Press, 2014), 73.
[20] Gardner, 'The Limits of Naturalism', 37, referring to Terry Pinkard, 'Speculative *Naturphilosophie* and the Development of the Empirical

that 'we' may then institute a treatment that is altogether insufficient-
ly absolute and objective, and thus leaves the position vulnerable to
hard naturalism:

> The hard naturalist will claim, once again, than no reason has
> been given for thinking that there is not a naturalistic explanation
> to be given for the emergence of normativity from nature, in the
> light of which it can be seen that *what* emerges is not *Geist*/nor-
> mativity as Hegelians conceive it – something with *real* auton-
> omy – but simply our *representing ourselves* in *geistig*, normative
> terms. The sophisticated naturalist may grant, furthermore,
> than an *appearance* of autonomy and absoluteness is built into
> the perspective of *Geist*/normativity, and then claim that it is
> this which leads to the (illusory) view that *Geist*/normativity is
> independent from nature in the strong, 'absolute' sense affirmed
> by Hegelians... [21]

Gardner argues, as we have seen, that for Hegel himself this problem
does not arise, as on his metaphysical conception of Geist as outside
and prior to nature, and as therefore absolute in itself, the kind of
value and normativity it institutes suffers from no such relativity –
but of course this requires a metaphysical and non-naturalistic
reading of Hegel's position that sets him at odds with the analytic
mainstream.

However, one assumption that both Gardner and his opponents
seem to share, is that on the Hegelian picture, value and normativity
are instituted by Geist on a natural world that is intrinsically non-
normative – where Geist is either understood in a deflationary
sense as 'us', or in an inflationary sense as 'absolute spirit'. Then
the issue is whether the former view can keep the axiological commitments of German Idealism in a sufficiently strong sense, or whether
this requires moving to the latter. But I would like to now question
this shared assumption: for I think it is possible to see value for
Hegel arising in a different, more Aristotelian, way, as relating to
claims about the natures of things, and how well or badly they
realize those natures.

To outline the view: on this sort of account, evaluative claims are
based on comparisons between objects as they actually are and the
kinds or types of objects they belong to, where the latter brings

---

Sciences: Hegel's Perspective', in G. Gutting (ed.), *Continental Philosophy
of Science* (Oxford: Blackwell), 23 and 30.
[21] Gardner, 'The Limits of Naturalism', 37–38.

with it normative implications. Given realism about such kinds, a view of this sort can then also claim to be realist about the normative judgements based on them, in a way that escapes Gardner's worries about value being tied to the human perspective, as needing to be imposed on a natural world that is alien to normativity. This also then counts as a metaphysical view, given the ontological commitments it involves. At the same time, however, it is a metaphysical view that perhaps at least has some chance of being made compatible with naturalism in some form – or at least, so contemporary proponents of this sort of approach (such as Philippa Foot and Michael Thompson) might lead one to expect. At any rate, there seems to be more room for hope here than with the appeal to Geist that is required on Gardner's view – where this may then make something like Bernstein's optimism regarding the rapprochement with analytic philosophy more plausible, though on grounds that are still very different from the ones he offers.[22]

So, it may turn out, both sides in this debate are partly right, but also partly wrong, so that each must make some concessions to the other: Gardner can keep a metaphysical reading of Hegel, but must move to a metaphysical reading that can build bridges with naturalism and hence analytic philosophy; Bernstein and his fellow 'deflationary' readers of Hegel must give up their non-metaphysical approach, but can retain their sense of optimism; and both sides are wrong regarding the view of value that Hegel wants to defend.

Let me say a little more regarding that view of value, as I understand it, where I think it can be seen most clearly in the third book of Hegel's *Logic*, and in his treatment of the Concept (Begriff), Judgement, and Syllogism. Here, Hegel essentially offers a hierarchy of forms of judgement and syllogism, based on how they see the relation between the conceptual 'moments' of universal, particular and individual. At the simplest and most basic level, judgements and syllogisms involve claims about individuals and their simple properties, such as 'This rose is red', or 'This rose is red; red is a colour; therefore this rose is coloured'. However, for reasons we cannot go into fully here, Hegel holds that it is not possible to rest at merely this level of judgement and syllogism, where it is necessary to bring in more sophisticated forms of thought, which involve more complex

[22]   Cf. Michael Thompson, *Life and Action: Elementary Structures of Practice and Practical Thought* (Cambridge, Mass.: Harvard University Press, 2008), 12: 'The project of an "analytic" or "analytical" Hegelianism or of an "analytical Marxism" (however well- or ill-advised such a thing might be) must see itself as aiming at a form of analytic Aristotelianism...'

conceptual structures. In particular, it is necessary to move to thinking of some individual objects as instantiating natural kinds which
characterize their essential natures, and where this introduces a significant evaluative element. For, to understand a concept as representing a natural kind is to understand individuals falling under
that kind in terms of certain characteristics, but where failing to
possess those characteristics is then a fault in the individual qua
member of the kind. So, for example, a rose that dies prematurely,
or which fails to attract sufficient bees to be pollinated, or is odourless
but belongs to a species with a scent, is a 'bad' rose – but where these
norms are not based on mere statistical generalizations, but reflect
claims about what it is for a rose of this species to be a proper exemplar
of the kind of thing it is. Thus, taking this approach, it can be argued
that for Hegel, value enters in as a consequence of his conception of
the relation between individuals and their fundamental natures,
where the question of their goodness or badness, and even of their
'truth' and 'finitude', for him seems to rest on this relation.

Here are two key passages to this effect, from different treatments
of the *Logic*:

> Here we have the *apodeictic* judgment (e.g., "*This* – the immedi-
> ate singularity – *house* – the genus – *being constituted thus and so* –
> particularity – is good or bad"). – *All things* are a *genus* (which is
> their determination and purpose) in a *single* actuality with a *par-
> ticular* constitution; and their finitude consists in the fact that
> what is their particular [way of being] may (or again may not)
> conform to the universal.[23]

> The subject of the apodeictic judgement (the house consti-
> tuted so and so is *good*, the action constituted so and so is *right*)
> has within it, first, the universal, what it *ought to be*, and secondly,
> its *constitution*; this latter contains the *ground* why a predicate of
> the Concept judgement applies or does not apply to the *whole
> subject*, that is, whether the subject corresponds to its concept
> or not. This judgement, then, is *truly* objective; or it is the
> *truth of the judgement* in general.[24]

[23] G. W. F. Hegel, *The Encyclopaedia Logic*, translated by T. F.
Geraets, W A Suchting and H S Harris (Indianapolis: Hackett, 1991),
§179, p. 256.
[24] G. W. F. Hegel, *The Science of Logic*, translated by A. V. Miller
(London: George Allen & Unwin, 1969), 661–2 (translation modified).

As far as I know, these are the only passages in the main part of the *Logic*, Hegel's key text, in which issues of value of this kind are addressed and explained.[25]

Now, passages such as these may then be set alongside the views of contemporary neo-Aristotelian naturalists, such as Foot, Thompson, and Rosalind Hursthouse, where the similarities should be clear. Thus, for example, Foot states that her key conception of 'natural goodness' is 'intrinsic or "autonomous" goodness in that it depends directly on the relation of an individual to the "life form" of its species',[26] thereby relating the individual to its kind in an Hegelian manner; and she also emphasizes how this gives normative claims an objectivity that they would otherwise be lacking:

> Thus, evaluation of an individual living thing in its own right, with no reference to our interests or desires, is possible where there is intersection of two types of propositions: on the one hand, Aristotelian categorials (life-form descriptions relating to the species), and on the other, propositions about particular individuals that are the subject of evaluations.[27]

A closely related view is taken by Thompson, who was a key influence on Foot in adopting her own:

> If, though, we want to apply 'normative' categories to sub-rational nature, and apart from any relation to 'our interests', then the question inevitably arises, and not so unreasonably: Where does the standard come from? What supplies the measure? The system of natural-historical propositions with a given kind or form as subject supplies such a standard for members of that kind. We may implicitly define a certain very abstract category of 'natural defect' with the following simple-minded principle of inference: *from*: 'The S is F,' *and*: 'This S is not F,' *to infer*: 'This S is defective in that it is not F'. It is in *this* sense that natural-historical judgments are 'normative', and not by each proposition's bearing some sort of secret normative infrastructure. The first application of concepts of good, bad, defect and

---

[25]   Cf. *Encyclopaedia Logic* §21, 52, for a related passage from the introductory material: 'When thinking is taken as active with regard to objects as the thinking over [Nachdenken] of something – then the universal, as the product of this activity – contains the value of the matter [Wert der Sache], what is essential [das Wesentliche], inner, true'.

[26]   Philippa Foot, *Natural Goodness* (Oxford: Oxford University Press, 2001), 27.

[27]   Foot, *Natural Goodness*, 33.

pathology is to the individual, and it consists in a certain sort of reference of the thing to its form or kind and the natural history that pertains to it.[28]

Finally, Hursthouse has adopted a similar approach, also emphasizing the objectivity of this way of accounting for value:

> First, the truth of such evaluations of living things does not depend in any way on my wants, interests, or values, nor indeed on 'ours'. They are, in the most straightforward sense of the term, 'objective'; indeed, given that botany, zoology, ethnology, etc. are scientific, they are scientific.[29]

Claims of this sort seem to echo Hegel's own account of value, and give us a way of understanding it that is neither Gardner's resolute anti-naturalism on the one hand, nor that of the 'soft naturalism' that he criticizes on the other.

Let me now try to say something about what I take to be distinctive of this sort of view, and also some potential problems with it, both in itself and as a reading of Hegel.

The following can be identified as key features of the view, as I would understand it. First, it counts as a broadly metaphysical reading, which gives us a realist account of value. It is metaphysical in that it relies on thinking of individuals as instances as kinds, and thus as having essential properties, where there is no suggestion that these kinds are 'constructions' of ours, which is why the claims about value they underpin ('this is a good horse and that is a bad one') are realist. Second, while this view may constitute a challenge to naturalism in some reductive and anti-metaphysical forms, and so it is dialectically more stable than the 'soft naturalism' which Gardner rejects, it is also not as wholly opposed to it as the conception of idealism that Gardner proposes. Third, this is a form of eudaimonism, as there is meant to be a conceptual link between being a proper exemplar of the kind and doing well or flourishing as an individual, such that if we were to treat X as a member of a kind but find that doing so in accordance with norms of that kind leads X not to flourish, then we would have to change our account of the kind to which X belongs: so if I treat this plant as a house plant, but it wilts and dies, then I have clearly got my classification wrong, and so should try treating it as another kind of thing instead – perhaps as a hardy

---

28 Thompson, *Life and Action*, 80–1.
29 Rosalind Hursthouse, *On Virtue Ethics* (Oxford: Oxford University Press, 1999), 202.

Robert Stern

perennial. Fourth, Hegel's position brings out the links between individuals, kinds, and value in a transcendental way: that is, to have the concept of an individual, one must see the individual as exemplifying a kind; to see it as exemplifying a kind is to see as doing so well or badly, and thus to see it in normative terms; so one cannot understand an individual without bringing in axiological considerations, which makes them fundamental to the understanding of the world, including nature itself. Fifth, it is less 'historicized' than someone like Bernstein would expect for a reading of Hegel: as I understand Hegel's position, the claims he wants to make about our essential nature and its link to our well-being do not concern a historical construct that might vary over time, although of course our understanding of it can.

However, of course, views of this broadly Aristotelian sort have been subjected to many sorts of criticism, and I do not have the time to consider them all here. But I want to consider those criticisms that relate most closely (it seems to me) to the naturalism/idealism debate that concerns Kemp Smith and Gardner, to see if it can be argued that in the end, naturalism even of this Aristotelian sort is as unstable as 'soft naturalism' and must either collapse into idealism or hard naturalism; where it then could be argued that as Hegel would have rejected the latter, we should think that it is plausible he would have adopted the former, thus re-instituting the divide that Gardner insists upon between Hegelian idealism and naturalistic analytic philosophy.

The criticisms of Aristotelian naturalism that I have in mind are as follows:

(1)   Aristotelian naturalism is implausibly biologistic, but to make it less so is to move from naturalism to idealism.
(2)   Aristotelian naturalism's conception of nature is incompatible with the modern conception of nature, particularly in this naturalism's commitment to teleological notions, and to save those notions it must move from naturalism to idealism.
(3)   Aristotelian naturalism will involve a degree of relativism when it comes to our moral practices, which is incompatible with the absoluteness of moral value and norms that then requires idealism for its defense.

The thought here is that each of these criticisms shows that Kemp Smith and Gardner can argue that Aristotelian naturalism needs to give way to idealism, and that Hegel and the other idealists saw this, and hence should no more be interpreted as Aristotelian naturalists than they should be interpreted as 'soft naturalists'.

Let me consider each point in turn:

The first objection is that Aristotelian naturalism is committed to an implausibly biologistic view of us as agents, as if as 'life forms' we could be understood in terms of purely biological imperatives such as reproduction, and the norms that arise from that.[30] More radically, it can be argued that even if Aristotelian naturalism worked for animals, we are a special case, as human beings can always transcend their biology and indeed any essentialist claims altogether: our existence precedes our essence, as Sartre said.[31] So, it could be argued, we cannot use this account when thinking about how value applies to us; rather, we create value through our own processes of self-creation, as the soft naturalist argues – or if we don't, value rests on spirit or Geist as something outside nature, as the idealist claims.

However, while it is true that Hegel moves beyond a purely biological conception of human flourishing,[32] it may still be that he is committed to Aristotelian naturalism more broadly conceived:[33] For Hegel arguably moves from thinking of us as *human*

[30]   Foot herself put this worry as follows: 'The questions remains, however, as to whether once we have made the transition from sub-rational to rational beings we may not need a new theory of evaluation. Surely, my critics will say, it must be so.... For such an evaluation [of sub-rational beings] is based on the general relation of this kind of feature to the pattern of life that is the *good of* creatures of this species. But how can we possibly see human good in the same terms? The life cycle of a plant or animal ultimately has to do with what is involved in development, self-sustenance, and reproduction. Are we really going to suggest that human strengths and weaknesses, and even virtues and vices, are to be identified by reference to such "biological" cycles?' (Foot, *Natural Goodness*, 41)
[31]   Cf. Foot, *Natural Goodness*, 37: 'There will surely be objection to the idea that a natural form of life characteristic of humankind could determine what you or I *ought* to do. What does it matter to me *what species* I belong to? Should we not protest on behalf of individuality and creativity against bringing in the human species when asking what I myself – this particular person – should do?'
[32]   This has been argued by Sebastian Rand in his article 'What Is Wrong With Rex? Hegel on Animal Defect and Individuality', *European Journal of Philosophy*, forthcoming (available online doi: 10.1111/ejop.12029).
[33]   In her discussion, Hursthouse makes biology central to the naturalist view, and hence resists talk of 'persons' or 'rational beings', so to this extent her form of naturalism would be opposed to Hegel's: 'But "ethical naturalism" is usually thought of as not only basing ethics in some way on considerations of human nature, but also as taking human beings to be part of the natural, biological order of living things. Its standard first premise is that

beings in a biological sense to thinking of us as *persons* or *rational agents*, precisely because we are more than just merely biological beings. However, as I think *The Philosophy of Right* makes clear, it is still the case that the notion of a person or agent brings with it its own kind of normativity when it comes to assessments of our behaviour, capacities and actions: for, persons are then understood by Hegel in terms of a kind of freedom that he takes to be distinctive of the human will.[34] Thus, to put his position very briefly, Hegel sees the will as a balance of competing elements, of particularism on the one side (roughly, your distinctive interests and concerns) and universality on the other side (roughly, your ability to step back from those interests and concerns and put them in question), where we can oscillate from one side to the other, so that if we take each side in isolation, the other will come back to bite us: so, if I try to focus on just what is of interest to me, the universal side of my will leads me to feel I am wasting my time; on the other hand, if I try to act in a purely universal way, for the 'good in general', I will find it impossible to act, as action requires willing something in particular. I thus need to find forms of action that will successfully balance both sides – and this, Hegel thinks, can only happen in a well ordered state, where on the one hand my interests are given a place, but where on the other my actions also have some relation to the good of other individuals within the social whole. There is thus a conception of what it is for an individual to properly function as an agent, as the kinds of beings we are, even though that is not something that biology alone can tell us, as with other creatures. This also explains why I think Hegel would reject a radical kind of Sartrean anti-essentialism, even for us, though it is an essentialism that takes us beyond our purely biological natures.

A second worry concerns the extent to which Aristotelian naturalism is committed to forms of teleological understanding of nature that themselves only make sense given some kind of underlying theistic idealism. Thus, Foot and Thompson have been criticized by 'hard naturalists' for blithely accepting the kind of teleology than Aristotelian naturalism seems to require, without seeing how this is

---

what human beings *are* is a species of rational, social animals and thereby a species of living things – which unlike "persons" or "rational beings", have a particular biological make-up and a natural life cycle' (*On Virtue Ethics*, 206).

[34] Cf. G. W. F. Hegel, *Philosophy of Right*, §§5–7.

at odds with the post-Darwinian conception of nature.[35] Of course, the idealist might be able to re-inject this teleological framework into nature, but this leave Aristotelian naturalism on its own looking unstable.[36]

Now, at a purely interpretative level, this may not look like such a worry when it comes to Hegel; for of course Hegel was writing before Darwinian ideas had taken hold, so *he* might have been a kind of Aristotelian naturalist and not felt any pressure towards idealism, simply because he was innocent of this kind of concern. However, this response is arguably too simple, for even if pre-Darwin, Hegel was still post-Newton, and as the example of Kant reminds us, teleology was already a fraught issue; so in this context, some of Hegel's easy acceptance of Aristotelian naturalism might be attributed precisely to the idealistic framework that makes the Aristotelian framework retain some plausibility in the modern world.

However, as some recent commentators have argued,[37] while Hegel did seem to feel more comfortable with teleology than Kant, this is arguably for reasons to do with explanatory concerns over mechanism, and thus on a broadly naturalistic basis; so Hegel's position might be compared to the kind of contemporary biologist who, even post-Darwin, defends the meaningfulness of a teleological conception of nature, rather than an idealist who feels the need to go beyond naturalism altogether to defend the place of teleology in our understanding.

A third and final objection may be put in terms of a comment made by Kemp Smith when he observes that 'Naturalism can now profess to meet idealism on more equal terms within its [idealism's] own field, that of our specifically human activities', because it can 'trace more distinctions to social conventions adopted for their beneficial consequences in forwarding the secular welfare of the individual and of

---

[35] Cf. James Lenman, 'The Saucer of Mud, the Kudzu Vine, and the Uxorious Cheetah: Against Neo-Aristotelian Naturalism in Meta-Ethics', *European Journal of Analytic Philosophy*, 1 (2005), 47.

[36] As Foot herself puts the worry: 'Philosophers are sometimes afraid of recognizing teleological language, thinking it must be left over from a worldview in which all nature was seen as reflecting the will of the deity' (Foot, *Natural Goodness* 32).

[37] Cf. James Kreines, 'The Logic of Life: Hegel's Philosophical Defense of Teleological Explanation of Living Beings', in Frederick C Beiser (ed), *The Cambridge Companion to Hegel and Nineteenth-Century Philosophy* (Cambridge: Cambridge University Press, 2008), 344–378, and *Reason in the World: Hegel's Metaphysics and Its Philosophical Appeal* (Oxford: Oxford University Press, 2015).

society'.[38] Thus, for example, Foot speaks of promising as a 'tool invented by humans for the better conduct of their lives',[39] much as hunting in packs improves the lives of wolves, or 'waggle dancing' improves the lives of bees by informing each other about sources of nectar, and thus that in the light of these practices, beings who fail to abide by them are bad or defective. However, it is clear from Kemp Smith's article that he thinks this naturalistic account of various practices such as promise making cannot achieve what the idealist is after, as it still leaves the values concerned too 'terrestrial' and relativistic, as presumably different creatures could have different needs or ways of going on, such that promising for them on this account would no longer be a norm, and lying no longer wrong; and one suspects Gardner might have similar misgivings. Thus, for example, Kemp Smith writes: 'the supreme concern of idealism is to show that the aesthetic and spiritual values have a *more than merely human significance*';[40] and 'Naturalism has to treat human values as merely relative; idealism interprets them as disclosing a richer and more comprehensive Universe than can be identified in scientific terms'; thus 'though man can, indeed, be studied only in his natural setting, for an understanding of his nature and destiny idealism refers to that wider reality which is depicted in poetry and the arts, and worshipped in religion, and which, though not yet scientifically known, can be philosophically discerned as conferring upon human life its standards and values'.[41] So, Kemp Smith argues, on the one hand the naturalist treats 'the aesthetic, spiritual, and social criteria' as 'so inextricably bound up with the civilization of our planet, that upon them no judgments having wider jurisdiction can legitimately be based',[42] while on the other hand for the idealist 'the human spirit [can] rise above its natural conditions' so that it 'finds its salvation not in independence of its animal conditions but in using them as instruments for the expression of desires and meanings that genuinely transcend them'.[43] Thus, for Kemp Smith, according to the idealist in contradistinction to the naturalist, '[man's] true self-knowledge is made possible by value and standards that constitute his humanity in distinction from the animals; and it is by their absoluteness that they deliver him from the limitations of

---

[38] Kemp Smith, 'The Present Situation in Philosophy', 6.
[39] Foot, *Natural Goodness*, 51.
[40] Kemp Smith, 'The Present Situation in Philosophy', 15 (my emphasis).
[41] Op. cit. 18.
[42] Op. cit. 20.
[43] Op. cit. 23.

strictly animal existence'.[44] For Kemp Smith, then, Foot's conception of 'natural goodness' is a contradiction in terms, to the extent that we are talking about the genuine moral goodness of promising, justice, benevolence and so on, which (Kemp Smith argues) must be more than tools for living flourishing lives as a species; rather, in becoming aware of these practices as valuable, we precisely looking beyond our natures into a more absolute realm of normativity that only idealism can account for in a proper manner.

Now, where does Hegel stand on this debate? I would like to suggest, based on the conception of flourishing of the person briefly mentioned previously, than in fact his account of ethical life in the *Philosophy of Right* can be understood in naturalistic terms, as precisely setting out a form of life and its associated practices that are best designed to realize the human good, understood in terms of the free will.[45] Whereas the standpoint of morality tends to think there is something distinctive and special in the moral, once we get to ethical life we see that our moral norms are simply part of a system of practices of ordering our lives together in a way that is conducive to collective human flourishing or self-realization, much as Foot argues concerning promising and our systems of rights, for example. Thus, just as the 'lone wolf' is defective qua member of his species and thus bad as a result, so too is the individual who fails to play their part in ethical life:

> Like the animals, we do things that will benefit others rather than ourselves: there is no good case for assessing the goodness of human action by reference only to good that each person brings to himself... And it will surely not be denied that there is something wrong with a free-riding wolf that feeds but does not take part in the hunt, as with a member of the species of dancing bees who finds a source of nectar but whose behaviour does not let other bees know of its location. These free-riding individuals of a species whose members work together are just as *defective* as those who have defective hearing, sight, or powers of locomotion.[46]

---

[44] Op. cit. 25.

[45] Cf. Axel Honneth, *The Pathologies of Individual Freedom: Hegel's Social Theory* (Princeton: Princeton University Press, 2001), 27: 'Hegel starts with the self-realization of the individual and derives the task of a modern legal system from these conditions of self-realization; the fact that in his case the communicative spheres come to the fore is due to the specific way in which he defines the structure of the freedom of the "free will"'.

[46] Foot, *Natural Goodness*, 16.

Taken in this way, Hegel's account of ethical life can be made compatible with Aristotelian naturalism.

However, the idealist like Kemp Smith, and perhaps also Gardner, might argue that this kind of account is still inadequate unless it introduces Geist at a higher level, in some quasi-theistic form. An argument of this sort is proposed by Cottingham, against the view the Aristotelian view that 'goodness is like health: the criteria for its attribution to objects and actions have to do entirely with the presence or absence of certain broadly natural features, such as the tendency to alleviate suffering, the promotion of sympathy and fellow feeling, respectful treatment, and the like'. Cottingham objects to this view as follows:

> But the normative status of the obligations connected with such types of behaviour is, as Kant famously pointed out, not simply instrumental, or hypothetical: we ought to do these things not just because we have contingently evolved to have certain inclinations, not because our society happens contingently to put a premium on certain goods, but rather because such behaviour is categorically right. Such behaviour is indeed, in the currently fashionable terminology, behaviour we have conclusive reason to pursue. And ultimately, for the theist, such conclusive reasons, riding free from the contingencies of our human development, will be interpreted in a way that makes reference to the moral teleology that permeates the whole cosmos.[47]

Thus, for Cottingham, as for Kemp Smith, unless our conception of the good is based on a theological conception, it is too relativistic and hypothetical to serve as the basis for a genuinely moral conception of value.

Now, this is a large issue which cannot be really settled here, but it seems to me that there are two responses the Aristotelian naturalist can give to Cottingham's challenge. First, to claim that conceptions of value relate to how well or badly the individual performs in relation to the life form of their species is not subjectivist or relativist in the sense it is just up to the individual or the group to decide on this how they like, but is tied to objective considerations, much as is the case for health or illness. Secondly, and relatedly, this makes the reasons to act categorical and not hypothetical, as the reasons for the wolf to hunt in a pack or for me to keep my promises are independent of our desires in such cases, and thus are categorical: the fact that as a wolf I don't *want* to hunt in a pack, or as a person that I don't *want* to keep my promises doesn't entail on the Aristotelian view that *qua* wolf or person I no longer

[47] John Cottingham, *The Spiritual Dimension: Religion, Philosophy and Human Value* (Cambridge: Cambridge University Press, 2005), 56–7.

now have a reason to do these things. The questions of relativity and hypotheticality seem to be red-herrings, therefore.

The real remaining issue then seems to be whether being just linked to the *human* good is enough to make such categorical reasons *strong enough* to be compelling or overriding, unless a link to some divine or higher spiritual source is forged, a link that is lost in Aristotelian naturalism. But how might the appeal to God (or a Geist in some quasi-theistic form) help here? This is Cottingham's answer:

> To spell it out more explicitly, if the pattern after which we are shaped, whether we like it or not, is one that allows us true fulfil-ment only if the love that is deep in our nature wells up and over-flows towards our fellow-creatures, only then have we the highest and most compelling reasons to live in accordance with that love.[48]

But what is striking about this response is how close it comes to Aristotelian naturalism: for the Aristotelian naturalist will equally claim that our self-realization as individuals is directly tied in with the moral life, and thus this seems something the naturalist can claim as much as the theist. And certainly, as many Hegelians have stressed, Hegel himself seems to have wanted to make this kind of connection, in a way that again draws him close to Aristotelian naturalism.[49]

But, of course, there is also a fundamental difference, which is that Cottingham holds that it is only within a *created* order that this good can *really* matter: we have to think that our pattern is something that has been 'shaped', by something that has a 'higher' value itself, where he quotes Tennyson: 'God [is] love indeed/and love Creation's final law'.[50] The challenge for the secular Aristotelian naturalist, therefore, is whether there can be value in a nature that is not viewed in theo-logical terms, as created.

Now, of course, this again is hardly something that can be settled here, while it is indeed true that Hegel (like virtually everyone in his time) would have assumed nature *was* created in some sense, and thus this may be taken as a background assumption to any of conceptions of

---

[48] Cottingham, *Philosophy of Religion*, 86.

[49] 'The rational state is an end in itself only because the highest stage of *individual* self-actualization consists in participating in the state and recog-nizing it as such an end. This means that Hegel's ethical theory is after all founded on a conception of individual human beings and their self-actual-ization' (Allen W. Wood, *Hegel's Ethical Thought* (Cambridge: Cambridge University Press, 1990), 21).

[50] Cottingham, *Philosophy of Religion*, 85. For a related attempt to move naturalism about value in a theistic direction, see Fiona Ellis, *God, Value, and Nature* (Oxford: Oxford University Press, 2014).

value he may have had. But the question is whether Hegel gave this idea any work to do in his axiology, of the sort Cottingham thinks is required, and which the Aristotelian naturalist thinks is not. For myself, I see no argument in Hegel that mirrors Cottingham's (though of course some might, perhaps including Kemp Smith and Gardner). But either way, if this is a central issue to which naturalism tends, Hegel is a figure to place at the heart of such debates, rather than on their periphery, thus making Hegel part of philosophy now.

5. Conclusion

In this paper, I have tried to argue for a cautious optimism in response to the question 'why Hegel now?': namely, that current philosophers are right to think that they will find in Hegel a position that answers to their concerns in a way that they can recognize. However, in order to do so, I have argued, they need to go beyond the picture of Hegel presented by Bernstein and others, while also being able to avoid the picture of him presented by Gardner. And the structure of my response concerning value would seem to mirror the structure of broader current debates on how we should read Hegel, where three main options are often played out across a range of issues: Namely, is Hegel a nonmetaphysical thinker who offers us a sophisticated form of Kantian antirealism; or a metaphysical thinker committed to a spiritualistic idealism; or a metaphysical thinker who offers us a kind of Aristotelian realism. When it comes to value, Gardner may be seen as rejecting the first option and so taking the second, where I have been urging the virtues of the third, as the best way to both read Hegel's position, and to explain how he should be taken up now, even if Bernstein is right that until recently it was in the more non-metaphysical approach that his relevance had seemed to lie.[51]

University of Sheffield
r.stern@sheffield.ac.uk

[51] I am grateful to those who responded to this paper when it was delivered as a lecture, and those who read it in draft form, particularly Joe Saunders. Related ideas are discussed in my forthcoming papers 'Does Hegelian Ethics Rest on a Mistake?', in Italo Testa and Luigi Ruggiu (eds), *I That Is We, We That is I: Contemporary Perspectives on Hegel* (Leiden: Brill, 2016), and 'Freedom, Norms and Nature in Hegel: Self-Legislation or Self-Realization?', in James Kreines and Rachel Zuckert (eds), *Hegel on Philosophy, History, and Modernity* (Cambridge: Cambridge University Press, 2016).

Is Nietzsche a Life-Affirmer?

SIMON MAY

Abstract

The question of how to affirm one's life in view of suffering and loss is central to Nietzsche's philosophy. He shows, I claim, that one can affirm – take joy or find beauty in – one's life *as a whole*, conceived as necessary in all its elements, while also despising parts of it. Yet he mostly pictures such life-affirmation as achievable only via an atheistic theodicy that relies on a key ambition of the very system of morality that he famously attacks: namely to explain or justify suffering in terms of a higher end to which it is essential. I argue that affirmation of one's life is more powerful without the crutch of any theodicy, and point to Job as a paragon of one who can affirm his life without seeking an answer to the question of the meaning or value of suffering – indeed who can dispense altogether with that question.

I'd like to start with a variant of an ancient question: how can evil, and all the suffering to which it gives rise, be explained, or even justified, so that, far from causing us to turn against our life, we are able to celebrate it?[1] In other words: what stance must we take towards so-called natural evil – illness, earthquakes, tsunamis – and moral evil – sadism, murder, concentration camps – such that we can affirm a life into which we are cast through no choice of our own? And indeed fill it with genuinely demanding ends and virtues to which we are strongly committed?

This sort of question has been asked with particular insistence (though by no means exclusively) by Christianity, beginning not so much with the Gospels as with the Church Fathers, and in particular with Augustine. One way of posing the question in Christian terms – the question that since Leibniz has been called the 'question of theodicy' – is this: why would an all-good and all-powerful God – the God whose very nature, John the Evangelist tells us, is love – place us in a world filled with so much evil and suffering? How do we

---

[1] This article is a reworking of, and contains extracts from, Simon May, 'Why Nietzsche is still in the morality game', in S. May (ed.), *Nietzsche's On the Genealogy of Morality: A Critical Guide* (Cambridge: Cambridge University Press, 2011), 78–100, © Cambridge University Press 2011, reproduced with permission. I am grateful to Bernard Reginster and to Ken Gemes for their penetrating comments on an earlier draft.

doi:10.1017/S1358246116000291   © The Royal Institute of Philosophy and the contributors 2016
Royal Institute of Philosophy Supplement **78** 2016   211

affirm the life and the world that this God has given us? Whether or not we hold that God created the possibility of evil. For even if you're a Manichean who believes that evil is an autonomous force, the handiwork of a rival deity, the fact is that our Creator decided to place us in a world where the possibility of evil exists.

What is at stake here is nothing less than men's and women's capacity to be reconciled to, indeed to affirm, their own lives and the world in which they are set, if only as something to be overcome. Moreover, the principal, but by no means the only, answer of mainstream Christianity to the question of theodicy is well known, and it is roughly this: 'free will is the cause of our doing evil', as Augustine puts it in the *Confessions*,[2] and free will gives us moral responsibility, which is integral to the full human dignity that God intends for us. The possibility of moral evil is therefore both explained and justified as flowing from the capacity for free will, a capacity that gives weight and substance to human dignity.

***

Now what interests me about this question of theodicy is not, for the moment, any particular answers that are given to it, or the theological terms in which it is posed – in other words how to justify the ways of a putatively all-good and omniscient God. Rather, I am interested in what the *question itself* presupposes. And I think that if we look at this question we will see that it presupposes at least two things. The first is that the existence of natural or moral evil, and the suffering that flows from it, can profoundly alienate us from the world of which it is an inextricable part, as a result of which we are in danger of fatally resenting our life, or indeed life as such. At the limit this assumption is sufficient to motivate Camus's famous claim in *The Myth of Sisyphus* that the only serious philosophical question – and decision – in life is whether to commit suicide.[3]

And a second assumption underlying the question of theodicy is that any answer must take the form of an explanation, or even a justification, of the possibility of evil in terms of a great good that could not have been achieved without it – a good of which the possibility of evil is constitutive or a precondition. In other words, an answer cannot just show that sometimes bad things result in good things – that some pain happens to lead to gain: for example, starting

---

[2]   Augustine, *The Confessions of St. Augustine* (Mineola, NY: Dover Publications, 2002), 107.

[3]   Albert Camus, *The Myth of Sisyphus* (London: Penguin, 1975), 11.

Is Nietzsche a Life-Affirmer?

a charity in the name of a dead loved one, writing a novel as catharsis for hardship, creating a successful company out of the experience of a failed one, and so on. The impulse behind theodicy is more ambitious than this: the possibility of evil, it demands, must be shown to be not just contingently a cause of good, but to be a precondition of good.

Theodicy, in other words, seeks to posit a supreme principle of good that cannot be attained without the possibility of the relevant evil; an ultimate standard of value that vindicates and *gives meaning* to the possibility of evil, and all the suffering with which it is associated, so that the world or a life of which it is a part can be affirmed and welcomed.

Now let me turn to Nietzsche, whose entire philosophy, it seems to me, is suffused by precisely these two presuppositions of the question of theodicy: that natural and moral evil can profoundly alienate us from our life and the world; and that evil and suffering can be tolerated, even welcomed, only by finding a meaning for them in terms of a supreme and demanding principle of good that *could not* be achieved without their possibility.

As he puts it in his conclusion to *On the Genealogy of Morality*: 'Man [...] does *not* deny suffering as such: he *wills* it, he even seeks it out, provided he is shown a *meaning* for it, a *purpose* of suffering.' (GM, III, 28).[4] How then, Nietzsche repeatedly asks, can we find a meaning for suffering that will enable us to affirm life wholeheartedly and unreservedly? How, through discovering such a meaning, can we maintain that fundamental trust in life without which we cannot flourish? (By 'life' he refers, I think, to our own life in particular and to life viewed as a whole – from our individual perspective and

---

[4] Following standard convention, I refer to the English translations of Nietzsche's works using the following abbreviations (references are to section numbers): *Beyond Good and Evil* (BGE), trans. W. Kaufmann (New York, NY: Vintage, 1966 [1886]); *The Birth of Tragedy* (BT), trans. W. Kaufmann (New York, NY: Vintage, 1966 [1872]); *Ecce Homo* (EH), trans. W. Kaufmann (New York, NY: Vintage, 1967 [1888]); *On the Genealogy of Morality* (GM), trans. C. Diethe (Cambridge: Cambridge University Press, 1997 [1887]); *The Gay Science* (GS), trans. W. Kaufmann (New York, NY: Vintage, 1974 [1882; Part 5: 1887]); *Twilight of the Idols* (TI) (1889), trans. W. Kaufmann, in *The Portable Nietzsche*, ed. W. Kaufmann (New York, NY: Viking, 1954); *The Will to Power* (WP), trans. W. Kaufmann and R. J. Hollingdale (New York, NY: Vintage, 1968); *Thus Spoke Zarathustra* (Z) (1883–1885), trans. W. Kaufmann, in *The Portable Nietzsche*, ed. W. Kaufmann (New York, NY: Viking, 1954).

Simon May

out of our individual experience, of course, rather than from nowhere or everywhere.)

These questions matter desperately to Nietzsche – they underlie his whole philosophy – because of his overwhelming conviction that suffering came in Western cultures to be regarded as so unacceptable that men and women turned against and denied life;[5] at the limit turning against everything about the world that causes suffering, such as time and transience and loss – which, for Nietzsche, means that they turned against the only world that exists. When this happened, suffering – experienced and, in various ways, detested by all human beings in all cultures – became 'the problem of suffering'[6] – experienced by human beings in very particular cultures, notably, he says, those permeated by Platonic/Hellenized Jewish/Christian thought and morality and, since the 18th century, by their secular successors.

Nietzsche's concern is therefore that in the modern age despair created by this intense awareness of the so-called problem of suffering has ended up either in a nihilism of ethical passivity, indifference and confusion, where none of our highest values hitherto seems achievable or remains authoritative for us; or in a still more radical nihilism in which no demanding higher values at all, and perhaps no possible groundings for such values, are ultimately authoritative.

The nihilism that really worries Nietzsche isn't, therefore, just one characterized by losing faith in God, or in one particular set of reigning values – a nihilism marked, affectively, by despair or confusion resulting from this loss and from uncertainty about what faith and what values are to replace it. The nihilism that disturbs Nietzsche most is much more thoroughgoing: it is a loss of trust in, a repudiation of, ultimately an indifference towards, *any* demanding values or ends along with a rejection of *any* feature of existence that is seen as entailing suffering. This is the nihilism that ends up in a vacuous 'religion of comfortableness' (GS, 338) in which suffering itself is regarded as so unacceptable that our supreme concern is only to keep going without pain and without hardship, and in which, for all our outward ambition and boldness and will to power, we have in fact detached ourselves from any ends, any project, any experience, any virtues, any philosophy, indeed any religion, that, because they are difficult and require uncompromising commitment, might risk suffering and so threaten our comfort.

---

[5] GM, Preface, 5; GM, III, 11.
[6] Just as evil became 'the problem of evil'.

The kind of person who pursues this nihilism of comfort – whose overriding aim is avoiding suffering – Nietzsche's Zarathustra calls the 'small man' (Z, II, 4) or the 'last man' (Z, 'Zarathustra's Prologue', 5). And though this last man, who no longer believes in God or in a transcendent domain, seems as far away as it is possible to be from a supreme metaphysician like Augustine, whose ethic is certainly structured by demanding higher values, he is in effect, for Nietzsche, an insipid version of the metaphysician. For both of them are slaves of what Nietzsche calls a 'will to nothingness'.

In other words, both are governed by a will characterized by 'an aversion to life, a rebellion against the most fundamental prerequisites of life' (GM, III, 28): a life-denying will that makes life's highest end the elimination or justification of suffering – for the sake of some state of affairs that is purified of it. For the last man this highest end is the 'happiness' of a life dedicated to career, health, comfort and the avoidance of risk and hardship. For Augustine it is a life beyond this world: a life of *quies*, or eternal and perfect rest, which he sees both as the nature of God and as the highest good for which, in his ethics, life can strive. This end, this striving, is well expressed in Augustine's famous call to God right at the beginning of the *Confessions*: 'thou hast made us for thyself and restless is our heart until it comes to rest in thee'.[7]

***

When Nietzsche addresses himself to the question 'How can we affirm our own life wholeheartedly and so avoid falling into nihilism of either or both of these kinds?' his most consistent answer turns on this idea: that to affirm our life is to experience it as beautiful. Or at least to experience as beautiful certain presuppositions of (one's) life, such as its necessity.

In his early work, *The Birth of Tragedy*, he famously proclaims that 'it is only as an *aesthetic phenomenon* that existence and the world are eternally *justified*' (BT, 5). In *The Gay Science*, a later work, we read that *amor fati* or being a Yes-sayer (*Ja-sagender sein*) – Nietzsche uses both these terms here – is 'to see as beautiful what is necessary in things' (GS, 276). Also in a middle period passage from *The Gay Science*, Nietzsche posits art as the 'counterforce' against the 'nausea and suicide' that honest looking at the nature of things would, he says, induce (GS, 107). *Twilight of the Idols*, a late work, posits 'art [as] the great stimulus to life' (TI, IX, 24), and this

---

[7] Op. cit. 1.

thought is echoed in unpublished notes where Nietzsche speaks of art as 'the great seduction to life [and] the great stimulant of life [...] the redemption of the sufferer' (WP, 853 – II). Only in his last published work, *Ecce Homo*, does affirmation get defined in terms that don't make explicit reference to beauty or art, or indeed to any sort of explanation or justification of suffering: *amor fati* is now expressed as 'wanting nothing to be different, not forward, not backwards, not in all eternity'. The goal here is not merely to bear what is necessary, still less to conceal it ... but rather to *love* it (EH, II, 10).

Such thoughts raise two initial questions about Nietzschean affirmation of life. Firstly, what exactly is the object of affirmation? And secondly, is this affirmation consistent with also hating, negating, rejecting, aspects of one's life and of the world?

On the first question – what exactly is getting affirmed here? – if we read these passages carefully we see that in almost all of them the direct object of affirmation isn't in fact every single thing and event, but is rather a whole or a principle of some sort. This is variously posited by Nietzsche as existence, or fate, or necessity, or world, or life in general, or one's own life in particular, or the narrative or poem or aesthetic unity that we make of our lives. In *The Birth of Tragedy* it is existence and the world that are the objects of eternal justification. In the passage from *Twilight of the Idols* that I just cited it is life. In both statements on *amor fati*, the one in *The Gay Science* and the other in *Ecce Homo*, the proximate object of love is again necessity. Nietzsche could have talked instead of love of all things, but he chooses, in the main, to speak of love of fate or necessity. And constitutive of loving fate or necessity is that I do not expect individual events and things to be other than they are, even if I negate or despise them.

But – turning now to my second question – is life-affirmation really consistent with negating or despising aspects of one's life and the world? The child who gets accidentally run over. The brick that drops on the passer-by and kills her. Auschwitz. The answer, it seems to me, is clearly Yes: life-affirmation is consistent with negating or despising aspects of one's life and the world. To love a whole does not entail that I separately love each and every one of its parts. I can love my child but not love or find beautiful everything that he does, from taking drugs to becoming a violent criminal. I can love life without loving the death camp. I can love a work of art, or life experienced as a work of art, and find beauty in the whole, without needing to do so in every one of its individual parts taken alone. Indeed not only is affirmation or love consistent with such negative attitudes; these negative attitudes arguably test love's resilience and genuineness. What I am suggesting, in other words, is that affirmation of life can only be an attitude towards life, or my life, considered as a whole – or towards some condition of the possibility of life as a whole – however we conceive that whole.

This is, I think, especially true of an aesthetic affirmation, such as Nietzsche avows again and again. Nor is he the first in the history of philosophy to offer an aesthetic affirmation of existence that sees beauty in the whole, and so can affirm the whole despite the undeniable horror of many of its parts. Again, no less a figure – and no less a seeming opponent of Nietzsche – than Augustine does just this. Nietzsche, whose thinking is saturated by Lutheran Protestantism, which is in turn heavily indebted to Augustinian thought, sounds remarkably like Augustine praising the beauty of Creation as a whole, which he regards as an ordered work of art of which even Hell and the eternal damnation of sinners is an indispensable part. 'That which we abhor in any given part [of the universe]', says Augustine, 'gives us the greatest pleasure when we consider the universe as a whole'.[8]

As it turns out, most of Nietzsche's thinking on the affirmation of life does go together (and is entirely consistent) with despising or saying No to particular events in life. Indeed, he himself obviously detests and says No to much about the world as he finds it – the motivations and functions of 'slave morality', the so-called 'last man', the 'religion of comfortableness' and a great deal besides – without, he claims (at least *qua* life-affirmer rather than *qua* revaluer of all values) wishing to have lived another life free of those realities. 'We immoralists', he says, though we make it 'a point of honour to be affirmers', do also negate, albeit 'not easily' (TI, IV, 6).

Nietzsche's wish to be an affirmer evidently doesn't commit him to saying that there is only one sort of value – namely, good – and that everything is good in one way or another. Not only does he disvalue a great many things; but, more fundamentally, his very project to revalue all values presupposes just such a No-saying – an ethical No-saying and an aesthetic No-saying – to much of the world in which he finds himself. Indeed he explicitly recognizes this, speaking of the task he set himself in *Beyond Good and Evil*:

> After the Yes-saying part of my task had been solved, the turn had come for the No-saying, No-doing part: the revaluation of our values so far [...] (EH, III, 'Beyond Good and Evil', 1)

***

[8] Augustine, *Of True Religion* (Chicago: Henry Regnery Company, 1959).

In short: there is clearly room within a Nietzschean ethic of affirmation for saying No to particular events and experiences. With a crucial proviso: that such No-saying does not go together with resentfully expecting those events and experiences to be, or to have been, otherwise, positing imaginary worlds in which they are indeed otherwise, inventing faculties or categories or realms like metaphysically free will or noumenal freedom that supposedly enable them to be otherwise, and ascribing moral guilt to agents for their failure to act upon such putative freedom to *do* otherwise. The morality that Nietzsche takes aim at is not defined by saying No to things about the world; it is defined by a will to nothingness that resentfully expects things to be other than they are, a will that at the limit demands a world purified of those fundamental preconditions of life, such as loss and transience, that give rise to suffering and hardship and boredom and whatever else we say No to; a will for which the horrors of life become an objection to life's own preconditions.

Now admittedly, in Nietzsche's characterization of the affirmer of 'eternal recurrence' – that is, of the idea that our lives and everything will be repeated identically to all eternity – it does seem that each individual event is indeed a direct object of affirmation. As Nietzsche puts it, 'The question in each and every thing, "Do you desire this once more and innumerable times more?" would lie upon your actions as the greatest weight.' But as so often with Nietzsche things aren't as clear as any single sentence might suggest. The very next sentence seems to claim that what is affirmed is my own self and life as a whole: 'Or how well disposed would you have to become to *yourself* and *to life* to crave nothing more fervently [...]?' (GS, 341, my italics).

Whatever affirmation of eternal recurrence really involves – and I am not much clearer on this than I was when I first read Nietzsche, though I am sympathetic to Heidegger's claim that it reflects a metaphysical manner of thinking – when we come to his formulations of *amor fati* we get the sense that what I affirm is, as I suggested, the *necessity* driving and structuring my life as a whole, and indeed all life – and that in affirming this necessity I *ipso facto* affirm particular events, even those I despise or say No to, insofar as they are inextricable parts of the whole.

This idea, that in affirming the whole – my life and its necessity; or my life as a unity, aesthetically or otherwise experienced – we can in a sense affirm even those particular events that we despise, seems to be explicitly articulated by Nietzsche in a passage from *Twilight of the Idols*. In discussing one of his highest types, Goethe, and what he calls 'the highest of all possible faiths', that of Dionysus, he identifies the core stance of this 'faith' as follows:

> only the particular is loathsome [...] all is [...] redeemed and affirmed in the whole. (TI, IX, 49)

So we seem to have it from Nietzsche in black and white: we can affirm our life – indeed affirm it in the 'highest possible' way – while hating particular events and experiences within it.

In other words, we take joy in the whole on account of its beauty as a whole or on account of seeing beauty in the necessity that has given rise to it. And, when viewed in the light of this beauty, whatever we loathe is redeemed in virtue of its belonging to the whole. Those particular events and experiences that we despise when we look at them individually can be affirmed, and to that extent redeemed, when – and only when – we become able to view them in the light of this beauty that we see in the whole or in the necessity governing the whole.

To be clear: what we despise is affirmed not because in the light of the whole we cease despising it in its particularity and instead come to see it as beautiful, but only because we now see its necessity to the whole. Ultimately we see that to will the whole is, *ipso facto*, also to will the individual events that make it up, though this doesn't mean that we would or could ever value or will them as individual events in their own right.

It is worth noting that, on this picture, determinism, in the full sense in which Nietzsche thinks of it, becomes a redemptive concept – just as in the old order 'free will' was such a concept. Whereas back then the capacity freely to choose a life dedicated to God over a life dedicated to profane goods, to pursue virtue over vice or *caritas* over *cupiditas*, to atone for one's sins, and the like, were all part of the conceptual apparatus of redemption, now the deepest possible acceptance of the determined necessity of life is what redeems the past, including all its losses and sufferings.

'Acceptance', we must emphasize too, is not the same as resignation, any more than affirmation is synonymous with valuation. It is experienced as the power to square up to reality, to look it in the face, to confront it – including its horror. When the music of a composer like Franz Schubert confronts the fact of death it does not speak of resignation in the face of death, and nor, evidently, does it seem to value death as a good thing that is preferable to the absence of death. Rather, acceptance of death's determined necessity as part of the order of life becomes a moving statement of vitality on the part of

Simon May

life, which understands that in valuing life as a whole it affirms the death that is inseparable from it.

***

To sum up where we have got so far: I believe that, at least in his middle and later work, from *The Gay Science* to *Ecce Homo*, Nietzsche offers us elements of a powerful conception of life-affirmation, though, as I will explain in a moment, not one that goes far enough, including by his own lights. Here is what he is telling us:

(1)   To affirm life is to love, or see beauty in, or take joy in, one's life as a whole, experienced as necessary (or fated) in all its elements.

(2)   The direct object of affirmation is the *necessity* of the individual's life. The life-affirmer experiences this necessity – this majesty of fate, as it were – as beautiful.

(3)   To affirm my life is consistent with loathing, or 'saying No' to, particular experiences or events within it.

(4)   Those experiences or events can nonetheless be affirmed *qua* inextricable parts of the whole.

(5)   Despite saying No to particular events or experiences the life-affirmer has no will to consider alternatives to the actual life he or she lives. This is crucial: insofar as we affirm necessity we cannot have expectations of living a life other than the one we live, and in that sense it is possible that life-affirmation and Nietzsche's project to revalue all values do come apart. To expect to be elsewhere, and especially in a radical elsewhere, where the preconditions that structure this life no longer obtain, is a paradigmatic symptom of the will to nothingness. Indeed, the type who exemplifies that will is the 'ascetic priest' – who, Nietzsche tells us, is precisely 'the incarnate wish for being otherwise, being elsewhere, indeed, he is the highest pitch of this wish, its essential ardour and passion' (GM, III, 13).

These five features of the affirmative stance are genuinely non-moral, in Nietzsche's own terms. But there are other aspects to his thinking on life-affirmation that remain tethered to precisely the moral world that he wishes to revalue – and to that extent are not themselves life-affirming.

Firstly, as we have seen, there is his repeated talk of needing to be seduced or stimulated to life – not, of course, through seeing life as a bridge to another world but rather through art or beauty (e.g. WP,

853 – II) – where art or beauty are used either to conceal reality, as in *The Birth of Tragedy*, or as a counterforce to the 'nausea and suicide' that honest looking at reality would induce, as in *The Gay Science* (GS, 107). Indeed, for Nietzsche, art plays a role in seducing us to this world and its trials that is closely analogous to the role that, according to him, God and his earthly agent, the priest, play in the Christian moral order.

Secondly, Nietzsche is, through much of his writing, determined to give suffering a meaning, to vindicate it, in terms of a higher good of which it is constitutive, or a precondition. In other words, he is determined to offer an atheistic theodicy, albeit one that explains or justifies suffering in terms of a good that he considers not to be motivated by the will to nothingness. Such a good is, paradigmatically, creativity in art and values, the achievement of personhood, and, in general, any 'enhancement' of humanity (BGE, 225).

As I mentioned at the outset, both of these closely related ways of thinking – the expectation that we need to be seduced to life and the employment of a theodicy-like explanation or justification of suffering for this purpose – are, in their conceptual form, right out of the playbook of traditional morality and especially Christian morality. Thus when Nietzsche says of 'great suffering' that 'only *this* discipline has created all enhancements of man so far' (*Ibid.*) he closely follows the traditional Christian argument, articulated by, for example, the Greek-speaking Church Father, St Irenaeus (c. 130–202 CE), that hardship and pain are needed for soul-making, for the self-creation of the individual, so that he or she may attain more perfect states of being.[9] Or when St Paul says 'we rejoice in our sufferings, knowing that suffering produces endurance, and endurance produces character, and character produces hope' (Romans 5:3–4),[10] his thinking bears more than a passing resemblance to Nietzsche's.

***

By contrast, I claim that a stance towards life that genuinely affirms it would not be so powerfully colonized by the desire to explain or justify suffering. Let me give three reasons why I take this to be so.

Firstly: if affirmation is to be conceived as a form of love, as it clearly is in Nietzsche's conception of *amor fati*, then we would not

[9]   John Hick, *Evil and the God of Love* (London: Macmillan, 1966), 211–215, 253–255.
[10]   Cf. II Corinthians 12:7–10. Cited in Hick, op. cit., 357.

expect it to depend critically on explaining or justifying whatever is being affirmed – my life, my vocation, my suffering – for example through a calculus of welfare that issues in an all-things-considered attitude to it. On the contrary we would expect the affirmative stance to evince *no* urge to engage in such assurances. Instead, it would take joy in the existence and reality, in the quiddity as it were, of its object – joy that is not underpinned by calculations of the ulterior value to us, or to it, of the object's failings, however painful or unsightly or regretful we find them. One motive, after all, for seeking to justify something is that we are unsure of our commitment to it, or we fear that there is something wrong with our commitment to it. The will to justify involves, experientially, detachment from, perhaps even mistrust of, its object (essential of course though that detachment is when we are reflecting on the worth of our goods and practices, on how to live our life best and so on). It is the position of the observer who stands back and reaches judgements. Crucially, it presupposes that justification *can* fail – and so that there is the alternative of saying No – in other words of negating.

The second problem with the urge to justify suffering is that it is, or can be, in effect yet another way of trying to do away with it – which is the very urge that Nietzsche rightly deems 'absurd' (BGE, 225). For suffering most fundamentally *isn't* about obstacles or pain *per se*. It is about desperate helplessness, vulnerability, uncertainty – in ourselves or witnessed in others. Why did it strike? Why me? How bad will it get? What consequences will it have? Will it ever end? To interpret suffering as Nietzsche comfortingly does – as constitutive, say, of creative activity, so that to will the latter is to will suffering – is still to be in the business of abolishing precisely the impotence, the interpretative vacuum, that gives suffering its bite, by telling ourselves that we have in fact willed it, that its consequences are desirable, and indeed that they are not merely desirable but perhaps belong to the greatest goods of which we can conceive. And to that extent it is, as I said, still to be in the business of abolishing suffering itself. For suffering interpreted as valuable and willed is no longer suffering.

Thirdly: it is in any case a fact that the suffering that poses the greatest challenge to affirming one's life is precisely that which cannot credibly be justified – and which goes on stubbornly resisting all attempts to discover its value or beauty. We can't deny that such suffering exists, whether of natural or man-made origin, such as disasters of a sufficient order to destroy all conditions for flourishing – an event, for example, that destroys an artist's entire ability to create; a mental illness that forces the writer to put down her pen forever; an accident in which all your children die. Not to mention such realities as Auschwitz or Pol Pot. The challenge of affirmation ultimately exists, and has always existed, because of, and in relation to, the existence of such horrors, and not those that can be shown to foster creativity and heroism and soul-making.

To see how to rise to *this* challenge of suffering that eludes all justification we should look not to Nietzsche but to Job. Job explicitly refuses the appeals of his wife and friends to justify or even explain the horrors that God has inflicted on him – for example to interpret these horrors as punishment for transgression against God, or as gaining Job in the end more than he lost. He also refuses to seek a distraction from – or, as Nietzsche would put it, a 'counterforce' to – the nausea he feels towards these undeserved horrors of life.

The point about Job's suffering is that it does not lead to any discernible higher or net good. He has lost all ten of his children, and though at the end of the story God finally gives Job peace and progeny in abundance – 'twice as much as he had before' (Job 42:10), we are told – these gifts cannot vindicate Job's losses; and, significantly, neither Job, nor God when he comes to speak, claims that they do vindicate them. And yet his immediate reaction is one of ebullient acceptance: 'Naked I came from my mother's womb, and naked shall I return there; the Lord gave, and the Lord has taken away; blessed be the name of the Lord' (Job 1:21).

Job's friends find this affirmation completely absurd. His suffering, they explain to him, must have a meaning. As one of them, Eliphaz, asks: 'Think now, who that was innocent ever perished? Or where were the upright cut off?' (Job 4:7). Meanwhile, his wife urges him to give up the struggle to live such a nightmarish life in such a nightmarish world, curse God and die, thus answering Camus's question about suicide in the affirmative. Indeed, she presents suicide as a matter of 'integrity' under the circumstances.[11] But he answers her with another statement of remarkable affirmation, saying simply: 'Shall we receive the good at the hand of God, and not receive the bad?' (Job 2:10). For those who live after the death of God, read 'fate' or 'necessity' instead of 'God'.

In other words, rather than searching for suffering's meaning or value, Job points to an ideal of how to be given the existence of suffering. This is the ideal of doing without answers to the questions, 'How can I find value in my suffering?' or 'What is the meaning of my suffering?', questions that Nietzsche insists *must* be answered. Indeed it is the even harder ideal, or better still disposition, of not

[11]   Job 2:9, where Job's wife asks: 'Do you still persist in your integrity? Curse God, and die.'

asking the question in the first place – of being strong enough to live without clinging even to the unanswered question – and instead accepting that the dreaded event has become another manifestation of the necessity that governs your life, a necessity that you celebrate.

***

There are, I think, few better examples of how Nietzsche struggles to overcome morality, with its guiding will to nothingness, than his philosophy of affirmation. As we have seen, he cannot go all the way in abandoning the conceptual forms of traditional Christian ways of affirming one's life or the world in spite of its horrors. In particular, he steadfastly insists on ascribing suffering a meaning and purpose (GM, III, 28). Only towards the end of his creative life does he seem to acknowledge, albeit not explicitly, that the challenge of affirmation is how to say Yes to the world without that Yes being secured either by veiling the world's horrors, or by finding a counter-force to them, or else by turning them via an atheistic theodicy from a negative into a positive. He achieves this fuller affirmation, in particular, in his formulations of *amor fati* and in what are almost his last published words, where he praises the capacity to look at unvarnished reality without seeking the protection of illusions: 'How much truth does a spirit *endure*, how much truth does it *dare*?' he asks. 'More and more that became for me the real measure of value [...] error is *cowardice*' (EH, Preface, 3).

No mention here of power, or will to power, as the ultimate standard of value, let alone of the value of falsehood and deception. The key is truth: without looking at things as they are – without being free of the urges to conceal, or beautify, or justify the horrors of the world, urges that he had previously celebrated – there is no genuine affirmation. Perhaps this is what Nietzsche is getting at in his Delphic remark a little later in this last work, in which affirmation seems to take a remarkably cognitive turn. The 'ultimate, most joyous [...] Yes to life', he says there, 'represents not only the highest insight but also the deepest, that which is most strictly confirmed and borne out by *truth and science*.' (EH, III, 'The Birth of Tragedy', 2, my italics).

This Yes to life, he tells us, is a 'Yes-saying without reservation', 'even to guilt, even to everything that is questionable' (EH, III, 'The Birth of Tragedy', 2) – including, one can only assume, even to everything that is questionable for Nietzsche, such as slave morality. Such unreserved Yes-saying must be in insoluble tension with the rebellious, critical drives – for example those that impel Nietzsche's hatred of morality and mediocrity, and his will to beautify the ugly and to revalue all values. We should resist the urge to reconcile his final ideal of affirmation, *amor fati*, with his rejection of morality in the name of life-enhancement – and, relatedly, the urge to attribute to him a neat ideal of a unitary self consistently governed by a stable master drive or disposition. Life-affirmation and life-enhancement are not necessarily reconcilable. For the disposition to say Yes to life entails, as Nietzsche himself recognizes, 'rejoicing [...] even in the very sacrifice of its highest types' (EH, III, 'The Birth of Tragedy', 3): those capable of maximizing life-enhancement. In other words, the life-affirmer will be prepared, at the limit, to rejoice in the destruction and sacrifice of everything she values most highly if, as Nietzsche puts it, she is to achieve this 'most wantonly extravagant yes to life' (EH, III, 'The Birth of Tragedy', 2).

***

In conclusion, I suggest that to affirm one's life is to take joy or pleasure, or to see beauty, in one's life as a whole conceived as necessary in all its elements. To affirm life in general is similarly to endorse life conceived as necessary in all its elements.

And the principal disposition of the life-affirmer is to be able to love his life without this love depending on successful explanation or justification of his sufferings – for example, as constitutive, or as a precondition, of his supreme good.

The stance of the life-affirmer can be further characterized as follows:

– The primary object of affirmation is the individual's whole life hitherto, or life viewed as a whole from the perspective of that individual.
– To affirm my life, or life in general, is consistent with loathing, or 'saying No' to, particular experiences or events within it.
– Those experiences or events can nonetheless be affirmed *qua* inextricable, or 'necessary', parts of the whole.
– Despite saying No to particular events or experiences the life-affirmer has no will to consider alternatives to the actual life he has.

The real challenge, it seems to me, is not to find yet another answer to the question of the meaning or purpose of suffering – an answer that, as Nietzsche repeatedly suggests, might be couched in terms of enhancing one's creativity, achieving selfhood, or other goods that are no longer structured by metaphysical dualism, in hoc to the ascetic ideal, or motivated by *ressentiment*. The real challenge is to stop being obsessed with the question itself. The very preoccupation with that question remains a symptom of life-denial – even if it results in a revaluation of suffering that now hails as good what was previously condemned as bad, or deems beautiful what was once denigrated as ugly. In many ways Nietzsche regards that preoccupation as part and parcel of the will to nothingness that has driven European morality and sensibility since Plato. And yet so much of his thinking remains enslaved to that very question. One wonders, therefore, what our ethics and sensibility would look like if the question were to be demoted – or even experimentally struck off the agenda altogether.

King's College London
simon.may@kcl.ac.uk

The Analytic Revolution

MICHAEL BEANEY

Abstract

Analytic philosophy, as we recognize it today, has its origins in the work of Gottlob Frege and Bertrand Russell around the turn of the twentieth century. Both were trained as mathematicians and became interested in the foundations of mathematics. In seeking to demonstrate that arithmetic could be derived from logic, they revolutionized logical theory and in the process developed powerful new forms of logical analysis, which they employed in seeking to resolve certain traditional philosophical problems. There were important differences in their approaches, however, and these approaches are still pursued, adapted, and debated today. In this paper I shall elucidate the origins of analytic philosophy in the work of Frege and Russell and explain the revolutionary significance of their methods of logical analysis.

1. Introduction

Analytic philosophy, as it is generally regarded today, is a complex tradition made up of various strands, some mutually reinforcing, some in creative tension with one another. As analytic philosophy has evolved over the last century or so, it has incorporated new ideas, methods and arguments, ramified into all areas of philosophy, and extended its influence right across the world. In an earlier period of its history, it was seen as having originated in the rebellion by Bertrand Russell (1872–1970) and G. E. Moore (1873–1958) against British idealism around the turn of the twentieth century. As it developed, however, especially in the work of Ludwig Wittgenstein (1889–1951) and the logical positivists (with their heyday in Vienna in the 1930s), the influence of Gottlob Frege (1848–1925) manifested itself to an ever increasing extent and Frege became recognized as one of the founders – together with Russell, Moore and Wittgenstein – of the analytic tradition.

Frege's significance is based on his creation of modern logic and the use that he made of this logic in analysing arithmetic. His life's project was to demonstrate that arithmetic is reducible to logic. After his rebellion against British idealism, this was a project to which Russell, too, dedicated himself in the first decade of the twentieth century. Russell also contributed to the development of logic itself and offered new logical analyses of his own, most famously, in

doi:10.1017/S1358246116000229

Michael Beaney

his theory of descriptions, which became a paradigm of analytic philosophy. In this chapter I will explain the new logic that Frege created and the kind of analyses that this logic made possible. I shall focus on Frege's and Russell's concern with the foundations of arithmetic, but I shall avoid undue technicality in order to bring out as clearly as I can the philosophical significance of their logical analyses.

In focusing on the origins of analytic philosophy in the work of Frege and Russell, I do not want to suggest that Moore did not also play an important role.[1] Nor do I want to deny that Wittgenstein was enormously influential in the subsequent development of analytic philosophy.[2] But I do think that Frege's creation of modern logic and the use that he and Russell put it to in the logical analysis of arithmetic lay at the heart of what can justifiably be regarded as the 'analytic revolution' that took place in philosophy in the decades around the turn of the twentieth century. This analytic revolution continues to inspire philosophers today, and although its significance and implications are as much debated as anything else in philosophy, its achievements and fecundity have changed the intellectual landscape irreversibly.

2. Frege's logical revolution

The analytic revolution has its origins in a logical revolution that can be given a precise date of origin: 1879. It was in this year that Frege published his first book, *Begriffsschrift*. The term 'Begriffsschrift' literally means 'concept-script' and was the name that Frege gave to his new logical system. This system was the first system of what we now call quantificational logic, which proved to be far more powerful than any system that had hitherto been developed. It opened up the semantic machinery, as we might put it, of a whole host of complex sentences that had resisted effective analysis up to that point.

To appreciate how Frege revolutionized logic we need to understand how he went beyond traditional, essentially Aristotelian logic. Crucial here was his use of function–argument analysis, which he extended from mathematics to logic. Analytic geometry provides us

---

[1] On Moore's contribution to analytic philosophy, see T. Baldwin, *G.E. Moore* (London: Routledge, 1990) and 'G.E. Moore and the Cambridge School of Analysis' in *The Oxford Handbook of the History of Analytic Philosophy* (ed.) M. Beaney (Oxford University Press, 2013), 430–50.
[2] For an account of Wittgenstein's influence, see P.M.S. Hacker, *Wittgenstein's Place in Twentieth-Century Analytic Philosophy* (Oxford: Blackwell, 1996).

with a simple example to illustrate the idea. In writing the equation for a line as $y = ax + b$, we exhibit y as a function of x, where a is the gradient of the line and b the point where the line cuts the y-axis on a graph. Let $a = 3$ and $b = 4$. If $x = 2$, then $y = 10$: we say that 10 is the value of the function $3x + 4$ for argument 2. Inserting different numerical values for x yields different numerical values for y, allowing us to draw the relevant line. Frege generalized this idea: not just mathematical equations but all sentences – and indeed, what those sentences express or represent – can be analysed in the same way, in function–argument terms.

Let us see how this works in the case of simple sentences such as 'Gottlob is human'. In traditional logic, such sentences were analysed as having subject–predicate form, symbolized by 'S is P', with 'S' representing the subject ('Gottlob') and 'P' the predicate ('human'), connected by the copula ('is'). Frege, however, analysed them as having function–argument form, symbolized by 'Fa', with 'a' representing the argument ('Gottlob') and 'Fx' the function ('x is human'), the variable x indicating where the argument term goes to complete the sentence. The sentence 'Gottlob is human' is taken to be the value of the functional expression 'x is human' for the argument term 'Gottlob'. At this simple level, though, the two analyses may not seem to differ much, beyond the incorporation of the copula ('is') into the functional expression ('x is human').

If we turn to the case of relational sentences, however, then the advantages of function–argument analysis start to become clear. Relational sentences, on Frege's account, are analysed as functions of two or more arguments. In 'Gottlob is shorter than Bertrand', for example, 'Gottlob' and 'Bertrand' are taken as the argument terms and 'x is shorter than y' as the relational expression, symbolized as 'Rxy' or 'xRy'. This form of analysis can be readily extended to more complex relational sentences, such as 'York is between London and Edinburgh', which can be symbolized as '$Rabc$'. This enables a unified account of relational sentences to be provided, something which is much harder to do using only subject–predicate analysis.

The greater power of function–argument analysis, however, is only fully revealed in the case of sentences involving quantifier terms such as 'all' and 'some'. Consider the sentence 'All logicians are human'. In traditional logic, this was analysed in the same way as 'Gottlob is human', the only difference being that the subject term was taken as 'all logicians' rather than 'Gottlob' and the copula as the plural 'are' rather than singular 'is'. On Frege's view, on the other hand, 'All logicians are human' has a very different and more

Michael Beaney

complex form, symbolized in modern notation as '$(\forall x)(Lx \rightarrow Hx)$', read as 'For all x, if x is a logician, then x is human'. Here what we have are two functional expressions, 'x is a logician' and 'x is human', joined by the propositional connective 'if ... then ...' (symbolized by '$\rightarrow$') and bound by the universal quantifier ('for all x', represented using an inverted 'A').

'Some logicians are human' is also analysed by Frege as having a more complex quantificational form, symbolized in modern notation as '$(\exists x)(Lx \,\&\, Hx)$', read as 'There is some x such that x is a logician and x is human'. Again what we have here are two functional expressions joined in this case by the propositional connective 'and' (symbolized by '&') and bound by the existential quantifier ('there is some x', represented using a backwards 'E'). In both cases there is nothing that directly corresponds to the subject term 'all logicians' or 'some logicians': these terms are 'analysed away', to use a phrase that Russell was to make famous in his theory of descriptions (as we will see).

Introducing a notation for quantification – in particular, to represent 'all' and 'some' – was Frege's key innovation in creating his logical system.[3] This enabled him to formalize sentences not just with one quantifier term but with multiple quantifier terms. Sentences involving multiple quantification had proved especially difficult to analyse within traditional logic. Since what inferences can be drawn from them depends on their quantificational structure, it is only when we can represent this structure that we can properly exhibit the relevant logical relations.

As an example involving two quantifier terms, consider the sentence 'Every philosopher respects some logician', which is actually ambiguous. Paraphrasing it out a little, it can either mean 'Take any philosopher you like, then there is some (at least one) logician whom they respect (not necessarily the same one)'; or it can mean 'There is some (at least one) logician (the same one or more) whom every philosopher respects'. Quantificational logic provides a neat way of exhibiting this ambiguity:

(1) $(\forall x)(Px \rightarrow (\exists y)(Ly \,\&\, Rxy))$.
(2) $(\exists y)(Ly \,\&\, (\forall x)(Px \rightarrow Rxy))$.

---

[3] In fact, Frege only introduced a notation for the universal quantifier, relying on the equivalence between 'Something is F' and 'It is not the case that everything is not F' to represent the existential quantifier. For an account of Frege's logical notation, see App. 2 of *The Frege Reader* (ed.) M. Beaney (Oxford: Blackwell, 1997).

The first can be read as 'For all x, if x is a philosopher, then there is some y such that y is a logician and x respects y'; the second can be read as 'There is some y such that y is a logician and for all x, if x is a philosopher, then x respects y'. The difference in meaning is reflected in the order of the quantifiers – either $\forall\exists$ or $\exists\forall$. Furthermore, there is an asymmetry in their logical relation: while the first can be inferred from the second, the second cannot be inferred from the first. Mistakenly thinking that the first implies the second is known as the quantifier shift fallacy. Quantificational logic allows us to expose the error and helps us to avoid it in our own reasoning.

We see here an excellent example of the power of Frege's logic. While the ambiguity can be clarified in ordinary language, the use of quantificational notation sharpens the expression and, more importantly, makes clear the relevant logical relations. It can then be proved, for example, that (2) implies (1) but that (1) does not imply (2). It was the revolution in logic that Frege effected in creating quantificational logic that made possible the analytic revolution.

3. Frege's use of logical analysis in logic

Frege's use of function–argument analysis in developing his logical system yielded new forms of logical analysis. To bring out the significance of the difference between function–argument analysis and subject–predicate analysis, let us return to the examples of 'Gottlob is human' and 'All logicians are human'. Traditional logic had treated them as essentially the same, the only difference being between what is taken as the subject: 'Gottlob' in the first case, 'all logicians' in the second. Frege, on the other hand, is insistent that they involve *different* logical relations: subsumption and subordination, respectively. To say that Gottlob is human is to say that a certain object, namely, Gottlob, is subsumed under – i.e., falls under – a certain concept, the concept *human*. To say that all logicians are human is to say that anything that falls under the concept *logician* also falls under the concept *human*, in other words, that the concept *logician* is subordinate to the concept *human*. The first involves a relation between an object and a concept, the second a relation between two concepts.

Another way to express the contrast is to say that while 'Gottlob is human' and 'All logicians are human' have a similar grammatical form, they have quite different logical forms. The task of logical analysis can then be described – in a way that became typical of analytic

Michael Beaney

philosophy – as the project of revealing the logical form of sentences. The point of this project, though, was not to reveal the logical form of sentences for its own sake, but to do so in solving philosophical problems. To illustrate this, let us take the problem of negative existential statements, which has puzzled philosophers from ancient times. Consider the (true) statement made by using the following sentence:

(U₁)   Unicorns do not exist.

If we analyse this in traditional subject–predicate terms, then we would take 'unicorns' as the subject and 'non-existent' as the predicate. If we wanted to make explicit how (U₁) has the form '*S* is *P*', then we could regiment it as:

(U₂)   Unicorns are non-existent.

But if this is the analysis, then we might find ourselves asking what these unicorns are that have the property of non-existence. Must not unicorns exist somehow for them to be attributed *any* property? (U₁) and (U₂), after all, are true (i.e., would be understood as typically used to make a true statement). But how can this be if the subject term does not refer? Alexius Meinong (1853–1920) is one philosopher who thought that we should grant unicorns some kind of being – *subsistence* rather than *existence* – to account for how such sentences can be true.

   In quantificational logic, on the other hand, (U₁) would be formalized using the existential quantifier as follows:

(U₃) $\neg(\exists x)\ Ux.$

This can be read as 'It is not the case that there is some x which is a U', where '$\neg$' is the sign for negation and 'Ux' abbreviates 'x is a U', with 'U' representing the concept *unicorn*. Here, as in the cases of sentences involving quantifier terms considered in the previous section, there is nothing that directly corresponds to the subject term in (U₁): it is 'analysed away' when we make use of function–argument analysis. (U₃) makes clear that what we are really saying when we say that unicorns do not exist is that nothing falls under the concept *unicorn*. This suggests that what our statement is really about is not unicorns (since there aren't any!) but about the *concept* of being a unicorn. What (U₃) makes clear could thus be expressed in ordinary language as:

(U₄)   The concept *unicorn* is not instantiated.

This in turn can be clarified by making use of another important distinction that Frege draws – between first-level and second-level

232

concepts. First-level concepts are concepts under which objects fall; second-level concepts are concepts within which first-level concepts fall.[4] So (U₄) is to be understood as saying that the first-level concept *unicorn* falls within the second-level concept *is not instantiated*.

An implication of this distinction between first-level and second-level concepts is that the quantifiers themselves are to be construed as second-level concepts. To say that something is F is to say that the (first-level) concept F is instantiated (i.e., falls within the second-level concept *is instantiated*). To say that nothing is F is to say that the concept F is not instantiated. To say that everything is F is to say that the concept F is universally instantiated. When we talk of 'some Fs' or 'no Fs' or 'all Fs', in other words, we are saying something about the concept F.

How, then, does this resolve the philosophical problem of negative existential statements? On Frege's analysis, the statement that unicorns do not exist turns out not to involve the attributing of a first-level property (non-existence) to an object or objects (unicorns) but the attributing of a second-level property (non-instantiation) to a first-level property (being a unicorn). We do not therefore need to suppose that unicorns must have some kind of existence ('subsistence') in order for us to say something true in using (U₁). To deny that something exists is just to say that the relevant *concept* has no instances: there is no need to posit any mysterious *object*. Negative existential statements only commit us to there being concepts (of the relevant kind), not to there being objects (to which the subject term somehow refers).[5]

---

[4] To make clear that there are two different relations here, between object and concept and between first-level and second-level concept, Frege distinguishes between *falling under* (subsumption) and *falling within*. But the two relations are analogous. See Frege 'Über Begriff und Gegenstand', *Vierteljahrsschrift für wissenschaftliche Philosophie* 16 (1892), 192–205; tr. as 'On Concept and Object' in *The Frege Reader*, 181–93, 189. Both relations are different from subordination (as explained in the previous section), which is a relation between concepts of the same level.

[5] As Frege himself makes clear (*Die Grundlagen der Arithmetik*, (Breslau: W. Koebner, 1884), §53 / *The Frege Reader*, 103), his analysis of existential statements also offers a diagnosis of what is wrong with the traditional ontological argument for the existence of God. In its most succinct form, this may be set out as follows: (1) God has every perfection; (2) existence is a perfection; therefore (3) God exists. In (1) we are taking 'perfections' to be first-level properties, but on Frege's view, 'existence' is not to be understood as a first-level property, so the argument fails.

Michael Beaney

We can see here how logical analysis can do genuine philosophical work: it can elucidate the logical structure of our thinking and reasoning and help clear up the confusions that may arise from misinterpreting statements we make. Before illustrating this further in considering how Frege used logical analysis in his logicist project, let me say something more to help clarify how logical analysis itself should be understood. It is common today to think of 'analysis' as primarily meaning 'decomposition'. Traditional subject–predicate analysis encourages this conception. When we analyse 'Gottlob is human' in subject–predicate terms, i.e., as having the form '*S* is *P*', we 'decompose' it into 'Gottlob', 'is' and 'human': these are quite literally the constituents. In the case of such a simple sentence, function–argument analysis works in a similar way: it yields the constituents 'Gottlob' (the argument) and 'is human' (the function), the copula being absorbed into the functional expression to constitute one 'unit' (of logical significance). But when we consider more complex sentences, function–argument analysis yields constituents that are different from what their surface grammatical form might indicate. As we have seen, 'All logicians are human' is analysed as 'For all *x*, if *x* is a logician, then *x* is human', formalized as '$(\forall x)(Lx \rightarrow Hx)$'. Here we have a quantifier, two functional expressions and a propositional connective.

This suggests that we should distinguish two conceptions of analysis: decompositional analysis and what I have called 'interpretive analysis'.[6] On the first conception analysis is indeed seen as decomposing something into its constituents. In the case of logical analysis, however, there is a first step that needs to be taken before the relevant constituents can be identified: the sentence to be analysed must be *interpreted* by rephrasing in some appropriate way. 'All logicians are human', for example, must be interpreted (in Frege's logic) as 'For all *x*, if *x* is a logician, then *x* is human' or (in more ordinary language) as 'If anything is a logician, then it is human'. This is interpretive analysis.

We can think of logical analysis, then, as proceeding in two steps. We first engage in interpretive analysis, rephrasing a sentence to reveal its logical (as opposed to merely grammatical) form, and only then do we apply decompositional analysis to identify its supposed (logically significant) constituents. Of course, our sense of

---

[6]   For fuller discussion of conceptions of analysis in the history of philosophy, and of the interpretive conception, which is what I think especially characterizes analytic philosophy, see M. Beaney, 'Analysis' (2009) in *The Stanford Encyclopedia of Philosophy*, online at: plato.stanford.edu/entries/analysis.

what these constituents should be may guide us in the interpretive analysis we offer, but we should nevertheless distinguish the two steps and not underestimate the importance of the first step. In logical analysis there is no decomposition without interpretation. We shall return to the significance of interpretive analysis later.

4. Frege's logicist project

Frege published three books in his lifetime, all of them directed at demonstrating that arithmetic is reducible to logic. In the *Begriffsschrift* of 1879 he developed the logical theory by means of which he could carry out the demonstration. In the third part of this work he also gave a logical analysis of mathematical induction, an important form of reasoning in mathematics. In *The Foundations of Arithmetic* of 1884 he offered an informal sketch of his logicist project, criticizing earlier accounts of arithmetic and elucidating his main ideas. In the *Basic Laws of Arithmetic*, the first volume of which appeared in 1893 and the second in 1903, he sought to provide the necessary formal proofs, with some modifications to his earlier logical theory. I shall concentrate here on the main ideas of the *Foundations*.

The central claim of the *Foundations* is that number statements are assertions about concepts (*Die Grundlagen der Arithmetik*, §§ 46ff.). We are already in a position to explain this claim. According to Frege, as we have seen, existential statements are assertions about concepts. But existential statements are just one type of number statement. When we say that unicorns do not exist, we mean that the concept *unicorn* is not instantiated, in other words, has 0 instances. When we say that horses do exist, we mean that the concept *horse* is instantiated, in other words, that it has at least 1 instance. When we say that there are two horses, we mean that the concept *horse* (in the relevant context) has exactly 2 instances, and so on. A statement about how many of something there are is an assertion about a concept.

Let us then consider one of Frege's own examples of the kind of number statement that we might make in everyday life (*Die Grundlagen der Arithmetik*, §57):

(J₁)   Jupiter has four moons.

It might be natural to interpret this, in accord with a subject–predicate analysis, as saying something about Jupiter, namely, that it has the property of possessing four moons. But this is a complex

Michael Beaney

property, which is itself in need of further analysis. What Frege argues is that (J_1) should be interpreted, instead, as saying something about the concept *moon of Jupiter*:

(J_2)   The concept *moon of Jupiter* has four instances.

More precisely, what this says is that the first-level concept *moon of Jupiter* falls within the second-level concept *has four instances*. So (J_1) is to be construed not as about the object Jupiter, as its surface grammatical form might suggest, but about the concept *moon of Jupiter*. The number statement is an assertion about a concept.

But how does this get us any further? Is the concept *has four instances* not just as much in need of further analysis as the supposed concept *has four moons*? It is indeed, but in this case we have the logical resources to provide the analysis. We have already seen how to define the second-level concept *is instantiated*, i.e., the concept *has at least 1 instance*. This is simply the existential quantifier: '$(\exists x)\ Fx$' means that the (first-level) concept F is instantiated. So we just need to build on this. To say that a (first-level) concept has four instances, i.e., is instantiated four-fold, is to say that there are exactly four objects that fall under it. So (J_1) can be formalized logically as follows, with 'M' representing the concept *moon of Jupiter*:

(J_3) $(\exists v, w, x, y)\ (Mv\ \&\ Mw\ \&\ Mx\ \&\ My\ \&\ v \neq w \neq x \neq y\ \&\ (\forall z)$
$(Mz \rightarrow z = v \lor z = w \lor z = x \lor z = y))$.

This can be read as 'There is some v, w, x and y such that v is M and w is M and x is M and y is M and v, w, x and y are all distinct from one other, and for all z, if z is M, then z is identical with either v or w or x or y'.

(J_3) is Frege's logical analysis of (J_1).[7] (J_1) thus has a more complex (quantificational) logical form than its surface (subject–predicate) grammatical form might suggest. Revealing such logical forms is precisely what logical analysis is all about, and demonstrating how *all* arithmetical statements can be analysed purely logically is precisely what the logicist project is all about.

This is not the place to give even a sketch of how Frege attempted to carry this through. Let us confine ourselves here to seeing how Frege defined the natural numbers themselves. For we do not just use number terms adjectivally, as in 'Jupiter has four moons', but also substantively, as in '(The number) 2 is the successor of (the

---

[7]   Frege does not, in fact, provide a logical analysis of precisely this example, and I also use here modern notation; but the analysis is in the spirit of his account in the *Foundations*.

number) 1'. So how do we define, purely logically, 0, 1, 2, 3, and so on? Here we need to introduce the idea of an *extension of a concept*, which is the class or set of things that fall under the concept. Under the concept *human*, for example, fall Frege, Russell, you, me, etc. All of these objects (all of us) are members of the class of humans – the extension of the concept *human*. This class or extension, according to Frege, is itself a kind of object, not a 'concrete' object (existing in the empirical, spatio-temporal world) but an 'abstract' object (an object of our rational thought), in this case a logical object, since the idea of a class has traditionally been seen as logical.

Leaving aside here the problem of what abstract objects are, let us accept that classes (extensions of concepts) are abstract, logical objects. Traditionally, numbers have also been regarded as abstract objects. Frege himself stressed that we talk of 'the number one', for example, indicating that it refers to an object (rather than a concept). So can numbers be regarded as *logical* objects? If so, then the obvious suggestion is to find appropriate classes with which to identify them, and this is just what Frege did.

If we are going to define the natural numbers as classes, understood as logical objects, then we need to find appropriate logical concepts. Two of the most fundamental concepts of logic are the concepts of identity and of negation. Take the concept of identity, or more precisely, the concept of being identical with itself. Every object is identical with itself, in other words, every object falls under the concept *identical with itself*. (It might be a strange thing to say, but seems to be trivially true.) So the corresponding class has as its members all objects. Now let us add the concept of negation to form the concept *not identical with itself*. Nothing is not identical with itself. (If every object is identical with itself, then no object is not identical with itself. Again, this might be a strange thing to say, but seems to be trivially true.) So the corresponding class here has no members at all. This is what logicians call the 'null class' (or 'null set'), and in this case, it has been defined purely by means of logical concepts, as the class of things that are not self-identical.

The obvious suggestion is then to identify the first of the natural numbers, namely, the number 0, with the null class. This is what is done in modern set theory and is the simplest definition. Frege, in fact, offers a more complicated definition, identifying the number 0 not directly with the null class but with the class of classes that have the same number of members as the null class; but we can ignore this complication here. For present purposes, let us accept that this gives us our first natural number, the number 0, defined

Michael Beaney

as the null class. We can then form the concept *is identical with 0* (i.e., the concept *is identical with the null class*). Here the corresponding class has just one member, namely, 0 (the null class itself). This class (the class of things that are identical with 0) is distinct from its sole member (0, i.e., the null class), since the former has one member and the latter has no members, so we can identify the number 1 with this class (the class of things that are identical with 0). We now have two objects, and can then form the concept *is identical with 0 or 1* (using, in this case, the additional logical concept of disjunction). This gives us a corresponding class which we can identify with the number 2, and so on. Starting with the null class, then, and using only logical concepts, we can define all the natural numbers.

The two cases we have just considered – Frege's analysis of 'Jupiter has four moons' and his definition of the natural numbers – should be enough to give a sense of the feasibility of the logicist project.[8] The key point here is to highlight the role that Frege's new logic – and the accompanying philosophical understanding of it – played in this project, without which it would scarcely have been thinkable. Unfortunately, however, as we will now see, there was nevertheless a fundamental problem in Frege's conception of his project, which is where Russell enters the story.

5. Russell's paradox

Like Frege, Russell was trained as a mathematician and became interested in the foundations of mathematics. After initially being attracted to British idealism, the philosophical tradition that was then dominant in Britain, he rejected it on the grounds that it could not do justice to mathematics,[9] and he then devoted himself, like

[8] I give a fuller sketch in Beaney *Frege: Making Sense* (London: Duckworth, 1996), chs. 3–4; and in comparing Frege's and Russell's logicist projects, in Beaney 'Russell and Frege', in *The Cambridge Companion to Bertrand Russell* (ed.) N. Griffin (Cambridge: Cambridge University Press, 2003), 128–70; Beaney 'Frege, Russell and Logicism' in (eds) M. Beaney and E.H. Reck *Gottlob Frege: Critical Assessments* (London: Routledge).
[9] For a detailed account of this, see Griffin *Russell's Idealist Apprenticeship* (Oxford: Clarendon Press, 1991); Griffin 'Russell and Moore's Revolt against British Idealism', in *The Oxford Handbook of the History of Analytic Philosophy* (ed.) M. Beaney (Oxford: Oxford University Press, 2013), 383–406.

Frege, to showing that arithmetic (and geometry, too, in Russell's case) could be reduced to logic. Russell's logicist views were first presented in *The Principles of Mathematics*, published in 1903, and those views were revised and a detailed formal demonstration offered in his main work, *Principia Mathematica*, published in three volumes between 1910 and 1913. This work was written with his former mathematics teacher at Cambridge, A. N. Whitehead (1861–1947), who was to become a significant philosopher in his own right.

Like Frege, too, Russell defined the natural numbers as classes, using only logical concepts. Unlike Frege, however, he came to believe that classes should not be taken as objects, whether logical or not. Rather, he argued, they are 'logical fictions'. In making sense of how we could nevertheless talk about such fictions in saying true things (not least in mathematics), he developed his most famous theory, the theory of descriptions, to which we will turn in the next section. To understand what motivated his views, however, we need to go back to Frege's conception of classes (extensions of concepts). Central to this conception was the principle that for every concept, there is a class of things that fall under it. (If nothing falls under it, then there is still a class – the null class.) Furthermore, if classes are objects (in any sense at all, it seems), then they can themselves be members of classes. All we need is a relevant concept under which these classes can be taken to fall. The concept *class* is obviously one such concept. This in turn means that it is possible for a class to be a member of itself, as indeed, the class of classes would be.

These ideas, however, lead to a contradiction, now known as Russell's paradox. Consider the class of horses. This class is not itself a horse, so the class is not a member of itself. Consider the class of non-horses. This class is not a horse, so the class *is* a member of itself. So classes divide into those that are members of themselves and those that are not members of themselves. Consider now the class of all classes that are not members of themselves. Is this a member of itself or not? If it is, then since it is the class of all classes that are not members of themselves, it is not. If it is not, then since this is the defining property of the classes it contains, it is. We have a contradiction.

Why should this contradiction trouble us? Why should we not just deny that there can be any such class as the class of classes that are not members of themselves? The problem is that the defining condition for such a class seems perfectly logical. If we allow the concepts of a class and of class-membership, then we can legitimately form the concepts of a class being a member of itself and of a class not being a member of itself. The concept of a class being a member of itself seems to determine a legitimate class – the class of classes that are members of themselves. (Is this class a member of itself or not? If it is, then it is; and if is not, then it is not; so no contradiction arises here.) So the concept of a class not being a member of itself ought also to determine a legitimate class – the class of classes that are not members of themselves. Yet it is the idea of this class that generates a contradiction.

Given that both Frege and Russell wanted to define numbers in terms of classes (and indeed, classes of classes), determined by logically legitimate concepts, Russell's paradox is potentially devastating. Russell discovered the contradiction in 1902 and wrote to Frege in June that year informing him of it. Frege immediately recognized its significance, replying that it threatened the very foundations that he had hoped to establish for arithmetic. At the time that Frege received Russell's letter, the second volume of his *Basic Laws of Arithmetic* was in press. He attempted to respond to the paradox in a hastily-written appendix, but he soon realized that his response was inadequate, and ended up abandoning his logicist project, focusing instead on the clarification of his logical ideas. Russell did not give up so easily, however, and devoted the next ten years of his life to solving the paradox and attempting to show how the logicist project could nevertheless be carried out.

Again, this is not the place for even a brief sketch of Russell's own logicist project. Let us simply highlight here the main idea behind Russell's response to the paradox before considering its implications for our concern with the nature of analysis. Essentially Russell denied that classes could be members of themselves, but he embedded this response in a theory – his so-called theory of types – that was intended to provide a philosophical justification of his solution to the paradox. On this theory, there is a *hierarchy* of objects and classes. At the most basic level, there are 'genuine' objects – objects such as horses, tables, chairs, and so on. At the next level, there are classes of objects – such as the class of horses and the class of non-horses (which contains all those genuine objects, such as tables and chairs, that are not horses). Then there are classes of classes of objects, and so on up the hierarchy. The key point is that something at any given level can only be a member of a class at a higher level. This automatically rules out any class being a member of itself; so no contradiction can be generated.

According to Russell, then, classes are not genuine objects. But what are they, and how can we apparently say true things about them (as we must do if we are to define numbers as classes)?

240

Russell came to argue that classes are 'logical fictions' or 'logical constructions': they do not 'exist' in any proper sense, but we can give a satisfactory logical analysis of our talk about them. A simple example (not Russell's own) can be used to illustrate the basic idea. Let us imagine making the following true claim:

(A₁)   The average British woman has 1.9 children.

Here there is no such person as the average British woman, and even if there were, she could hardly have 1.9 children! So how could any such claim be true (or indeed false, as the case may be)? It is clear what we mean here, which might be unpacked by expressing it as follows:

(A₂)   The total number of children of British women divided by the total number of British women equals 1.9.

(A₁), then, is really just a disguised claim about all British women. It offers us a useful abbreviation of (A₂), enabling us to compare more easily the situation in different countries, for example. We can say such things as 'While the average British woman has 1.9 children, the average Chinese woman has 1.5 children'. 'The average British woman' and 'the average Chinese woman' are *logical fictions*. No such women exist, but the terms provide a convenient way of talking, enabling us to make true statements more simply.

Talk of classes can be analysed in a similar way. Consider, for example, the following true claim:

(C₁)   The class of horses is a subclass of the class of animals.

Do we need to suppose that such classes 'exist' in order for this statement to be true? Not at all, on Russell's view. (C₁) can be analysed as follows:

(C₂)   Anything that falls under the concept *horse* falls under the concept *animal*.

This is a claim about concepts, not classes, readily formalized in logic as:

(C₃) $(\forall x)\,(Hx \rightarrow Ax)$.

As we have seen, this says that one concept (the concept *horse*) is subordinate to another (the concept *animal*). We need only to suppose that concepts 'exist', therefore, not classes as well.

Given the close connection between classes and concepts, as captured in the principle that for every (legitimate) concept there is a class determined by it, talk of classes can be translated into talk of their corresponding concepts. Concepts can thus be regarded as 'ontologically prior' to the classes they determine. It is this idea that lies behind Russell's claim that classes are logical fictions or logical constructions. Talk of classes is 'constructed' out of our talk of concepts, in a similar way to how talk of 'the average woman' is constructed out of our talk of actual women.

6. Russell's theory of descriptions

Russell's concern with solving the paradox that bears his name, in pursuing his logicist project, is the background against which to understand his theory of descriptions.[10] For what the paradox raises is the problem of how definite descriptions, i.e., terms of the form 'the F', can contribute to the meaning and truth-value of sentences in which they appear even when they lack a referent. 'The class of all classes that are not members of themselves' seems meaningful and yet there can be no such class. If all classes are logical fictions, as Russell came to believe, then all class terms lack referents, yet we can say true things using such terms. So analysis of talk of classes is clearly called for.

Let us consider Russell's own famous example of a sentence involving a definite description:

(K_1)   The present King of France is bald.

If we were to treat this sentence as having the form 'S is P', in accord with traditional subject–predicate analysis, then we would regard 'the present King of France' as the subject term. But if there is no King of France, then what is the sentence about? A non-existent – or 'subsistent' – object? How can we understand such a sentence if the subject term lacks a referent? Can it have a truth-value in such a case? Traditional subject–predicate analysis seems to raise many questions when the subject term fails to refer.

---

[10]   There has been a huge amount written both on the theory of descriptions itself and on its history, and I can do no justice to any of this here. A full understanding would have to recognize, for example, how the theory improved on Russell's own earlier theory of denoting (as presented in *The Principles of Mathematics* of 1903). For discussion, see e.g. Hylton *Russell, Idealism, and the Emergence of Analytic Philosophy* (Oxford: Clarendon Press, 1990); Hylton, 'The Theory of Descriptions', in *The Cambridge Companion to Bertrand Russell* (ed.) Griffin, N. (Cambridge: Cambridge University Press, 2003); Linsky 'Russell's Theory of Descriptions and the Idea of Logical Construction', in *The Oxford Handbook of the History of Analytic Philosophy* (ed.) M. Beaney (Oxford: Oxford University Press, 2013).

In 'On Denoting', published in *Mind* in 1905, Russell introduced his theory of descriptions to answer these questions.[11] On the account he offered, (K_1) is analysed into a conjunction of the following three sentences, each of which can be readily formalized in quantificational logic (given in square brackets afterwards), with 'K' representing the concept *King of France* and 'B' the concept *bald*:

(K_a) There is at least one King of France. $[(\exists x)\, Kx]$

(K_b) There is at most one King of France. $[(\forall x)\,(\forall y)\,(Kx \,\&\, Ky \rightarrow y = x)]$

(K_c) Whatever is King of France is bald. $[(\forall x)\,(Kx \rightarrow Bx)]$

Each of these constituent sentences has a quantificational structure, and can be interpreted as saying something about a concept, not an object. The first says that the concept *King of France* is instantiated (by at least one object), and the second says that the concept *King of France* is instantiated by at most one object.[12] Taken together they say that the concept *King of France* is uniquely instantiated. The third says that whatever instantiates the concept *King of France* also instantiates the concept *bald*.

Putting all three together, we have:

(K_2) There is one and only one King of France and whatever is King of France is bald.

Formalizing this (and simplifying) yields:

(K_3) $(\exists x)\,(Kx \,\&\, (\forall y)\,(Ky \rightarrow y = x) \,\&\, Bx)$.

Reading this as saying something about a concept gives us the following interpretive analysis of the original sentence (K_1):

(K_4) The concept *King of France* is uniquely instantiated and whatever instantiates this concept also instantiates the concept *bald*.

With this analysis we can now answer our earlier questions. The surface grammatical form of (K_1) is misleading: it has a much more complex logical form. The sentence is not about a non-existent (or subsistent) object, but about a concept; and all we need to grasp to

---

[11]   Russell had first tried to answer these questions in his earlier theory of denoting (see the previous note). But for various reasons which we cannot address here, he soon became dissatisfied with his answer.

[12]   Very roughly, it could be read as saying that were it to seem as if two objects fell under the concept *King of France*, then they would actually be one and the same.

Michael Beaney

understand the sentence are the two relevant concepts, the concept *King of France* and the concept *bald*, as well as the relevant logical ideas (conjunction, implication, identity, and existential and universal quantification). Where there is no King of France, i.e., where the subject term has no referent, the first conjunct of the analysis – (K_a) – is false, thereby making the original sentence – (K_1) – false. So (K_1) still comes out as having a truth-value.

Russell's theory of descriptions has often – and rightly – been regarded as a paradigm of analysis. But we should recognize that all the materials for his analysis were already present in Frege's work. As we have seen, Frege construed existential statements as assertions about concepts and interpreted sentences such as (K_c) as involving the subordination of concepts. To make this clearer, we could thus rephrase (K_1) further as follows:

(K_5) The concept *King of France* is uniquely instantiated and subordinate to the concept *bald*.

This might seem to be saying something rather different from what we thought was being said by (K_1), but that it does have this interpretation is precisely what is implied by its formalization into quantificational logic within Russell's theory of descriptions.

7. Interpretive analysis

As we have seen, both Frege and Russell use interpretive analysis, drawing on the new resources of quantificational logic. It is the role played by interpretive analysis that I think is especially distinctive of analytic philosophy, and it was the logical revolution that Frege inaugurated that made possible the analytic revolution that took place in philosophy around the turn of the twentieth century.

This is not to say, however, that Frege and Russell use interpretive analysis to do the same kind of philosophical work. Certainly, they were both concerned to demonstrate logicism, and interpretive analysis played an essential role in this. But their philosophical conceptions of logicism were rather different. By defining numbers as classes (extensions of concepts), Frege saw his analyses as showing that numbers are logical objects. Russell, on the other hand, in responding to the contradiction he discovered in Frege's work, came to reject the view that classes are objects, arguing instead that they are logical fictions. Such fictions may be useful in demonstrating logicism but they must ultimately be recognized for what they are.

244

What is characteristic of Russell's use of interpretive analysis, then, is its role in a philosophical project that is not just *reductivist* (like Frege's) but *eliminativist*. Numbers are not just 'reduced' to classes but 'eliminated' as mere logical fictions. Talk of numbers is nevertheless shown to be logically legitimate by interpreting or rephrasing sentences involving number terms: this is also what is meant when Russell describes numbers as logical constructions. It was Russell's theory of descriptions that gave him the confidence to take this philosophical line. As Russell himself put it in explaining that theory, definite descriptions are 'analysed away'. When a sentence involving a definite description – such as (K_1) – is interpreted in accord with the theory, the definite description disappears. In (K_2), for example, the term 'the present King of France' is not used, only the concept word 'King of France'. In itself, according to Russell, the definite description is meaningless, although it may nevertheless contribute to the meaning of a sentence in which it appears.[13]

Whose approach is right: Frege's or Russell's? Philosophers today still debate the issue and take sides in their own work. To explore the issue a little further, let us return to one of our earlier examples:

(J_1)   Jupiter has four moons.

We saw that this can be analysed into:

(J_3) $(\exists v, w, x, y)\,(Mv$ & Mw & Mx & My & $v \neq w \neq x \neq y$ & $(\forall z)$
$(Mz \rightarrow z = v \lor z = w \lor z = x \lor z = y))$.

Here the number term 'four' is analysed away, so this might seem to support Russell's approach. We have no need to suppose that 'four' denotes an object; indeed, it hardly seems to do so when used adjectivally as in (J_1).

Frege,[14] on the other hand, noted that (J_1) could also be taken to express an identity statement:

(J_4)   The number of Jupiter's moons is (the number) four.

For him, the possibility of such rephrasal or 'interpretation' – and the perceived equivalence between (J_1) and (J_4) – showed that numbers should indeed be seen as objects. His thinking was very simple. Assuming that (J_1) is true and that it is equivalent to (J_4), then (J_4) is true. But (J_4) can only be true if the terms flanking the identity sign, i.e., 'the number of Jupiter's moons' and 'the number four' have

[13]   Russell, 'On Denoting', 488; *My Philosophical Development* (London: George Allen and Unwin, 1959), 64.
[14]   *Die Grundlagen der Arithmetik*, §57.

245

Michael Beaney

meaning (*Bedeutung*). But such terms, i.e., terms of the form 'the *F*' only have meaning, according to Frege, if they stand for objects.

For Frege, then, interpretive analysis was not part of an eliminativist project; on the contrary, it was employed to support a form of Platonism: numbers must be conceived as existing in a realm of abstract objects. However, from what we have already seen, Frege's actual use of interpretive analysis nevertheless has an implicit eliminativist dimension. His analysis of 'Unicorns do not exist', for example, readily suggests that we do not need to posit any objects for this sentence to be true. All that we need be ontologically committed to is the existence of the relevant concept – the concept *unicorn* (which might in turn, though, be analysable into the concepts of a horse and of a horn), together with the logical concept of negation and second-level concept *is instantiated*.

It was left to Russell, however, to properly appreciate the eliminativist potential of interpretive analysis. But does this mean that Russell is right to claim that numbers, as classes, are logical fictions? If calling something a 'fiction' implies that it does not exist, then this is misleading. For it suggests that numbers lack something that they could have. But numbers are not the kind of thing that could exist (in the empirical, spatio-temporal world). Denying that they exist, though, makes them seem more mysterious than they actually are. What we want to understand is our use of number terms, and trying to decide whether or not numbers 'exist' is to become distracted by the real issue. It is better, then, to use Russell's other term and talk of numbers as logical constructions. What is it to claim, for example, that Jupiter has four moons? It is indeed to claim that the concept *moon of Jupiter* is instantiated by one object, another object distinct from the first, another object distinct from either of the first two, a further object distinct from any of the other three, and by no other object. This is exactly what (J_3) captures. We can abbreviate this by saying that the number of Jupiter's moons is four, helping us to compare more easily the numbers of other types of things, such as the number of seasons in a year – in just the same way as talk of 'the average woman' may help us make comparisons across different countries.

However, the main point here is not to take sides on the dispute between Frege and Russell but just to illustrate the different uses that interpretive analysis can be put. The logical revolution may have made possible Frege's and Russell's logicist projects, but it also opened up the use of interpretive analysis for a whole range of other philosophical projects, as the subsequent history of analytic philosophy has shown.

8. The paradox of analysis

Frege's attempt to reduce arithmetic to logic was undermined by
Russell's paradox, and a natural response is to reconceive interpretive
analysis as playing more of an eliminativist role. But there is also a
paradox that threatens to undermine the very possibility of interpretive analysis. This is the paradox of analysis, which was first given this
name in discussion of Moore's philosophy in the 1940s, but which in
fact was formulated by Frege himself in 1894, in responding to criticisms that Husserl had made to the logicist analyses he had offered in
The Foundations of Arithmetic.[15]

The paradox can be stated very simply. Call what we want to
analyse (the *analysandum*) '*A*' and what is offered as the analysis
(the *analysans*) '*B*'. Then either '*A*' and '*B*' have the same
meaning, in which case the analysis expresses a trivial identity and
is uninformative; or else they do not, in which case the analysis is
incorrect, however informative it might seem. So no analysis can be
both correct and informative. Let us illustrate the problem by returning to one of our earlier examples:

(L₁)   All logicians are human.

In quantificational logic, this is formalized as follows:

(L₂) $(\forall x)(Lx \rightarrow Hx)$.

In explaining this formalization, we might offer various interpretive
analyses, including, for example:

(L₃)   If anything is a logician, then it is human.
(L₄)   For all x, if x is a logician, then x is human.
(L₅)   The (first-level) concept *logician* is subordinate to the (first-
       level) concept *human*.

All of these, we want to claim, are equivalent. But if we take, say, (L₅),
can we really maintain that this has the same meaning as (L₁)? Surely
someone can understand (L₁) without understanding (L₅)? They
may never have come across the idea of one concept being subordinate
to another (or appreciate the distinction between first-level and
second-level concepts).

[15]   For details, see Beaney *Frege: Making Sense* (London: Duckworth,
1996), ch. 5; Beaney 'Sinn, Bedeutung and the Paradox of Analysis' in
Gottlob Frege: Critical Assessments (eds) M. Beaney and E.H. Reck
(London: Routledge, 2005).

Michael Beaney

Clearly, on some conceptions of meaning, (L_1) and (L_5) – or any of the other analyses – do not have the same meaning. But there must be something they have in common if the analysis is indeed to be taken as correct. A minimum requirement is that they are are logically equivalent, in the sense that one implies the other, and vice versa. Now without trying to specify an appropriate criterion for sameness of meaning here, on which there has been great controversy,[16] let me defend the legitimacy of analysis and respond to the paradox by stressing the *dynamic* nature of the process of analysis. Of course, someone can understand (L_1) without understanding (L_5), but once they are brought to appreciate what (L_5) means, they thereby come to recognize that (L_5) captures what is going on, conceptually, in (L_1). An analysis is informative by being transformative.

In offering an analysis we provide richer conceptual tools to understand something. This is exactly what Frege and Russell did in drawing on the powerful resources of the new logic. In coming to appreciate – or being convinced by – an analysis, we learn to use these conceptual tools ourselves in deepening our own understanding. Learning what is meant in talking of the subordination of concepts, for example, gives us a deeper insight into the logical relations between concepts and the statements we make. Consider once again the claim that Jupiter has four moons – (J_1). What underlies our understanding of (J_1) is our abilities to count and to apply concepts to objects. This is what is made explicit in (J_4): that one object and a second object and a third object and a fourth object, and no further objects, fall under the concept *moon of Jupiter*. (J_4) may have a much more complex logical form, but it is precisely this that reflects the complexity of the logical and arithmetical abilities that underpin our use of sentences such as (J_1).

In giving and understanding analyses, then, we typically utilise richer conceptual tools. In the case of logical analysis, we invoke concepts such as those of subsumption, subordination, instantiation, first-level and second-level concepts, and so on. In thinking about – or indeed, analysing – these analyses themselves, we invoke further concepts, such as those of meaning, reference, equivalence, and so on. All these logical and semantic concepts and relations might themselves be seen as logical constructions, which emerge in our activities of analysis. Logical construction permeates all of our conceptual and logical practices.

---

[16] I discuss the issue in Beaney *Frege: Making Sense* (London: Duckworth, 1996), ch. 8.

9. Conclusion

What does 'analytic philosophy', as it is generally used today, mean? The obvious answer is that it is philosophy that accords a central role to analysis. But 'analysis', in one form or another, has always been part of Western philosophy, from ancient Greek thought onwards.[17] So this answer says little. I have suggested in this lecture that what is especially distinctive of analytic philosophy, at least of that central strand that originates in the work of Frege and Russell, is the role played by interpretive analysis, drawing on the powerful resources that the new quantificational logic provided.

This brought with it – or crystallized – a new set of concepts, which opened up a new set of questions concerning meaning, reference, and so on, that Frege and Russell began to explore but were especially taken up by the next generation of analytic philosophers, including Wittgenstein and the logical positivists. This gave rise to the so-called linguistic turn, heralded in Wittgenstein's *Tractatus*, published in 1921. Here, too, though, the roots of the linguistic turn lie in the analytic revolution that Frege and Russell effected. And my main concern here has just been to shed some light on this analytic revolution.

Humboldt-Universität zu Berlin
King's College London
michael.beaney@kcl.ac.uk

[17] I offer an account of the different – but related – conceptions and practices of analysis in the history of philosophy in Beaney 'Analysis', in *The Stanford Encyclopedia of Philosophy* (2009), online at: plato.stanford. edu/entries/analysis.

Ramsey's Cognitivism: Truth, Ethics and the Meaning of Life[1]

CHERYL MISAK

Abstract

Frank Ramsey is usually taken to be an emotivist or an expressivist about the good: he is usually taken to bifurcate inquiry into fact-stating and non-fact stating domains, ethics falling into the latter. In this paper I shall argue that whatever the very young Ramsey's view might have been, towards the end of his short life, he was coming to a through-going and objective pragmatism about all our beliefs, including those about the good, beauty, and even the meaning of life. Ethical beliefs are not mere expressions of emotion, but rather fall under our cognitive scope. They can be assessed as rational or irrational, true or false.

1. The Shape of the Debate in 1920's Cambridge

In 1925, the 22 year old Frank Ramsey read a provocative paper to the Apostles titled 'On There Being No Discussable Subject'. Many of the papers presented to this 'Cambridge Conversazione Society' were not terribly serious, and most have left minimal trace. But after Ramsey died in 1930 just shy of his 27th birthday, this paper (and not one of the many other, more serious papers he presented to the Apostles) was pulled from his manuscript remains by Richard Braithwaite, and printed in the posthumously-published *The Foundations of Mathematics,* under the title 'Epilogue'. A snappy passage from it has been taken to express Ramsey's view on ethics:

> most of us would agree that the objectivity of good was a thing we had settled and dismissed with the existence of God. Theology

---

[1] This paper will also be published by the Transactions of the Charles S. Peirce Society, in a volume honoring Chris Hookway. It has benefitted from comments from audiences at the Ecole Normal Supérieure, The Idea of Pragmatism Workshop at Sheffield University, the Peirce Centennial Conference, The Institute of Education at UCL, Royal Holloway University, the Royal Institute of Philosophy, the Moral Sciences Club, Queen's University, and from Griffin Klemick, Tom Hurka, and Sergio Tenenbaum.

doi:10.1017/S1358246116000308

and Absolute Ethics are two famous subjects which we have realized to have no real objects.[2]

Alasdair MacIntyre, A.J. Ayer, and R.M. Hare thus assert that
Ramsey is one of the 'modern founders of emotivism'.[3] They take
him to argue that our beliefs about the good do not state facts, but
rather are expressions of emotions.

While Ramsey might have been at times attracted to emotivism,[4] I
shall suggest that by the time he wrote this paper, he was already starting to articulate what would eventually become his through-going
and objective pragmatism about all of our beliefs, including beliefs
about the good, the beautiful and perhaps even the meaning of life.
I shall argue that the standard reading of the cheeky 'On There
Being No Discussable Subject' is not careful enough, and when we
build on a careful reading by drawing on Ramsey's unfinished the
book manuscript, we can get a glimpse of a promising naturalist,
pragmatist account of how our value judgments might be genuine
beliefs aimed at truth.

Emotivism was very much on the scene in 1920's Cambridge. It
was a reaction against Moore's view of the good as a simple, unanalyzable property. But I shall argue that by 1929, Ramsey was inclined to
reject *all* of the received views, including emotivism, and was carving
out his own brand of pragmatic naturalism. In the book he was
writing at the time of his death, titled *On Truth*, Ramsey in effect
set out the options in the following way:

(i)   the good is a simple and indefinable property (Moorean
       realism)
(ii)   the good is irreducibly complex (idealism)

---

[2]   F. P. Ramsey, 'On There Being no Discussable Subject', in *F. P. Ramsey: Philosophical Papers* as 'Epilogue', 245–250, ed. D. H. Mellor (Cambridge: Cambridge University Press, 1990), 246–247.

[3]   Alasdair MacIntyre, *After Virtue* (London: Duckworth, 1981): 20. See also R. M. Hare, 'Broad's Approach to Moral Philosophy', in *The Philosophy of C. D. Broad, Library of Living Philosophers*, ed. P. A. Schlipp (New York: Tudor, 1959), 570.

[4]   Braithwaite, for instance, in his obituary of Ramsey, asserts that he was. Richard Braithwaite, 'Frank Plumpton Ramsey', *Cambridge Review*, Jan 31, 1930. See Misak, *Cambridge Pragmatism: From Peirce and James to Ramsey and Wittgenstein* (forthcoming) for consideration of all the evidence and for a more sustained argument about what Ramsey was really up to.

(iii)   there is no such subject as ethics (emotivism, which is one kind of naturalism)
(iv)   his own position (another kind of naturalism)

He dispatches idealism without much argument:

> With regard to the meaning of any concept of value such as goodness, ~~beauty~~, truth or validity there are three main schools of opinion which may, perhaps, be called idealist, realist and naturalist. With the idealists such as Green, Bradley, and Bosanquet I shall not deal; their writings seem to me to be almost entirely nonsense; the living issue is between the realists and the naturalists.[5]

With respect to Moorean realism, he argues against the idea that *any* property might be objective and unanalyzable. For instance, with respect to Keynes' view that probability relations are like that, he simply but disarmingly points out: 'I do not perceive them, and ... I ... suspect that others do not perceive them either'.[6] He thought that Moore's definition of good as objective and unanalyzable was similarly flawed. Indeed, Ramsey objected to the entire realist, logical atomist picture of Moore, Russell and the Tractarian Wittgenstein that backstopped the idea that the good might be a simple and indefinable property. He calls it a kind of 'scholasticism'.[7] Ethical beliefs do not correspond to simple facts, because *nothing* does. That is not the right way to talk about truth and our standards for achieving it.

This rejection of the picture that underpins realism has an implication for Ramsey's attitude towards the third option, emotivism. He refused to stand on the ground that emotivism is built upon. If we don't have something like a logical atomist picture as a contrast, we will not be tempted to see ethics as non-referring and merely expressive of emotion.

Moore's student Austin Duncan-Jones called emotivism 'out and out naturalism' – in fact, 'the most extreme kind of naturalistic theory which could be found.'[8] He had in mind the wave of

[5]   F. P. Ramsey, *On Truth*, ed. N. Rescher and U. Majer (Dordrecht: Kluwer, 1991), 82. The original has the strikethrough marked by brackets.
[6]   F. P. Ramsey, 'Truth and Probability', in *F. P. Ramsey: Philosophical Papers*, 52–94, ed. D. H. Mellor (Cambridge: Cambridge University Press, 1990), 57.
[7]   F. P. Ramsey, 'Philosophy', in *F. P. Ramsey: Philosophical Papers*, 1–7, ed. D. H. Mellor (Cambridge: Cambridge University Press, 1990), 1–2.
[8]   Austin Duncan-Jones, 'Ethical Words and Ethical Facts', *Mind* 42:168 (1933), 499.

emotivism sparked by Ogden and Richards who in 1923 published *The Meaning of Meaning.* They too claimed that Moore had it all wrong, and instead argued that:

> the word ['good'] stands for nothing whatever, and has no symbolic function. Thus, when we use it in the sentence, *'This* is good', we merely refer to *this,* and the addition of 'is good' makes no difference whatever to our reference ... it serves only as an emotive sign expressing our attitude to *this,* and perhaps evoking similar attitudes in other persons, or inciting them to actions of one kind or another.[9]

Ramsey was not on board with this extreme position. He did want to opt for a naturalist alternative, but he was looking for a different, more expansive kind of naturalism, more like the one he found in a certain kind of classical American pragmatism. On Ramsey's view, 'the rightness of actions is related to', but not reduced to, 'the intrinsic value of their consequences'.[10] I shall argue that he thought that beliefs about what is right and wrong, and perhaps even those about what is beautiful and about what is meaningful in life have such consequences, are responsive to experience and are aimed at truth.

2. Ramsey's Pragmatism

Ramsey's brand of naturalism was heavily influenced by one of the founders of pragmatism, C.S. Peirce. For one thing, he very much liked Peirce's idea that logic, ethics and aesthetics are 'normative sciences': they tell us *how* we ought to think.

And of course, in all the sciences, we are trying to discover *what* we ought to think. Thus, in the very first paragraph of his book manuscript, *On Truth,* Ramsey asserts that each of the sciences, including the normative ones, must answer for its own domain the question 'what is true?':

> in regard to the primary logical value of truth, all the logician can do is to determine its meaning; it is for him [alone] to tell us what truth is, but which opinions are true we shall learn not merely from logic but from all the sciences, each in its own domain.[11]

---

[9]   C. K. Ogden and I. A. Richards, *The Meaning of Meaning: A Study of the Influence of Language upon Thought and of the Science of Symbolism* (New York: Harcourt Brace, 1923), 228.
[10]   Op. cit. note 4, 82.
[11]   Op. cit. note 4, 81.

Ramsey thinks the debate about realism, idealism and emotivism in ethics must start with the idea that in all areas of inquiry, we are interested in the evaluation or appraisal of our beliefs. In step with all the classical pragmatists, he declines to start with a contrast between fact and value that sets up the question so that value judgments are at the outset bound to fail to meet the bar. It may be in the end that we decide that these statements should not be included under the scope of truth and rationality, but Ramsey does not prejudge the issue.

The pragmatism that was well-known, and unloved, in Ramsey's Cambridge was that of William James. Russell wrote something critical and devastating on Jamesian pragmatism every year from 1908 to 1912. James had suggested in 'The Will to Believe' that if the belief in God's existence is good for one's life, then it can be taken as true for that person, or if an alpine climber needs to jump a chasm, he is justified in taking it to be true that he can do so. Thus, on at least some expressions of James' pragmatism, truth is what works, and what works can be what works in making my or your life better.

Russell and Moore were appalled by this, and by James's more general statements in *Pragmatism* along the following lines:

> Any idea upon which we can ride ... any idea that will carry us prosperously from any one part of our experience to any other part, linking things satisfactorily, working securely, simplifying, saving labor, is ... true instrumentally'. 'Satisfactorily', he says, 'means more satisfactorily to ourselves, and individuals will emphasize their points of satisfaction differently. To a certain degree, therefore, everything here is plastic.[12]

James pragmatist colleagues in America were just as unhappy. Santayana says:

> Why does belief that you can jump a ditch help you to jump it? Because it is a symptom of the fact that you could jump it, that your legs were fit and that the ditch was two yards wide and not twenty. A rapid and just appreciation of these facts has given you your confidence, or at least has made it reasonable ... otherwise you would have been a fool and got a ducking for it.[13]

[12] William James, *Pragmatism: A New Name for Some Old Ways of Thinking*, ed. F. H. Burkhard, F. Bowers and I. K. Skrupskelis, (Cambridge, MA: Harvard University Press, 1975 [1907]), 35.

[13] George Santayana, *The Genteel Tradition in American Philosophy' and Character and Opinion in the United States,* Edited by James Seaton (New Haven: Yale University Press, 2009 [1920]), 61.

Peirce thought that James's account of truth amounts to: 'Oh, I could not believe so-and-so, because I should be wretched if I did'.[14]

Ramsey, to his credit, saw that James' pragmatism was not the only version on offer:

'What is ludicrous, is not the general idea' of pragmatism but 'the way in which William James confused it especially in its application to religious beliefs'.[15]

He went instead with Peirce's pragmatism, beginning with a dispositional account of belief and its evaluation, and coming to a unified view of the truth of various kinds of belief. Peirce had argued that beliefs are in part 'that upon which a man is prepared to act' - they are 'habits of mind', which are 'good or otherwise', or 'safe' or otherwise.[16] A belief is true if would be 'indefeasible'; or would not be improved upon; or would never lead to disappointment; or would forever meet the challenges of reasons, argument, and evidence.[17] Importantly, against James and with Santayana, Peirce argued that a belief must not be determined by a method 'extraneous to the facts'. It was this Peircean position that attracted Ramsey.

Notice the absence of talk about the physical world *making* a belief true, and the presence of talk of the more vague 'fact'. Peirce had a very broad account of experience, as that which impinges upon us. On his view, when a belief is about the world, it needs to be responsive to the experience that arises from our senses. The hypothesis about God's existence, he thought, is about what exists in the world, and so it needs to cash out in empirical experience, not in whether it makes my life go better. In mathematics and logic, he argued that experience can be had in diagrammatic contexts, as we manipulate proofs and come to surprising observations. He went some distance to explaining how his position worked in this domain, developing a

---

[14] C. S. Peirce, *Pragmatism and Pragmaticism*, volume five of *The Collected Papers of Charles Sanders Peirce*, ed. C. Hartshorne and P. Weiss (vols. i–vi), A. Burks (vols. vii and viii) (Cambridge, MA: Belknap Press, 1931–1958), §377.

[15] Op. cit. note 4, 91.

[16] Op. cit. note 14, §12. See Cheryl Misak, *The American Pragmatists* (Oxford: Oxford University Press, 2013), for a much more sustained account.

[17] C. S. Peirce, *Scientific Metaphysics*, volume six of *The Collected Papers of Charles Sanders Peirce*, ed. C. Hartshorne and P. Weiss (vols. i–vi), A. Burks (vols. vii and viii) (Cambridge, MA: Belknap Press, 1931–1958), §485.

first order quantified logic at the same but independently of Frege's, on which we experiment upon diagrams.

Ramsey fully adopted the Peircean position that a belief is a habit or disposition to behave, and is to be evaluated in terms of whether those habits are successful. He says his belief that the Cambridge Union is in Bridge Street doesn't flicker across his consciousness very often, but it 'is frequently manifested' by his turning that way when he wants a book from the Union Library. He goes there 'habitually', without having to think.[18] He sees that this account of belief and how it is evaluated leads to a Peircean account of truth:

> We have ... to consider the human mind and what is the most we can ask of it. The human mind works essentially according to rules or habits ... We can therefore state the problem of the ideal as 'What habits in a general sense would it be best for the human mind to have?'[19]

This, he sees, is 'a kind of pragmatism: we judge mental habits or beliefs by whether they work'.[20]

But Ramsey thinks we have to be careful with the idea of success or what works. In his most lively articulation of the point, he starts out:

> To say a man believes in hell means, according to the pragmatists that he avoids doing those things which would result in his being thrown into hell.[21]

So far, so good for the pragmatist – this is the dispositional account of belief Ramsey shares with them. He continues:

> Such conduct will be useful to the man if it really saves him from hell, but if there is no such place it will be a mere waste of opportunities for enjoyment. But besides this primary utility there are other ways in which such conduct may or may not be useful to the man or others; the actions from which a belief in hell would cause him to abstain might bring disasters in their train either for him or for others even in this present life. But these other consequences of the belief, whether useful or not, are clearly not relevant to ... truth ... William James ... included explicitly these further kinds of utility and disutility, which must obviously be excluded if pragmatism is to have any plausibility, and thought that the truth of the belief in hell depended not on whether

---

18   Op. cit. note 4, 44–45.
19   Op. cit. note 5, 90.
20   Op. cit. note 5, 93–94.
21   Op. cit. note 4, 91.

hell in fact existed but on whether it was on the whole useful for men to think it existed.[22]

Like Peirce and Santayana, Ramsey thinks that a belief is useful only if it is connected to the facts.

There is much to say about Ramsey's account of truth, and elsewhere I try to say it.[23] But its core insight is perhaps best put by Oliver Wendell Holmes, the eminent Supreme Court Justice, who was in on the founding of pragmatism. In 1929 he looks back half a century:

> Chauncey Wright a nearly forgotten philosopher of real merit, taught me when young that I must not say *necessary* about the universe, that we don't know whether anything is necessary or not. So I describe myself as a *bet*tabilitarian. I believe that we can *bet* on the behavior of the universe in its contact with us.[24]

Having a belief is taking an evaluable bet on the future. As Ramsey puts it, a belief is a habit or rule with which we meet the future.[25] In day-to-day life we are placing countless bets: Ramsey bets that the Union is on Bridge Street; the civil engineer bets that her calculations are accurate and fit for the purpose of holding up the bridge; and the critical care physician bets that a certain treatment will save the patient. These bets or beliefs will come with different probabilities attached, and it might be that the critical care physician, faced with low probabilities, has a warranted and even true belief despite the fact that her patient dies (a belief along the lines: 'The treatment most likely to save this patient is Extracorporeal Membrane Oxygenation').

The question Ramsey in effect asks is: Might one also place evaluable bets that it is wrong to torture; wrong to cheat on one's taxes; right to keep one's promises, and so on? Might we have genuine beliefs aimed at truth in ethics, and in other domains that have so

---

[22] Op. cit note 4, 91–92.

[23] See Cheryl Misak, *Cambridge Pragmatism* (Oxford: Oxford University Press, *forthcoming*).

[24] This is from a letter from Holmes to Pollock, reprinted in Mark DeWolfe Howe (ed.), *Holmes–Pollock Letters: The Correspondence of Mr. Justice Holmes and Sir Frederick Pollock, 1874–1932*, Volume 2, (Cambridge MA: Harvard University Press, 1941), 252.

[25] F. P. Ramsey, 'General Propositions and Causality', in *F. P. Ramsey: Philosophical Papers*, ed. D. H. Mellor (Cambridge: Cambridge University Press).

often been taken to be the province not of truth and rationality, but of emotion and desire? He is tempted to answer 'yes':

> The three normative sciences: Ethics, Aesthetics and Logic begin ... with psychological investigations which lead up, in each case, to a valuation, an attribution of one of the three values: good, beautiful, or rational, predicates which appear not to be definable in terms of any of the concepts used in psychology or positive science. I say 'appear' because it is one of the principal problems of philosophy to discover whether this is really the case ...[26]

Ramsey thinks that it's possible that we might get different answers for different kinds of value – 'for instance, that whereas goodness and beauty could be defined in terms of our desires and admirations, rationality introduced some new element peculiar to logic, such as indefinable probability relations'.[27] But we have seen that this last idea does not appeal to him. And he is generally down on the idea that we might get different answers for the different sciences of value: 'the arguments that can be used are so much the same ... any normal mind is likely to make the same choice in all three cases'. Ramsey would prefer a holist cognitivist account, but he does not want to prejudge this 'principal problem' for philosophy. Trying to solve the problem will involve a careful consideration of whether ethical beliefs, for instance, really are evaluable.

One thing we can say is that these evaluations will be complex matters, bringing into play all sorts of reasons, many of which anchor the traditional ethical theories of which states are intrinsically good – reasons having to do with utility, respecting preferences, the kinds of implicit or explicit contracts we enter, and perhaps even the kinds of agreements we would make were we to make them under conditions of ignorance about our actual circumstances.

Notice that one problem would disappear for the Ramseyan cognitivist. It had been noticed, in 1921, by Guy Cromwell Field, that on Moore's view, it is unclear how we could be motivated by the good:

> Mr. Moore is compelled to say that the goodness of a thing must be thought of as a reason for aiming at it. But on his theory how can this be so? How can it be a motive for action? We are told that it is a simple quality which we perceive immediately. But our mere cognition of it cannot move us to action.[28]

---

[26] Op. cit. note 4, 4.
[27] Op. cit. note 4, 4.
[28] Guy Cromwell Field, *Moral Theory: An Introduction to Ethics*, (London: Metheuen, 1921), 56–7.

Cheryl Misak

On Moore's view, says Field, 'it must be "merely a matter of taste whether we desire what possesses this simple, indefinable quality or not, just as it is whether we like a particular colour or not".'

For Ramsey, though, motivation in ethics is not a special problem in need of a special solution. There is an internal connection between an ethical belief and a disposition to behave, and that's because there is an internal connection between *any* belief and a disposition to behave. Ramsey sees that this will be a complex connection:

> no particular action can be supposed to be determined by this [particular] belief alone; [a believer's] actions result from his desires and the whole system of his beliefs, roughly according to the rule that he performs those actions which, if his beliefs were true, would have the most satisfactory consequences.[29]

But it is a connection nonetheless.

3. Is There Really Nothing to Discuss?

So what are we to make of that 1925 Apostles paper? Was Ramsey an emotivist until 1926 only to undergo a pragmatist epiphany? The answer, in short, is 'no'.

In the paper, Ramsey runs through some arguments for the idea that there is there is no longer any subject suitable for discussion – suitable for discussion *by the Apostles*. The topic was likely prompted by Wittgenstein's 1912 dismissal of the Apostles on the grounds that they had nothing to discuss and that the meetings were futile. The first argument Ramsey trots out is: 'there is nothing to know except science' and since most of us are ignorant about most of the sciences, we cannot really discuss them.[30] Out go the sciences as a subject matter the Apostles can discuss. Then: 'the conclusion of the greatest modern philosopher is that there is no such subject as philosophy; that it is an activity, not a doctrine; and that, instead of answering questions, it aims merely at curing headaches'.[31] There goes philosophy as a subject matter for discussion, courtesy of Wittgenstein. Then we get that infamous dismissal of ethics in which 'Theology and Absolute Ethics are two famous subjects which we have realized to have no real objects.'[32]

---

29   Op. cit. note 4, 45.
30   Op. cit. note 1, 245.
31   Op. cit. note 1, 246.
32   Op. cit. note 1, 246–247.

The purported argument for the infamous claim is that when we discuss ethical matters 'what we really like doing' is to indulge in a comparison of our own experiences and feelings. Our arguments (in ethics, but also in aesthetics and psychology) are 'feeble' and 'we are still at the stage' in which one person says he would feel guilty if he were inconstant in his affections, and another says he wouldn't feel guilty at all.[33] Ramsey's point is that we are not *inclined* to discuss these matters in a serious way, not that we *cannot* discuss them.

It is interesting that in one of the passages quoted earlier, Ramsey crosses out beauty. He wavers, that is, about whether aesthetics is part of our natural, yet evaluable body of knowledge. And that seems perfectly appropriate. If any judgment is an expression of taste or emotion – like 'chocolate ice cream is nicer than strawberry' – it might be aesthetic judgment. On the other hand, perhaps we are right to hold people responsible for the consistency of their aesthetic beliefs, to argue pro or con, to give evidence for or against, and to incur commitments to behave in particular ways, all of which suggests that here, too, we might have an genuine belief aimed at truth. We don't know if Ramsey would have mounted such an argument, had he lived to finish his book. But he was certainly right to say that one of the principal problems of philosophy to discover whether this is really the case.

Ramsey considers one other domain in which preference seems to rule or to be the relevant criterion – questions about the meaning of life. His treatment of the issue is set in the context of Russell's 'What I Believe' and 'A Free Man's Worship'. Here is Russell:

> ... all the labours of the ages, all the devotion, all the inspiration, all the noonday brightness of human genius, are destined to extinction in the vast death of the solar system, and ... the whole temple of Man's achievement must inevitably be buried beneath the débris of a universe in ruins ... Only within the scaffolding of these truths, only on the firm foundation of unyielding despair, can the soul's habitation henceforth be safely built.[34]

He was trying to forge an ethical position for atheists. Ramsey was just as much a non-believer as Russell, also in search of a way of understanding morality and the meaning of life in a Godless, scientific

[33]   Op. cit. note 1, 247.
[34]   Bertrand Russell, 'A Free Man's Worship', in *Contemplation in Action*, volume 12 of *The Collected Papers of Bertrand Russell* (London: Routledge, 1985), 66–67.

world. He finishes his own paper with a statement of where he differs from 'his friends'. It is worth quoting at length:

> My picture of the world is drawn in perspective, and not like a model to scale. The foreground is occupied by human beings and the stars are all as small as threepenny bits. I don't really believe in astronomy, except as a complicated description of part of the course of human and possibly animal sensation. I apply my perspective not merely to space but also to time. In time the world will cool and everything will die; but that is a long time off still, and its present value at compound discount is almost nothing. Nor is the present less valuable because the future will be blank. Humanity, which fills the foreground of my picture, I find interesting and on the whole admirable. I find, just now at least, the world a pleasant and exciting place. You may find it depressing; I am sorry for you, and you despise me. But I have reason and you have none; you would only have a reason for despising me if your feeling corresponded to the fact in a way mine didn't. But neither can correspond to the fact. The fact is not in itself good or bad; it is just that it thrills me but depresses you. On the other hand, I pity you with reason, because it is pleasanter to be thrilled than to be depressed, and not merely pleasanter but better for all one's activities.[35]

Of course, Ramsey really did believe in astronomy. His point, I suggest, is as follows. The fact that the world will cool and die is a ethically neutral fact about the world, a fact that is neither good nor bad. Our beliefs about what meaning life holds for us, given that fact, can nonetheless be evaluated. They are assessed in terms of whether they 'are more admirable or more conducive to a happy life'. At the end of the last sentence in the long passage quoted, he wrote and struck out 'which go more smoothly'. *It is better to be optimistic than depressed, as our activities will go more smoothly.*

That is, even when it comes to the meaning of life, Ramsey can give reasons for his attitude or feelings, and he can give reasons for pitying Russell and Wittgenstein for their despair. We can deliberate about whether there is meaning in life and if so, what it consists in. But *here* James is right that 'satisfactorily' includes 'more satisfactorily to ourselves, and individuals will emphasize their points of satisfaction differently'. The evaluation of a particular, and small class of our beliefs, that is, involves a Jamesian kind of consequence. For with respect to this class of beliefs we are pretty sure that there are

[35]   Op. cit. note 1, 249–250.

many conflicting but correct views of what makes life 'go best'. Each person to some extent determines the relevant standard for himself. We can ask: does the focus on the human rather than the astronomical angle result in more satisfaction for me?

Ramsey happens to answer 'yes', although, as with any matter, he might be wrong about that. All sorts of reasons will be in play, including ones that pull against his belief. For instance, perhaps someone would argue that such optimism leads to our not caring enough about the environment. The point is that even here, even when we allow the success of an attitude to include an emotional satisfaction, our attitudes are to some extent evaluable. Wittgensteinian quietism, on which a form of life, or a way of understanding the meaning of life, stands *protected* from the give and take of reasons is not the only option. Perhaps this important question for philosophy – the question of whether questions about the meaning of life, in which Jamesian consequences are relevant – will indeed be the quietist answer. But Ramsey hated Wittgensteinian quietism, and presents us with what I hope to have shown is a promising alternative.

University of Toronto
cheryl.misak@utoronto.ca

Wittgenstein and the Illusion of 'Progress': On Real Politics and Real Philosophy in a World of Technocracy

RUPERT READ

Abstract
'You can't stop progress', we are endlessly told. But what is meant by "progress"? What is "progress" *toward?* We are rarely told. Human flourishing? And a culture? That would be a good start – but rarely seems a criterion for 'progress'. (In fact, *survival* would be a good start...)

Rather, 'progress' is simply a *process,* that we are not allowed, apparently, to stop. Or rather: it would be futile to seek to stop it. So that we are seemingly-deliberately demoralised into giving up even trying.

Questioning the myth of 'progress', and seeking to substitute for it the idea of real progress – progress which is actually *assessed* according to some independent not-purely-procedural criteria – is a vital thing to do, at this point in history. Literally: life, or at least civilisation, and thus culture, may depend on it.

Once we overcome the myth of 'progress', we can clear the ground for a real politics that would jettison the absurd hubris of liberalism and of most 'Leftism'. And would jettison the extreme Prometheanism and lack of precaution endemic to our current pseudo-democratic technocracy. The challenge is to do so in a way that does not fall into complete pessimism or into an endorsement of the untenable and unsavoury features of conservatism. The challenge, in other words, is to generate an ideology or philosophy for our time, that might yet save us, and ensure that we are worth saving.

This paper is then a kind of reading of Wittgenstein's crucial aphorism on this topic: 'Our civilization is characterized by the word *progress*. Progress is its form rather than making progress being one of its features.'

Our civilization is characterized by the word 'progress'. Progress is its form rather than making progress one of its features. Typically it constructs. It is occupied with building an ever more complicated structure.[1]

---

[1] The quote continues: 'And even clarity is only sought as a means to this end, not as an end in itself. For me on the contrary clarity, perspicuity are valuable in themselves. I am not interested in constructing a building, so much as in having a perspicuous view of the foundations of typical buildings.' *Culture and Value* (ed. G. H. von Wright; transl. Peter Winch; Oxford: Blackwell, 1980), 7–8.

doi:10.1017/S1358246116000321   © The Royal Institute of Philosophy and the contributors 2016
Royal Institute of Philosophy Supplement **78** 2016   265

Rupert Read

This piece is a reading of what I think is Wittgenstein's greatest aphorism on the topic of progress: 'Our Civilisation is characterised by the word "progress". Progress is its form rather than making progress being one of its features.' Somebody reading that aphorism superficially might think that what Wittgenstein is saying is that progress is a feature of our civilisation and isn't that just great? But that's exactly what he's not saying – it's the opposite of what he is saying – and I will aspire to bring that out.

Wittgenstein was very sceptical, as we shall see, about the idea of progress. And he thought that the way in which this aphorism was true reflected very badly on our civilisation.

In order to start seeing how and why, I want to turn straight away to another quote from Wittgenstein (in fact, from Nestroy), the epigraph for *Philosophical Investigations*:[2] 'It is in the nature of progress that it is always less than it seems'. What is Wittgenstein telling us by putting this at the front of his great later work, the *Philosophical Investigations*?

Well, the standard professed reading of this aphorism, in so far as there is one – people don't often pay it a lot of attention, which is interesting and telling in itself – is that what Wittgenstein is saying here is that the progress between his own early work and later work is much less than it seems. And I am in favour of that interpretation of this aphorism.

But, on most readings of Wittgenstein, it is impossible to understand how to take that interpretation seriously. Most readings of Wittgenstein, at least until recently, have suggested that Wittgenstein had 'two distinct philosophies', and that the later was a massive advance on the former, which had been refuted.

I would like to go so far as to say that, in recent years, I think we have started taking seriously this remark of Nestroy's *as* the epigraph to the *Investigations* for the first time. And this has been part of the so-called 'New Wittgenstein' interpretation that I and others have developed,[3] which suggests that it's a radical misunderstanding of Wittgenstein to think that in his early work he proposed a theory, and then in his later work he said, 'No, that theory is wrong', and proposed another theory, or even the-absence-of-a-theory as a new idol.[4]

---

[2]   *Philosophical Investigations* (London: MacMillan, 2009/1953).

[3]   See my and Crary's edited collection, *The New Wittgenstein* (London: Routledge, 2000).

[4]   On this last point, see Martin Stone's essay in my and Crary's (ibid)., 'Wittgenstein on deconstruction', and my own 'A no-theory theory?', *Philosophical Investigations* 29:1 (2006), 73–81.

Wittgenstein and the Illusion of 'Progress'

He didn't propose any theory in his early work; his early work was already dedicated to the complete overthrow of philosophical theories. And the progress between his early work and later work, in my view, is basically a (deep) question of style and presentation and depth and detail.[5] And enriching, as he put it famously, our diet of examples, in a way that was not present in his early work, the *Tractatus*, where his diet of examples was very very thin. He was undernourished with examples in his early work, and that's one of the key changes between the early work and the later work, according to our 'New Wittgenstein' interpretation, which is also sometimes called the 'Resolute Reading' of Wittgenstein.

The idea is that Wittgenstein, *throughout* his life, was resolutely opposed to philosophical theorising, and resolutely determined to overcome the philosophical theories that he saw gripping contemporaries and antecedents, without replacing them with *anything* of the same form, or even with anything of the same form as the 'gap' which their passing seemed to leave.

So I believe that (t)his epigraph is intended by Wittgenstein as a way of introducing the *Philosophical Investigations* and saying, in effect, in advance prophylactical warning, 'Don't make the mistake of thinking that the progress I've made here on my earlier work is very great'.

But I also want to put it to you that this epigraph is doing a lot more than that. I think it would be a mistake, a serious mistake, to see this epigraph as narrowly self-regarding on Wittgenstein's part. It's not just about his own work.

The transition from the *Tractatus*, his earlier work, to the *Philosophical Investigations,* his later work, and his thought that, 'You should try to see this as a case where actually, there is very little progress, much less has changed than might meet the eye', is intended by him, I believe, as *an example*. It's an example of a much broader phenomenon. It's an example of, if you like, the way in which we tend, drastically, and dangerously, and in a dubiously self-congratulatorily mode, to overestimate the progress that we have made as individuals, as a discipline, as a society, and as a civilisation.

Wittgenstein wanted to suggest, with regard to authors who are tempted say, 'In my early work I thought this and then I realised it was wrong and now I've got these brilliant new ideas to replace

5 For detail, see my and Rob Deans's 'The possibility of a resolutely resolute reading of the *Tractatus*', in my and Matt Lavery's *Beyond the Tractatus Wars* (London: Routledge, 2011).

those old rubbish ideas with', that there is something dangerous
about that attitude on their part.[6]

And in the same kind of way, he thinks that when we as a society
say, 'In the old days we were primitive, and now we're modern and
we've got all these brilliant ways of organising everything that
shows so clearly how we've progressed, from the dark depths of our
ancestors, from the 'Dark Ages'', that we are engaging in self-back-
patting behaviour of a dubious kind. (It's funny how people virtually
never say, 'We're living in a dark age'. The 'Dark Ages' are almost
always sometime long ago.)

Wittgenstein intends this epigraph (to *Philosophical Investigations*)
to bring to our attention his own small progress, as an example of a
much broader phenomenon of the way we're inclined to overestimate
the nature of progress, and about how this is dangerous. About how
the idea of progress – the tacit *ideology*, as I shall put it to you that it is,
of progress – is, as he famously puts it elsewhere, a picture that holds
us captive. He wants to help release us from this captivity. He wants to
suggest that we need to be much more judicious in measuring or
assuming or claiming progress.

Before I consider progress as a general unthinking societal ideology, and as a phenomenon that Wittgenstein thinks is less real than
it seems, I want to dwell just a moment more on Wittgenstein on progress in philosophy. So here's a third quotation from Wittgenstein:

'Philosophy hasn't made any progress? – If somebody scratches the
spot where he has an itch, do we have to see some progress? Isn't
genuine scratching otherwise, or genuine itching itching? And can't
this reaction to an irritation continue in the same way for a long
time before a cure for the itching is discovered?'[7]

I think this is a wonderful way of – as Wittgenstein not-infrequent-
ly does – demystifying or puncturing the nimbus of grandiosity that
we sometimes build around philosophy. He likens philosophy, the
history of philosophy, to scratching an inch. This is quite a
radical – disruptive – move to be making.

Most of the history of philosophy consists in scratching an itch.
And of course scratching an itch can make it worse; it doesn't necessarily create progress at all. It can also, when at works, be at least

---

[6] My own view is that Wittgenstein *himself* did not succeed in fully overcoming this tendency in himself. See my essay in Beyond the *Tractatus* wars
(ibid.), for explication. (In other words: I think that Wittgenstein in his later
work became if anything slightly too hard on his early work.) But at least he
drew our attention powerfully to the tendency.

[7] *Culture and Value*, 86.

temporarily satisfying. Well, that might be figured as a kind of progress. But, as he says, 'Do we have to see some progress?' *Real* progress in philosophy, for Wittgenstein, is in another register entirely; it doesn't consist in what we are inclined to think of as progress. Real progress is discovering a cure: no longer needing to scratch the itch. Or simply no longer itching. And those are what Wittgenstein did, or (at least) that's what he thought he did, and I agree with him.

It's also – and this is very important – not just what he did in his later work and earlier work; it's also what many of his great predecessors had done. People such as Descartes, Berkeley, Hume, Kierkegaard, Nietzsche, Frege.

It's a mistake to think that what Wittgenstein thinks about these figures that came before him is that they're all almost idiots, or all to be simply jettisoned. He didn't think that at all. He thought these people were great deep thinkers, wrestling with great deep problematics. And he thought that at their best, unlike many of their interpreters and followers, they did actually succeed in offering clues towards a cure of the desire to philosophise.

I think it's clear how one can see this at moments in the work of people such as Nietzsche and Frege – I'll come back to them, shortly. Gordon Baker, one of my teachers, famously argued this in reinterpreting Descartes, alongside Katherine Morris.[8] Cora Diamond, another of my teachers, has argued the same for Berkeley.[9] I've argued the same for Hume.[10] James Conant has argued the same for Kierkegaard.[11] We 'New Wittgensteinians', one of the things we like to do is to go back into the history of philosophy and say, 'From a Wittgensteinian point of view, these people were not idiots; it's not that they were just down there primitively in the dirt and we've made this huge progress now'. No.

Very roughly: *They were already seeking to do the very thing that Wittgenstein succeeded just a little bit better in doing.* And it's not like he's completed the job either. People sometimes think, 'Didn't Wittgenstein end philosophy? Or thought he'd ended philosophy?'

---

[8]   Gordon Baker and Katherine Morris, *Descartes's dualism* (London: Routledge, 2002).

[9]   In the title essay of *The Realistic Spirit* (Cambridge, MA: MIT, 1991).

[10]   See my 'The new antagonists of "the New Hume": on the relevance of Wittgenstein and Goodman to the "New Hume debate"', in my and Ken Richman's *The New Hume Debate* (London: Routledge, 2007).

[11]   See e.g. his masterly 'Must We Show What We Cannot Say?' in *The Senses of Stanley Cavell*, ed. R. Fleming and M. Payne (Bucknell University Press, Lewisburg: 1989), 242–283.

Rupert Read

No, he didn't think that and there are numerous places in his texts where you can see that he didn't think that.[12] What he thought was that, when you were in philosophy seriously, you must be seeking in some sense to end the process or pain of itching. But he didn't complacently or hubristically assume that he had arrived at that place where he no longer had any itches, nor that doing so could be achieved by *any* kind of frontal assault, any broadly 'linear' or 'progressive' method.

So, a crucial point: looking back on the history of philosophy, what we see when we look at the great philosophers at their greatest moments is something broadly similar. Look at Frege, for example, at his deepest, when he says things like 'The reader needs at this point in my work to give me a pinch of salt, there is something here that I want to say but I can't quite succeed in saying it';[13] or, at Nietzsche when he gets to the moment close to the end of the *Genealogy of Morality* (and in book five of *The Gay Science*) when he, as I see it, successfully shows us, in relation to the very people who he is criticising, Christian thinkers *etcetera*, that he is, in a way, an extreme example of that very same mode of thinking.[14] He's trying to bring something to an end but it's very difficult to do so. This kind of 'real progress', this kind of cure, as opposed to just scratching an itch, is not achievable by aping science. Nietzsche is telling us that he has achieved far less progress than meets the eye over asceticism. Frege is telling us that he his new way of doing philosophy (that launched 'analytic philosophy') is far less securely founded than meets the eye, and that it is not (as most of his 'successors' have taken it to be) a new invulnerable quasi-scientific enterprise. This is great: for a philosopher to acknowledge their own limits, to push up-front their not having made a progressive bound, but having rather made a painful small and not-of-the-kind-as-usually-understood shuffle forward beyond the greatness of what came before. For us to understand how Nietzsche has improved on what has gone before, we have to see the profound level of the commonality he has with his supposed enemies. For us to understand how Frege has improved on what has gone before, likewise.

---

[12] See e.g. *Zettel* (Berkeley: U. Cal. Press / Blackwell, 1967) section 447. See also my reading of 133, a passage often (wrongly) adduced to impute an 'end of philosophy' philosophy to Wittgenstein: 'The real philosophical discovery', *Philosophical Investigations* 18:4 (1995), 362–369.
[13] See my reading thereof in Chapter 1 of my *A Wittgensteinian Way with Paradoxes* (New York: Lexington, 2013).
[14] I offer this reading in Chapter 10 of my (ibid).

Wittgenstein and the Illusion of 'Progress'

Science: the quintessentially progressive subject, or set of subjects. This is what a lot of my work in recent years has been about: How various subjects such as, most strikingly, the 'social sciences', but also philosophy itself, are subjects that do not progress as science undoubtedly does. Science progresses, most strikingly, for example, in the way that, as Thomas Kuhn famously describes to us: there is the process of 'normal science'. In which, what science consists of is essentially puzzle-solving, working away at a set of problems which are widely accepted, filling out a paradigm, filling out a theory which is already present and making it better, making it more accurate, filling in the holes in it. That's progress. That is a way in which it makes good sense to talk about progress.

But just because science has been successful does not imply that other subjects can or (even 'ideally') should progress in the same way. And in particular, a great deal of the history of philosophy, especially in recent years, has been occupied by people thinking, 'Hell if only we could make our subject into a subject like science and progress like science does, wouldn't that be great?' And the answer is: no; it's a farrago, it's a disaster. This is one of the key things that Wittgenstein sought to show us. Philosophers have tried to progress typically by answering questions, metaphysical questions, epistemological questions, logical questions. Answering questions is the right thing to do *when* it's clear that there are questions to ask, and that the questions have been framed aright. Just what isn't ever clear, in philosophy.

This – scientism, the idea that every discipline should proceed and *progress* by answering questions, solving puzzles – isn't the way Wittgenstein taught us to make any real progress in philosophy. On the very contrary: one needs rather to interrogate the questions, to question the questions. And to interrogate the tacit ideologies that generate these questions in our mind. For example, the ideology of scientism itself, the ideology that says that: every real problem should be answered by the methodology of science. Scientism is a justification, a would-be justification, for technophilia, for the dogmatic love of technology, and for the ideology of progressivism that I am going to talk more about in a moment.

Actually, the justification doesn't work even if scientism were right (which it isn't), because it doesn't follow from the fact that there is scientific progress, that there is in the same sense technological progress. Scientific progress is about us coming to know more about the world; technological progress is about us being able to do more to the world. But just because we can do more to the world, it doesn't necessarily mean that we *ought* to do more to the world.

Rupert Read

Barring certain extreme cases where questions of ethics arise, no-one can really complain – there is nothing to be said against it – when scientists learn something they didn't know before; but when a new technology is created it's *always* an open question whether we should complain. I am going to suggest that sometimes we should and that sometimes it is *essential*, indeed, for us to do so.

In this way, and this is a central idea of my lecture, we need an independent criterion to assess technological progress by means of. Just because a new technological innovation has occurred, it does not mean that we should *really* describe that as progress.

So, as I say, in the Twentieth and Twenty-first century in particular, philosophy, especially in the English-speaking world, has tended to embrace one form or another of scientism unfortunately. Wittgenstein has mounted a heroic rear-guard action against scientism, as manifested especially in so-called analytic philosophy, a 'discipline' in which we make progress; we make progress allegedly on the mind-body problem, on the problem of our knowledge of the so-called external world; and so on and so forth.

Let me attempt an adaptation of the aphorism with which I began, applying it now specifically to our subject of philosophy. I put it to you that Wittgenstein could have said about that specific topic, 'Our discipline is characterised by the word progress; progress is its form, rather than making progress being one of its features.' And in saying that, he would have been mounting the most powerful *criticism* of our discipline, philosophy, as it views itself. For that is an incoherent way of understanding what philosophy is, but it is the dominant understanding of what philosophy is in a country like this, or in the United States, today.

So as I say, and as I said earlier, think about what Wittgenstein is saying about progress as being about his own philosophy, and about philosophy in general, but about these things as an example of a much broader phenomenon, a phenomenon that effects our entire civilisation. When people say things like, 'You can't stop progress' they have in mind exactly a version of progress that Wittgenstein is criticising, when he says that 'our civilisation is characterised by the word progress; progress is its form, rather than making progress being one of its features.'

Such people are implying there is no need for, there is no room for, an independent criterion by means of which we can assess the degree, or otherwise, to which there has been progress. Progress is *what our society does* by definition. (What the engines of technological and economic change do. The accumulation of information, knowledge, power.) And I want to counterpoise against that the idea of real progress.

Wittgenstein and the Illusion of 'Progress'

But before I tell you more about what real progress would mean, let me dwell a little bit more on the way that the term 'progress' generally functions when people say things like 'We can't stop progress', and what is wrong with this. Progress in this sense is, among other things, crucially, I put it to you, synonymous with 'growth'; or, more specifically, economic growth (growth in 'GDP'). And with technological expansionism, and with the concept of 'development', as in, 'sustainable development'; as in, the idea that when we have a load of new houses being built, on a flood plain, or in a green belt, that's development – after all, that's simply what it's called.

There is a new 'development' going up around Cambridge, say. Is that really a *development*? You can't ask that question. Because development, by definition, is what 'development' is. 'It is progress'; that is what we're told without it even being needed to be made explicit. The idea is that these things are somehow inevitable and that destiny says that we are moving ever onward and upward, that there is no end to this process. Again, this is what Wittgenstein is criticising in the aphorism which this lecture is focussed around reading. And I want to say that he is right.

Other voices who are pointing in the same direction as me at the present time in this country include the interesting, quasi-conservative, philosopher, John Gray, who is I think right to challenge the myth of progress, which he has done explicitly. I will return to Gray below. Mayer Hillman, Emeritus Fellow of the Policy Studies Institute, is another, arguing, at the present time, that the likelihood now is that our children and our grandchildren will inherit worsening conditions of life relative to ourselves, which is not something that we're used to. This is a new phenomenon; it doesn't fit the ideology that we've been brought up with.

Almost certainly, by the way, this point of worsening has already begun. It's very hard to measure these things – there's a philosophical question about the extent to which measurement as such is a worthwhile aspiration, when it comes to happiness, etc. . But, in so far as these things *can* be measured, it looks as if there is some evidence to believe that things have got worse in countries like this and the United States and much of Europe. Since about the 1950s, and certainly since the 1970s, it appears that things have gradually started getting worse.[15] 'In spite of' the economy continuing to grow, and new technologies continuing to become available.

---

[15] See e.g. http://news.bbc.co.uk/1/hi/programmes/happiness_formula/4771908.stm.

We have, I believe, to junk the idea of progress as inevitable. Any hard won *real* progress has to *be* real. We need an independent criterion to measure it by.

Because technological progress is not an independent criterion. Technological progress is simply what occurs 'naturally', if scientists and engineers and investors and so on are allowed and facilitated to act as they tend to, in a society like ours. Technological progress is simply what our society *does*. This is what Wittgenstein is saying. But that *by no means* implies that such progress is always to be welcomed.

What about Gross Domestic Progress? Does an increase in GDP – 'economic growth' – connote a measure of (real) progress? Can it be an independent criterion by which to measure our society? Of course not, for the reasons I've given: An increase in GDP is simply what our economy is expected to do 'naturally'. It doesn't actually mean that things really are getting better: for lots of things increase GDP while actually making things worse. A classic example, so incredible that it serves in itself as a kind of reductio ad absurdum of economic-growthism, is the apparent fact that the judgement of expert economists is that the most-harmful-ever oil spill, the BP Gulf of Mexico disaster of 2010, was actually 'beneficial' to the economy, increasing GDP...[16]

So: What might such an independent criterion actually be? Well, as implied above, perhaps something like well-being. Do people actually have a stronger sense of well-being than they did before? One might generalise and talk about the flourishing of all beings, including non-human beings. Are we the only species that matters? And indeed future people, our descendants: they matter, too.[17] I believe that a return to one-planet living, to living as if we have one planet – at the moment we're living in this country as if we have about 4; so that's about 3 more than area actually available – is not only non-negotiable; I believe that such a return to one-planet living must be part of the independent criterion I am referring to, by means of which we assess whether we are *actually* making *progress*. Because I don't see how we can be making progress, if we are overshooting the limits to growth and eating into the life-support-conditions of our children.

I want to put it to you that real progress probably requires the opposite of most of what is currently called progress. It probably

---

[16]   See e.g. section 6 of http://useconomy.about.com/od/suppl1/tp/BP_Oil_Spill.htm.
[17]   See on this my 'On Future People', in *Think* 10:29, 43–47: http://journals.cambridge.org/repo_A83AqV93.

requires, for example, an end to 'economic growth'. At this point people often say, 'But then, what are you going to do about all the people living in poverty?'

In order to solve poverty in a world where we are awash in riches and wealth, which most of us are experiencing in this country at a level of all-time historical decadence, where there are people who are poor, surely the answer is that the rich need to give up a bit of what they have and share it with them. Once that's done the need for growth is (to say the least) by no means clear any longer.

Sometimes, people recently say things to me in objection along the following lines: 'Ah yes, but haven't you read Thomas Piketty? The great Thomas Piketty has told us that the world is dreadfully unequal and becoming more unequal'. Piketty's dead right about that. But Piketty has also suggested that a key part of the problem is that we don't have as much economic growth as we used to. And my response to Professor Piketty at that point is to say, 'If you're really wanting to inherit the mantel of Karl Marx, wouldn't it behove you to talk rather less about growth and rather more about sharing?'[18]

Progress, growth: these are obstacles to our thinking. They imprison us. We need freedom from them. We need what Wittgenstein called 'liberation' from them, unless we radically reconceive what they are. We have, in particular, to give up the idea that these things are linear, or that they are endless, *or that they are intrinsically desirable*. Now there is a certain sense in which there is a linearity to progress; there is a wonderful fact about human beings, which is not true of most other animals – I say 'most' because it is now clear that there are modicums of what we call culture present in the lives of some of our primate cousins, including chimpanzees, bonobos and some monkeys, and in many cetaceans. The wonderful fact is that we as human beings, to a much greater extent than they, are historical beings. This is a marvellous thing, that we can learn and in some ways we always do learn from our mistakes in history, from what happened before. Often of course, not as much as we should (or nothing at all; or less than nothing!). I.e. this process is not guaranteed.

Think of the Middle Ages where it appears that, while we learned some things, we also lost quite a lot of knowledge. There was a gradual loss of knowledge, texts gradually deteriorated as they were copied *etcetera etcetera*... We can lose knowledge. And of course it

---

[18] My full response to Piketty can be found here, in *Radical Philosophy* 189: 'Green economics versus growth economics', https://www.radicalphilosophy.com/commentary/green-economics-versus-growth-economics.

can go much further than that; societies can collapse.[19] And in fact what we find if we look at societies that have collapsed, is that most often they've collapsed if they've sought to progress endlessly...

If we turn to the term 'growth', then of course one thing which is important to notice is that the term growth is a term that is taken from a biological original meaning. Growth in biology is something organic. It involves circular rhythms: something grows, it matures, it decays, it dies, it decays completely, it becomes raw material for something else to grow. When we think of it in that way, as a lifecycle, one question one might ask is, 'Does that mean that economies are doomed to collapse?' I don't think they're doomed to collapse, I don't think we're doomed to collapse. But we have to think beyond the box of endless growth if we're going to escape that doom. And that economies are (hopefully) not doomed to collapse is itself an indicator of the serious limits and hazards of the 'growth' metaphor...

And we should note furthermore that that the very idea of economic growth is a kind of bastardisation, a dangerous projection of biology onto the inorganic. Because it fantasises the economy as an organism, while trying to extricate from the idea of being an organism the idea of it achieving any kind of maturity and being subject to any kinds of limits. The ideology of endless growth is a profoundly anti-biological ideology, and this is a profound problem.

Now in the past, when societies have collapsed the people who survived those collapses, if any, have learnt from those collapses; they've learned how to be more 'sustainable', as the current jargon has it.[20] Tim Flannery, explains this process wonderfully in his book *The Future Eaters*.[21] He explains how we can resolve the paradox that, on the one hand we want to say indigenous peoples are these wonderful paragons of ecological virtue, and on the other hand, indigenous peoples destroyed all their mega-fauna. *Both* are true.

Basically the process, as Flannery describes it, is that typically what's happened in our deep pre-history is that indigenous peoples, our deep ancestors, have destroyed many of the conditions for their own lives. And have then learned from that destruction and have

---

[19] See on this Jared Diamond's important book, *Collapse* (London: Penguin, 2011).
[20] For my objections to that jargon, see the section on '"Sustainability"?' in my chapter on 'Post-growth common-sense' in John Blewitt and Ray Cunningham's *The Post-Growth Project* (London: London Publishing Partnership, 2014).
[21] *The Future Eaters* (Kew: Reed Books, 1994).

learned ecological wisdom that we then sometimes found them with when we encountered them.

The problem of course is that we can't afford to learn from our own collapse, because if our own collapse occurs, it will be global and probably completely terminal. We must instead take a fundamentally precautionary attitude, we must learn from the mistakes of others before committing mistakes of the same gravity. This requires a giving up of the delusions of 'endless progress', 'growth', 'development' before it's too late. We must learn from *their* collapses and ecological disasters, *not* our own.

And this brings us to what is the terrible irony of the ideology of progressivism (and similar ideologies such as modernism): it is thoroughly out of date. It might have been an appropriate ideology in the eighteenth century or the nineteenth century – that is something we can debate – but it is not, now. The one fundamental way in which modernists are not modern is in regard to the relevance now of their own ideology! One fundamental way in which progressivists are not entitled to the term 'progressive' at all is that they don't understand how real progress now would mean precisely giving up the delusion of progressivism... It is paradoxical but true: progressivism is a defunct, out-of-date ideology. The idea that we must always be more modern is itself thoroughly past its sell-by-date.

This brings us to the vexed and vexing question of Wittgenstein and his relation to conservatism. There is a famous essay by J.C. Nyiri, *'Wittgenstein's later work in relation to Conservatism'*,[22] it caused an academic storm many years ago now. Because many people, and I think rightly, were concerned at the implication in the essay, that the implication of thinking through Wittgenstein's thinking, in something like the way I've done, led one to some very pessimistic and problematically politically-conservative conclusions.

Wittgenstein *was* quite culturally pessimistic. And there are other things that he did have in common with conservatism, and I think rightly so. I think that there are things that conservatism has got right. Most crucially the resistance to theory in conservatism. The resistance to the idea you can have a grand plan for completely remodelling society from the ground up. An idea which is fundamental to many forms of socialism and communism. An idea which is also found on the radical right in people like Hayek – Hayek in this way

---

[22]   In Anthony Kenny & Brian McGuinness (eds), *Wittgenstein and His Times* (University of Chicago Press, 1982).

is not a conservative as indeed explained in his famous essay, '*Why I am not a Conservative*'.[23]

Insofar as conservatism resists the delusional ideology of progress, then Wittgenstein and I are for it. But I think it is wrong to think Wittgenstein is a conservative if by 'conservative' one means anything at all like what we have in this country that is called the Conservative Party. Because the Conservative Party in this country has basically nothing whatsoever to do with conservatism anymore. The Conservative Party is a fundamentally neoliberal party. It is committed to endlessly more growth and 'modernisation', as well as to what it would claim as fiscal rectitude before all else.

And also we should remember that Wittgenstein was profoundly attracted by socialism and by communism, at least as profoundly attracted to them as he was by conservatism – the same is true of me.[24] What we have to do, I believe, is try to find out, using something like the independent criterion that I sketched a little earlier, what is living and what is dead in the ideologies that we have inherited. Once we dispense with the delusional ideology of progressivism, of growthism, and once we dispense with developmentality,[25] what is left?

Well let's quickly look then at the great ideologies that we have inherited and see how they fare on this score. So, take conservatism, represented today in this country by John Gray and Roger Scruton – although I would say that unfortunately both of those thinkers are still not conservative *enough*, in the sense that they've both been infected, in my view, to some considerable extent, by neoliberalism (They have, that is to say, too great a prejudice in favour of 'the free market'). Conservatism, gets right, as I say, a fundamental resistance to theory, and a belief that there is something in our historical institutions that is worth preserving – in institutions, for example, such as the common law, in community, and of course in advocacy of conservation.

This is what I believe is living in conservatism. What is dead in conservatism, is its apologia for elites, its apologia for privilege, in particular its apologia for inherited privilege. None of these are tenable any more I think in our time today. A time which is (or

---

[23] Found as a post-script to his *The Constitution of Liberty* (London: Routledge, 1960).

[24] For detail, see my 'How ecologism is the true heir of both socialism and conservatism': http://blogs.lse.ac.uk/politicsandpolicy/how-ecologism-is-the-true-heir-of-both-socialism-and-conservatism/.

[25] On which, see Debal Deb, *Beyond Developmentality* (London: Earthscan, 2009).

rather: aspires to become), profoundly-rightly I believe, a democratic one.

What about socialism? What is living in socialism? What I think is living in socialism is its fundamental idea of the social and of society, and tied in with that, the great dream, the great aspiration, the great goal: of equality, of human equality, as something to realise. (This connects directly with the importance of *meaning* democracy – thus, of democracy in the workplace – and with the placing centrally of the social, of society.) What is dead in socialism, as I already implied, is its ambition for a grand overarching *plan* that can reconstruct everything from the ground up. As was shown to disastrously fail, in the times when it was, to some extent, tried in Russia and other countries.

And liberalism? What is living in liberalism is the idea of intellectual freedom, which is an idea profoundly important for Wittgenstein when he talked about the absolute importance of finding *liberating words*, of trying to liberate our minds from the ways in which they were held captive by inherited ideologies, which most of the time we are not even aware of.

And what is living in liberalism also, is the importance of civil and political liberties.

But what is dead in liberalism, and in its bastard child which is now ruling us, neoliberalism, is individualism, which has been a profound disaster for our world, a profound wrong direction that we've moved in. And in so far as individualism triumphs, then there will be no future for the human race. And this can be connected with Wittgenstein's opposition to philosophical scepticism and to solipsism I believe; I've written on this elsewhere.[26] There is, in Wittgenstein's philosophy and in the philosophy of some other great philosophers, some of whom I mentioned earlier, material for a profound resistance to the individualism which is a dominant and unquestioned ideology of our time.

Something I like to do in my classes sometimes – I admit, it's a little bit cruel – is to say to students, 'What do you think is the most important thing about *you*?' and very quickly someone will say, 'It's that I'm an individual'. And then often what will happen is that somebody else in the class will say 'Yes, it's the same for me!' And then they'll sometimes get swiftly to the point where

---

[26] See Chapter 8, 'Swastikas and Cyborgs: The Significance of PI 420', of my *A Wittgensteinian Way with Paradoxes* (Plymouth: Lexington Books, 2013), for a Reading of Wittgenstein's Philosophical Investigations as a 'war book'.

Rupert Read

somebody will say 'We are all above all individuals', which some of you may recognise is a 'quote' (sic.) from a famous movie, *The Life of Brian:* 'We are all individuals'. 'So the thing about you that most quintessentially sums up who you are is that you are all individuals?', I ask; and they all shout, in unison, in earnest, 'Yes!' I've really done this, quite often, and it's frightening how easy it is to do.

This is a disastrous feature of our times. We have never been individuals. We are mammals, we are quintessentially social animals, and linguistic animals. Moreover, we are in fact, of course, far more entangled than we've ever been before. Globalisation, thought through properly, ought to be the final death knell of the individualistic fantasy that lies at the heart of liberalism.

I suggest that we try to put aside what is dead in conservatism, in socialism, and liberalism, and bring together what is living in them. And bring together all of them under the banner of what's been called in recent years ecologism. An ideology, a philosophy that takes as its fundamental starting point the truth that we now, even if we possibly didn't have to before (though Tim Flannery and Jared Diamond would beg to differ), must take seriously that we are all completely beholden to our ecological conditions of possibility. That has to be the starting point and the ending point, the *ground*, for all of our political and philosophical thinking.

Let me reciptulate. 'You can't stop progress', we are constantly told. But what is meant by 'progress'? What is progress toward? Is it progress toward human flourishing, as Aristotle would have it? Is it towards wisdom, as Socrates would want? Towards a culture, not just a civilisation? Wittgenstein says, 'Our civilisation is characterised by the word progress.' There is another famous aphorism where he says, 'We have a civilisation; one day we may have a culture.'[27] For Wittgenstein 'civilisation' wasn't a very positive term, not as positive as in the famous quip of Gandhi's on western civilisation. Wittgenstein believed that our having something that we could call honorifically a culture is something that we should aim attain; and we have not attained it yet. He thought this partly because of the extent to which he saw our society has been dominated by scientism. And was, very worryingly, becoming more dominated by it, not less.

If progress was towards Aristotle's goal, or Socrates', or Wittgenstein's, that would be great. That would be real. But that very rarely seems a criterion for how the word 'progress' is actually typically applied in our society today.

---

[27]   *Culture and value*, 64 (my translation).

Wittgenstein and the Illusion of 'Progress'

In fact, of course, one could have a more basic starting point. Before we even get to thinking about human flourishing, the flourishing of other beings, attaining wisdom, creating a culture out of our civilisation, it would be good to be at least reasonably confident that our civilisation was going to survive the next hundred years. But we cannot be confident of that. We can be less confident of that, the less we are prepared to give up on the ideologies of 'progress' and 'growth'. In our society, progress – and similarly growth – are taken for granted. They are the accepted 'wisdom' (sic.) of our media, our politics, our economics. We are suffering from the complete hegemonic taking-for-grantedness of the goal of economic growth – although we're finally starting to see a few little chinks in it now,[28] and I'm hoping to create another one here.

'Progress' or 'growth' are simply a process that we are not allowed apparently to stop. Or that it would be futile to try to seek to stop, so that we are seemingly deliberately demoralised into giving up on even trying. We are prevented from thinking that we might even try. Questioning the myth of progress and concomitant myth of economic growth, and the basically synonymous myth of development is then a great task for intellectuals in our time.

Let me just take a moment on 'development', for it's such an unbelievably awful hubristic idea. What they tell us is that we live in a developed country and that there are all these other countries in the world that are 'developing'. So what we're supposed to believe is that all the other countries in the world are trying to, and ought to try to, aspire to be like us. As if we've arrived at the end of history and they are still in some kind of mini-dark age.

Moreover, what this idea of us being developed occludes is the point that we are endlessly continuing to develop, i.e: creating more and more 'development' – building over more and more of the green belt, ripping things down, putting things up,[29] with ever-increasing speed,[30] everything allegedly getting better and more modern and so on all the time. In that sense, it is very obvious that

---

[28]   To mention one example, it is worth looking at Bhutan's goal: http://www.grossnationalhappiness.com.

[29]   The quotation that I have employed as an epigraph for the present essay includes this telling sentence: 'Typically, it [our 'progressive' civilization] constructs'. For Wittgenstein, building was not to be equated with progress. It might be (look say at the house he built); but often it was a substitute for thinking, for looking, for attending, for describing, for pausing, for dwelling.

[30]   Think for instance of the untenable 'life-cycle' of mobile phones, today.

we are, even on their own terms, a developing country.[31] So we're a developing country in that sense; but no, we're apparently a developed country. This is a profoundly dangerous self-contradictory ideology, an ideology which was created in its explicit form essentially by powerful Americans in the wake of the Second World War, in order to try to reinforce the system, which they were determined to remain at the heart of as decolonisation etc. happened.[32]

Questioning the myth of progress and growth and development, and seeking to substitute for it the idea of real progress, progress which is actually assessed according to some independent, non-purely-procedural criterion, is a vital thing to do at this point in history. Literally life, or at least civilisation and the chance of culture in the future, may well depend on it. Sanity certainly depends on it. It is literally insane to seek to grow forever.

Understanding this creates, as I have sought to make clear, some difficulties for the Left in politics because it brings into question the catch-all understand of leftism as 'progressive'. It brings into question absolutely directly the ideology of 'productivism', which has historically been central to socialism: the dominant concept in socialism has typically been about making things, converting more and more of the earth into capital and into products for the masses. What I've been doing radically brings into question whether being 'progressive', in this sense, is actually a good thing.

Once we overcome the myth of progress, we can clear the ground for a real politics that would jettison the absurd hubris of liberalism, of individualism, and of much leftism. And would jettison the extreme Promethianism and lack of precaution endemic to our current pseudo-democratic technocracy.

The challenge is to do so in a way that does not fall into complete pessimism. I am by no means seeking to foment despair or a cynical spectatorial stance: what I'm hoping to do is open up space in which we can actually think what the alternative might be to all of this. The challenge, as I say, is to do what I've just described in a way that does not fall into complete pessimism, nor into an endorsement of the untenable features of conservatism. Most crucially, its apologia for elites and hierarchies.

The challenge, in other words, is to generate an ideology or philosophy for our time that might yet save us and ensure that we are

[31] I owe this point to Jonathan Essex: see his important essay on 'How to Make-Do and Mend our economy', in Blewitt and Cunningham (op.cit.).
[32] For detail on this, see Wolfgang Sachs (ed.), *The Development Dictionary* (New York: Zed, 1992).

Wittgenstein and the Illusion of 'Progress'

worth saving. That we don't just have bare life, but rather flourishing, a culture, wisdom. This is what ecologism, seeking to integrate conservatism, socialism and liberalism – what remains of those, what is not dead in them – and to put them on a sound foundation of one-planet living, might offer us.

In conclusion, then. For Wittgenstein, 'progress' is not a *feature* of the main current of European/American civilization, but its *form*. That is to say: It is regarded as sufficient justification for any technological or economic innovation, to say 'That's progress'. Or 'You can't stop progress.' There is no possibility (or at least, has not been until very recently) endemic to the main cultural traditions of the West in recent centuries of questioning whether these changes really are progress. 'Of COURSE' they are. The only question is how they are to be best *used*. (Thus John Rawls for instance, the leading philosopher of contemporary liberalism, treats technology as a 'standing resource' for humanity, and treats the Earth the same way. There is no question of whether or not we might have fundamentally the wrong attitude to these things.)

For greens, the same is true as for Wittgenstein, on this point. That is to say: greens take issue with the mainstream, in that we ask, heretically, whether many of the changes that we have undergone or are undergoing are *really* progress. Is it really progress for instance to have built (as Wittgenstein figures it) an ever more complicated societal and industrial structure? Perhaps globalisation, and longer and longer supply lines, are *not* progress. Is it really progress, in the 'developed' world (a hubristic term that, as outlined above, needs in any case to be severely interrogated) to have more and more income and wealth, while happiness levels decline and the future itself is bankrupted?

And so this lecture can be heard, and I hope you are able now to hear it, as a kind-of reading of what I've argued is Ludwig Wittgenstein's (most) crucial aphorism on this topic:

'Our civilisation (note not culture, 'our civilisation', what we actually have, which is profoundly problematic) is characterised (and this is a central feature of that problematic) by the word progress; progress is its form, rather than making progress being one of its features.' If we were to bring in an independent criterion to say what progress, real progress, actually was, a criterion that we cannot just take for granted, that doesn't just go without saying and escape interrogation, then we would be changing from that situation. Progress then would potentially be a feature of our society, and this would be a good thing; whereas at the present time it is our society's form, and this is a bad thing.

283

Rupert Read

But we cannot take for granted, as I've sought to explain, that real progress will be or has been achieved. We are vulnerable creatures, profoundly vulnerable social beings,[33] and our hubristic breaking of the limits to growth is making us more vulnerable every day. In this context, Wittgenstein's wisdom on the unwisdom of the ideology of progress is philosophy that our time most profoundly needs.

In the darkness of this time, Wittgensteinian thinking is a light that can give us direction.

University of East Anglia
rupertread@fastmail.co.uk

---

[33] This, again, conservatism gets right.

Index of Names

Index of Names

For EU product safety concerns, contact us at Calle de José Abascal, 56–1°, 28003 Madrid, Spain or eugpsr@cambridge.org.

www.ingramcontent.com/pod-product-compliance
Ingram Content Group UK Ltd.
Pitfield, Milton Keynes, MK11 3LW, UK
UKHW020356140625
459647UK00020B/2508

* 9 7 8 1 3 1 6 6 2 6 2 6 9 *